Focused Daily on God's Best

A Daily Devotional

PRISCILLA DOREMUS

SEVEN BEARS
PUBLISHING

SEVEN BEARS
PUBLISHING

Copyright © 2017 Priscilla Doremus.

All rights reserved. No part of this book may be used or reproduced by any means, graphic, electronic, or mechanical, including photocopying, recording, taping or by any information storage retrieval system without the written permission of the author except in the case of brief quotations embodied in critical articles and reviews.

Scripture quotations are taken from the Holy Bible, New Living Translation, copyright ©1996, 2004, 2007, 2013, 2015 by Tyndale House Foundation. Used by permission of Tyndale House Publishers, Inc., Carol Stream, Illinois 60188. All rights reserved.

Scripture quotations marked (TLB) are taken from The Living Bible copyright © 1971. Used by permission of Tyndale House Publishers, Inc., Carol Stream, Illinois 60188. All rights reserved.

Scripture taken from the New King James Version®. Copyright © 1982 by Thomas Nelson. Used by permission. All rights reserved.

ISBN: 978-1-7361474-5-0 (paperback)

Publishing and Design Services: MelindaMartin.me

DEDICATION

*This book is dedicated to you, the reader.
May God bless you as you seek to focus your life on Him.*

I don't mean to say that I have already achieved these things or that I have already reached perfection. But I press on to possess that perfection for which Christ Jesus first possessed me. No, dear brothers and sisters, I have not achieved it, but I focus on this one thing: Forgetting the past and looking forward to what lies ahead, I press on to reach the end of the race and receive the heavenly prize for which God, through Christ Jesus, is calling us.

—PHILIPPIANS 3:12–14

JANUARY 1

Something Old, Something New

And now that I am old and gray, don't forsake me. Give me time to tell this new generation (and their children too) about all your mighty miracles.

—Psalm 71:18 (TLB)

Here you are, considering the dawn of a brand-new year.

As you reflect on the previous year, do you find it to have been a year in which you recognized the goodness of God?

Was it a difficult year?

What about miracles? God's miracles are always mighty, but often we fail to recognize them all around us.

Looking back, can you see the mighty hand of God moving in your life and in the lives of those around you?

As you begin this year, I challenge you to do something new. Take the time to find and declare the mighty miracles of our heavenly Father to those around you. Don't keep Him to yourself.

Someone needs to hear of the goodness of God today.

Psalm 96:2 tells us, "Sing to the Lord; praise his name. Each day proclaim the good news that he saves" (NLT).

This year, let God take your old self and do something new and beautiful in you.

JANUARY 2

Not Your Every Day Fruit-of-the-Month Club

Then the angel showed me a river with the water of life, clear as crystal, flowing from the throne of God and of the Lamb. It flowed down the center of the main street. On each side of the river grew a tree of life, bearing twelve crops of fruit, with a fresh crop each month. The leaves were used for medicine to heal the nations.

—Revelation 22:1–2 (TLB)

I am always astounded at the perfect planning of God. He works things out down to the smallest detail to bless mankind. Each plant and tree blossoms and provides its goodness at just the right time. Lemons ripen during cold and flu season. Peaches ripen in summer giving us extra beta carotene to protect us from sun damage and giving us extra energy in the heat. Simply amazing.

In the new Jerusalem, there will be a tree of life bearing twelve crops of fruit, a fresh crop each month, on each side of the river of life. This scripture tells us that the leaves from the tree of life will be used as medicine to heal the nations.

It is a picture of all the fullness of life with Christ—both now and forever. That tree of life, once guarded from Adam and Eve to protect them from dwelling in sin for eternity, now full of life-giving fruit for all of Christ's followers to partake.

Are you hungry for the fruit of the Holy Spirit? Are you thirsty for the river of life?

May we come to the Bread of Life and believe, that we may never be hungry or thirsty again (John 6:35).

JANUARY 3

Dry Bones

The power of the Lord was upon me and I was carried away by the Spirit of the Lord to a valley full of old, dry bones that were scattered everywhere across the ground. He led me around among them, and then he said to me: "Son of dust, can these bones become people again?" I replied, "Lord, you alone know the answer to that."

—Ezekiel 37:1–3 (TLB)

Have you ever felt as though things in your life were hopeless? If so, know that Israel did, too.

In this passage of scripture, the Holy Spirit brings Ezekiel out into the middle of a valley filled with bones. The bones are very dry, with not even the slightest hint that there was ever life in them.

These dry, lifeless bones represent the nation of Israel. The people of Israel felt dead and lifeless, as though there was absolutely no hope for them or their nation. But the Holy Spirit asked Ezekiel whether or not these dry, lifeless bones could live again. Do you believe that the dry, lifeless pieces of your life can live again?

Clearly, all things are possible with God (Matthew 19:26). He can make even dry, lifeless bones come to life again. He is the giver of hope to the hopeless (1 Peter 1:3).

Psalm 42:8 reads, "But each day the Lord pours his unfailing love upon me, and through each night I sing his songs, praying to God who gives me life" (NLT).

May you pray, giving all the hopeless pieces of your life to the Father, and may He breathe His life-giving hope into every part of you this day.

JANUARY 4

These Bones are Gonna Rise Again

Then he told me to speak to the bones and say: "O dry bones, listen to the words of God, for the Lord God says, 'See! I am going to make you live and breathe again! I will replace the flesh and muscles on you and cover you with skin. I will put breath into you, and you shall live and know I am the Lord.'"

—Ezekiel 37:4–6 (TLB)

Everything God does is awesome and miraculous. His care for His own, as demonstrated in the passionate way in which He pursues, chastens, and loves the nation of Israel, serves as an excellent reminder of how He deals with us. We often fail to realize just how much He cares for us in the midst of our hopelessness and despair.

Let's dissect this passage of scripture together.

God speaks to Ezekiel,

commanding him to prophesy to the despairing, hopeless nation of Israel. The word God commands Ezekiel to impart to the nation of Israel is first to hear the word of the Lord. God wants Israel to stand up and take notice, to listen, to pay attention, and to *really hear* Him. They must stop wallowing in their own self-pity long enough to notice God. Once God has their attention, He tells them that He will fill them with the breath of life, that their hope will be renewed and their spirits will be reinvigorated.

But God doesn't stop there. He says that He will attach tendons and flesh and skin. God is restoring the people and renewing them with hope and all the fullness of life in Him.

Can you relate to the nation of Israel? May we remember the words of Isaiah 61:3 today: "To all who mourn in Israel, he will give a crown of beauty for ashes, a joyous blessing instead of mourning, festive praise instead of despair. In their righteousness, they will be like great oaks that the Lord has planted for his own glory" (NLT).

JANUARY 5

The Simplicity of Obedience

So I spoke these words from God, just as he told me to; and suddenly there was a rattling noise from all across the valley, and the bones of each body came together and attached to each other as they used to be. Then, as I watched, the muscles and flesh formed over the bones, and skin covered them, but the bodies had no breath.

—Ezekiel 37:7–8 (TLB)

In this passage of scripture, we find that Ezekiel is obedient to God's command and prophesies as God has commanded. As a result, God begins to fulfill His promise to the nation of Israel.

That is all God ever requires from us—simple obedience and trust in Him. He will always do the rest.

John 3:36 tells us, "And anyone who believes in God's Son has eternal life. Anyone who doesn't obey the Son will never experience eternal life but remains under God's angry judgment" (NLT).

Our obedience to Christ is a demonstration of our love and commitment to Him. It is the evidence of our salvation.

Ezekiel's prophecy is a demonstration of his love for and commitment to God. It is the evidence of his relationship to the Father. The Father takes care of the rest.

Are you in need of the Father's action on your behalf?

Your part is really very easy. Walk in simple and complete obedience to God. He will take care of the rest.

JANUARY 6

Breath of Heaven

Then he told me to call to the wind and say: "The Lord God says: 'Come from the four winds, O Spirit, and breathe upon these slain bodies, that they may live again.'" So I spoke to the winds as he commanded me, and the bodies began breathing; they lived and stood up—a very great army.

—EZEKIEL 37:9–10 (TLB)

Ezekiel prophesied to the breath, as God commanded, calling from the four winds to come into the dead so that they might live again. This breath of heaven accomplished its purpose: the dead were raised to life.

God breathes new life into old, dead lives every day. He replaces cold, stony hearts with soft new ones, renewing hope and restoring faith.

Sometimes living in a fallen world can cause us to lose our God-given focus. We can become distracted and forget the life-giving power of God at work in the world around us. We can forget the life-giving power of God at work within us.

But God's Word never loses its power in our lives. As Isaiah 55:11 reminds us, "So My Word which goes from My mouth will not return to Me empty. It will do what I want it to do, and will carry out My plan well" (NLT).

May the breath of heaven fill you with renewed life, hope, peace, joy, love, and power today, and may you join the vast army of God's soldiers imparting light to the world around you.

JANUARY 7

New Lives for Old

Then he told me what the vision meant: "These bones," he said, "represent all the people of Israel. They say: 'We have become a heap of dried-out bones—all hope is gone.' But tell them, 'The Lord God says: My people, I will open your graves of exile and cause you to rise again and return to the land of Israel.'"

—Ezekiel 37:11–12 (TLB)

Have you ever felt as though you wanted to give up on life completely and just end it all? Many in the Holy Bible felt that way. Consider the story of Elijah as recounted in 1 Kings 19. Elijah had killed all the prophets of Baal, among other things, in accordance with God's instruction. When Jezebel received word of all that Elijah had done, she sent this message to him: "May the gods strike me and even kill me if by this time tomorrow I have not killed you just as you killed them."

Elijah was terrified and fled into the wilderness. First Kings 19:4 tells us, "He sat down under a solitary broom tree and prayed that he might die. 'I have had enough, Lord,' he said. 'Take my life, for I am no better than my ancestors who have already died'" (NLT).

Have you ever felt like that?

That is how Israel felt in Ezekiel 37. Their hope was completely gone. But notice God's response. It is glorious how He loves us. He brings the dead up from the grave, giving hope to the hopeless and lifting them from the pit of despair. He gives them new lives for old.

Our Savior can work the same miracle for you if only you will let Him today.

JANUARY 8

There Is a Fork in My Road, but I Asked for a Spoon

If you want favor with both God and man, and a reputation for good judgment and common sense, then trust the Lord completely; don't ever trust yourself. In everything you do, put God first, and he will direct you and crown your efforts with success.

—Proverbs 3:5–6 (TLB)

Who's in charge of your life today? Is it God, or are you still trying to run the show? Perhaps you are at that proverbial fork in the road, unsure of which way you should go.

In the summer before my senior year of high school, God called my father to pastor a church in Regina, Saskatchewan, Canada. Saskatchewan is a long way from Trinity, Texas, and it wasn't in *the plan*, as far as I was concerned. I wasn't born with a silver spoon in my mouth—it was stainless steel. But I didn't care, as long as it kept shoveling good things my way. In this particular situation, I thought that God and I had a deal. He was going to make me valedictorian of my senior class. In return, I would give Him all the glory for the accomplishment. *We* had forged the deal in fifth grade, and I considered it cemented solid as if we had made a blood oath or had pinky sworn. Everything, so far, was going according to my—I mean, *our*—plan. Daddy being called to a new church—in Canada, no less—was not part of the deal. It was adding a couple of unwanted prongs to my spoon.

I never was valedictorian. I didn't even finish high school. But God's plan was far better than mine. It still is. It is important for us always to remember that God's ways are not our ways (Isaiah 55:8) and that He has plans to prosper us, not to harm us (Jeremiah 29:11).

Are you seeking His will in all you do? He will show you which path to take.

JANUARY 9

The Life of Faith

When I saw what was happening and that they weren't being honest about what they really believed and weren't following the truth of the Gospel, I said to Peter in front of all the others, "Though you are a Jew by birth, you have long since discarded the Jewish laws; so why, all of a sudden, are you trying to make these Gentiles obey them?"

—Galatians 2:14 (TLB)

The life of faith—the life God calls us to—has little room for tradition. It is a life of total and complete dependence upon Him.

In this passage of scripture, Peter is shown as not following the gospel. The man whom God said was the rock upon which He would build His church (Matthew 16:18) had again denied the truth, as he had done at least three times before (Matthew 26:75). And here Peter was again, struggling with his faith and trying to make the Gentiles follow the Jewish traditions that he himself had already discarded.

We are no different. Often during life's struggles, we toss aside our faith and return to that which is comfortable—our personal tradition, our habit of choice. O we of little faith. But God loves us too much to allow us to stay there without being confronted by our sin. In this scripture, Paul steps in to confront Peter and to lovingly set him straight.

Do you have a Paul in your life, a person who lovingly tries to set you straight on the course God would have you to take? How do you treat the Paul in your life? Do you listen to that person, or do you dismiss him or her? Peter knew that Paul was right, and he listened. What about you?

May we listen to the voice of faith when it speaks to us, lovingly correcting and guiding us along this journey called life.

JANUARY 10

Make It Right

You and I are Jews by birth, not mere Gentile sinners, and yet we Jewish Christians know very well that we cannot become right with God by obeying our Jewish laws but only by faith in Jesus Christ to take away our sins. And so we, too, have trusted Jesus Christ, that we might be accepted by God because of faith—and not because we have obeyed the Jewish laws. For no one will ever be saved by obeying them.

—Galatians 2:15–16 (TLB)

We hear folks say it every day: "If I just do enough good, then God will let me into heaven." But that's not the way it works.

In Matthew 7:22–23, Jesus said, "On judgment day many will say to me, 'Lord! Lord! We prophesied in your name and cast out demons in your name and performed many miracles in your name.' But I will reply, 'I never knew you. Get away from me, you who break God's laws'" (NLT).

The passage of scripture above in Galatians tells us that no one will ever be made right with God by obeying the law. So how do we reconcile the two passages? It's really very simple. Our obedience to God is the result of, the evidence of, and the proof of our faith.

In Matthew 3:8, Jesus tells us, "Prove by the way you live that you have repented of your sins and turned to God" (NLT). Our faith makes us *want* to obey God. It steers us toward Him, like a moth to a flame.

"And it is impossible to please God without faith. Anyone who wants to come to him must believe that God exists and that he rewards those who sincerely seek him" (Hebrews 11:6 NLT).

"For it is by believing in your heart that you are made right with God, and it is by openly declaring your faith that you are saved" (Romans 10:10 NLT).

May you declare your faith in Jesus Christ every moment of every day.

JANUARY 11

Yo-Yo Christianity

But what if we trust Christ to save us and then find that we are wrong and that we cannot be saved without being circumcised and obeying all the other Jewish laws? Wouldn't we need to say that faith in Christ had ruined us? God forbid that anyone should dare to think such things about our Lord. Rather, we are sinners if we start rebuilding the old systems I have been destroying of trying to be saved by keeping Jewish laws.

—Galatians 2:17–18 (TLB)

Change can be difficult sometimes just because it's change. We like the familiar, even when a particular change is obviously and overwhelmingly better for us. Sometimes our spiritual eyes are blind to all that God is doing. We long for the good old days when things were familiar to us. Ecclesiastes 7:10 says, "Don't long for 'the good old days.' This is not wise" (NLT).

I recall a time when I accepted a new job that was better in every way than my previous one, yet the change was difficult. There were weeks when I longed for the familiar ways of old, even though I knew God wanted me in the new position. I was being a yo-yo.

Being a yo-yo displays a lack of faith. What it says is, "I don't trust God to know what's best for me." But has God ever let us down? Has He broken any of His promises? God proves Himself to us every moment of every day. Even so, choosing to believe in Him is an act of the will.

Romans 6:16 says, "Don't you realize that you become the slave of whatever you choose to obey? You can be a slave to sin, which leads to death, or you can choose to obey God, which leads to righteous living" (NLT).

May you put the yo-yo days of Christianity behind you by exercising your faith and believing in Jesus Christ today.

JANUARY 12

The Masterpiece

Because of his kindness, you have been saved through trusting Christ. And even trusting is not of yourselves; it too is a gift from God. Salvation is not a reward for the good we have done, so none of us can take any credit for it. It is God himself who has made us what we are and given us new lives from Christ Jesus; and long ages ago he planned that we should spend these lives in helping others.

—Ephesians 2:8–10 (TLB)

The Master Artist, Jesus Christ, is at work in your life painting a glorious masterpiece on the canvas of your heart. The day you accepted Him as your personal Lord and Savior, He began a new work on the canvas of your heart, mixing just the right shades of color and putting them together in a manner more beautiful than you or I could ever imagine. This work is unique to you, one of a kind. There will be nothing like it when the Artist is done.

Though the canvas may fall off of the easel or become damaged by the elements, the Master Artist picks up the fallen canvas, carefully cleans it off, and lovingly sets it back upon the easel to begin again.

He never makes a mistake, as He chooses each hue with absolute care and seamlessly glides each stroke across the canvas with impeccable finesse, knowing all the while its remarkable purpose.

The canvas can take no credit for the beauty that may be found there, created there—it is all the Artist's doing.

May you have the faith to believe in God, the will to depend on Him, and the spiritual eyes to see the masterpiece He is creating upon the canvas of your heart and life today.

JANUARY 13

Beautiful Dreamer

Until God's time finally came—how God tested his patience!

—Psalm 105:19 (TLB)

Do you ever feel as though your life is in a holding pattern of sorts? Perhaps there are circumstances in your life that you would like to see changed. You continue to pray about the situation, yet day after day things appear to be unchanged.

Take heart. God hasn't forgotten you. He knows your dreams. The very hairs upon your head are all numbered (Matthew 10:30).

God works behind the scenes in our lives to orchestrate His grand plans, plans that will bring glory and honor unto Him.

Psalm 37:4 tells us, "Take delight in the Lord, and he will give you your heart's desires" (NLT).

Consider the story of Joseph in Genesis 37. Joseph endured many trials. Through each and every one of these, God refined and tested him, preparing him for the fulfillment of the dreams he'd had many years before.

Are you in the midst of trial?

May your character, like that of Joseph, prove to be true and worthy of the calling God has placed upon your life and of the beautiful dreams He has placed in your heart.

JANUARY 14

Crime and Punishment

And who were those people I speak of, who heard God's voice speaking to them but then rebelled against him? They were the ones who came out of Egypt with Moses their leader. And who was it who made God angry for all those forty years? These same people who sinned and as a result died in the wilderness. And to whom was God speaking when he swore with an oath that they could never go into the land he had promised his people? He was speaking to all those who disobeyed him. And why couldn't they go in? Because they didn't trust him.

—Hebrews 3:16–19 (TLB)

There was no denying it. Clearly, it was God's chosen people—his favored ones—who had disobeyed and disappointed Him. And, as comes with the territory, there was punishment for their many crimes, their acts of disobedience, their failure to believe and trust in God's perfect plan and care for them.

They thought *their* plan was better than God's, so they missed out on His perfect plan and His blessing. Instead they received punishment.

What about you? Do you think your plan is better than God's? Are you busy doing what *you* want to do with your life instead of what God wants?

It's not too late to give Him *all* the pieces of your life. Don't hold anything back. He can put them together perfectly.

And you can experience the peace that passes all understanding, unspeakable joy, and the everlasting blessing He has promised.

JANUARY 15

His Promised Rest

Although God's promise still stands—his promise that all may enter his place of rest—we ought to tremble with fear because some of you may be on the verge of failing to get there after all. For this wonderful news—the message that God wants to save us—has been given to us just as it was to those who lived in the time of Moses. But it didn't do them any good because they didn't believe it. They didn't mix it with faith. For only we who believe God can enter into his place of rest. He has said, "I have sworn in my anger that those who don't believe me will never get in," even though he has been ready and waiting for them since the world began.

—Hebrews 4:1–3 (TLB)

God promised the Israelites a place of rest, a land flowing with milk and honey, when they left the tyranny of Egypt. But they didn't believe it, and as a result they missed out.

God promises you and me a place of rest where there will be no more death or sorrow or crying or pain. All these things will be gone forever (Revelation 21:4). Do you believe it?

If we listen to the world, we will end up like the Israelites, in rebellion against God and determined to go our own way. And we will miss out on the glorious blessing that God has promised us, His chosen ones. Yes, *we* are His chosen ones if our heart is right with Him and if we seek to please Him and only Him (Romans 2:29).

God promises rest, an eternal rest that has been ready since the world began, for those who believe in and follow Him. The scripture above says that we ought to tremble with fear at the thought that some of us might fail to experience God's promised rest.

Are you trembling? May you forsake your own way to follow God's way today.

JANUARY 16

Don't Be Too Late

We know he is ready and waiting because it is written that God rested on the seventh day of creation, having finished all that he had planned to make. Even so they didn't get in, for God finally said, "They shall never enter my rest." Yet the promise remains and some get in—but not those who had the first chance, for they disobeyed God and failed to enter. But he has set another time for coming in, and that time is now. He announced this through King David long years after man's first failure to enter, saying in the words already quoted, "Today when you hear him calling, do not harden your hearts against him."

—Hebrews 4:4–7 (TLB)

Today is the day of salvation (2 Corinthians 6:2).

Now is the time to follow Him, turning away from sinful habits, giving Him everything that you have and are.

We are not guaranteed tomorrow.

My father tells the story of a man to whom he witnessed at the behest of the man's wife, but the man replied, "Not today, preacher. I'll accept Christ sometime, but I'm not ready just yet. One day I will be."

But one day never came for this man. Three days later, he was tragically killed in a car accident. His wife asked my father to officiate the funeral service. They both agreed that the plan of salvation should be central to the service, reminding others of the brevity of this life. It was the only funeral service at which I can recall an individual accepting Christ as Savior, and it was a beautiful thing to witness.

Do you know someone without Christ today? May you share Christ with that person today. Tomorrow may be too late.

JANUARY 17

Nothing Is Hidden

He knows about everyone, everywhere. Everything about us is bare and wide open to the all-seeing eyes of our living God; nothing can be hidden from him to whom we must explain all that we have done.

—Hebrews 4:13 (TLB)

Nothing is ever hidden from God, neither our sins nor the sins of others. He sees it all. Everything.

Perhaps you're experiencing a difficult time in your life. Maybe someone is mistreating you, or is repeatedly doing wrong and never seeming to get caught. It's not an excuse for you to sin.

Have you forgotten that God still sees? He sees what you are going through. He also sees your response.

The people of Israel disobeyed Him repeatedly, and He saw. And there were consequences to their disobedience. Namely, they failed to enter His place of rest.

There are consequences to our sin, too. This passage tells us that if we disobey God, we will fall. It's not about legalism. It's about whom we allow to control our lives.

May we be diligent in our obedience to God, allowing the Holy Spirit to control our lives so that we may enter His eternal rest.

JANUARY 18

The Power of the Written Word

After Jeconiah the king, the queen mother, the court officials, the tribal officers, and craftsmen had been deported to Babylon by Nebuchadnezzar, Jeremiah wrote them a letter from Jerusalem, addressing it to the Jewish elders, priests, prophets, and to all the people.

—Jeremiah 29:1–2 (TLB)

Letters can be powerful. They can, and often do, serve as lasting records of truth. Jeremiah wrote an important letter that did just that.

There had been a lot said to and about the Jewish people who had been exiled to Babylon—a lot of lies. Some of these lies had even come from those claiming to be prophets, like Hananiah, who told the people that God was planning to return the exiles, restore King Jehoiachin, and return the stolen vessels to the temple in Jerusalem—all in less than two years' time.

But that was not God's plan.

Jeremiah needed to set the record straight. The best way to combat the liars and false prophets, leaving no room for misinterpretation, was to put it all down in a letter. The letter would serve as a record of God's plan for His people, and it would also give credence to Jeremiah's divine appointment as a true prophet. The message would be proven true, silencing the false prophets.

Today, God's Word is full of letters. They are lasting records of truth. And these letters will silence the liars and false prophets all around us if we will but use them today.

JANUARY 19

A Charge to Us All

The Lord Almighty, the God of Israel, sends this message to all the captives he has exiled to Babylon from Jerusalem: Build homes and plan to stay; plant vineyards, for you will be there many years. Marry and have children, and then find mates for them and have many grandchildren. Multiply! Don't dwindle away! And work for the peace and prosperity of Babylon. Pray for her, for if Babylon has peace, so will you.

—Jeremiah 29:4–7 (TLB)

It is a letter I still cherish after more than twenty years. The letter was written by my ninety-five-year-old grandmother just one week before her death and one month before I was to be married. The letter was a charge to work hard, build a home, bear children, live in peace, enjoy all that God provides, and above all, serve God with every ounce of my being—making daily prayer and Bible reading a priority always.

In much the same way, Jeremiah gave a charge to the Israelites. They were being punished, humbled for their rebellion against God. Yet God did not want the Jews in exile to become discouraged. God knew that one day they would be restored, though it would take seventy years and see three generations. The strength of this Jewish remnant would determine the strength of generations to come.

The same charge is applicable to us today. The strength of our families, the strength of our relationships, and our prosperity or failure will impact many generations to follow in ways we can never fully comprehend or imagine.

May we pray for the peace of Jerusalem, and for peace in our own homes, as well.

JANUARY 20

Wolves

The Lord Almighty, the God of Israel, says: Don't let the false prophets and mediums who are there among you fool you. Don't listen to the dreams that they invent, for they prophesy lies in my name. I have not sent them, says the Lord.

—Jeremiah 29:8–9 (TLB)

There are many wolves in the world that we must be on guard against—many in the church, too. Perhaps you've met a few.

It was no different in Jeremiah's day. There were prophets and fortune-tellers claiming to have God's message, but their messages were all lies. They told of all good things and spoke of a quick return from captivity and exile. I wonder, why would they lie? Why would they distort God's message?

Clearly, if the Jews had believed these false prophets, they would have easily lost heart and become discouraged. Patience would not have done its perfect work in their lives. James 1:4 tells us, "But let patience have its perfect work, that you may be perfect and complete, lacking nothing" (NKJV).

Matthew 7:15 says, "Beware of false prophets, who come to you in sheep's clothing, but inwardly they are ravenous wolves" (NLT).

Matthew 10:16 tells us, "Behold, I send you out as sheep in the midst of wolves. Therefore be wise as serpents and harmless as doves" (NLT).

May we heed the words of Jesus, being wise as serpents and harmless as doves, testing the words we hear to ensure they line up with scripture, and guarding our hearts and lives against the many wolves we encounter in life today and every day.

JANUARY 21

Our Future Hope

The truth is this: You will be in Babylon for seventy years. But then I will come and do for you all the good things I have promised and bring you home again. For I know the plans I have for you, says the Lord. They are plans for good and not for evil, to give you a future and a hope.

—Jeremiah 29:10–11 (TLB)

Have you ever been in a situation or faced a circumstance that you felt would never change? Perhaps you are there now, and it feels as though you have been in this place—this place not of your choosing—forever. That is exactly how the exiles in Babylon felt. They were being disciplined and humbled by a loving heavenly Father. It was a necessary part of their spiritual growth, although they didn't quite realize that yet. Hebrews 12:6 tells us, "For the Lord disciplines those he loves, and he punishes each one he accepts as his child" (NLT).

Still, God promised to bring the exiles home again. He promised to do good things for them, to give them a future and a hope. He promises the same thing to you and me.

Times of discipline, pain, and suffering are a necessary part of our spiritual growth and development, although we don't often understand what's going on when we're in the midst of the firestorm. If we will have faith, we will triumph in times of difficulty.

Romans 5:3b–5 tells us, "But we also glory in tribulations, knowing that tribulation produces perseverance; and perseverance, character; and character, hope. Now hope does not disappoint, because the love of God has been poured out in our hearts by the Holy Spirit who was given to us" (NLT).

May we never doubt the glorious plan that God has for each and every one of His children.

JANUARY 22

The Devil Is in the Details

One day Samuel said to Saul, "I crowned you king of Israel because God told me to. Now be sure that you obey him. Here is his commandment to you: 'I have decided to settle accounts with the nation of Amalek for refusing to allow my people to cross their territory when Israel came from Egypt. Now go and completely destroy the entire Amalek nation—men, women, babies, little children, oxen, sheep, camels, and donkeys.'"

—1 Samuel 15:1–3 (TLB)

The Lord was very specific and detailed in His instructions to Saul. Saul was not to spare anything or anyone.

God is very specific when He gives instructions to us, too. Much like Saul, if we listen to the voice of Satan, we often gloss over those details, or think that perhaps God didn't *really* mean them. And so we take liberties—arrogant liberties—not realizing that those liberties will have devastating consequences.

Satan loves to muddy the details of our lives with all sorts of lies and trickery. He puts thoughts in our mind to call into question the clarity of God's voice—the voice we know to be truth. With regard to God's instruction, the slightest change in detail can have a monumental impact on our life and the lives of others.

Do you recall a time when you didn't obey God completely? Partial obedience is not obedience at all. It is disobedience.

Remember that God blessed all the nations of the earth through Abraham's descendants, all because Abraham obeyed God (Genesis 22:18) and had a right relationship with Him—the kind that can only come through faith (Romans 4:13).

May we be fully obedient to God today, not just for ourselves but also for others, so that they may receive the blessing as well.

JANUARY 23

Father Knows Best

Then Saul butchered the Amalekites from Havilah all the way to Shur, east of Egypt. He captured Agag, the king of the Amalekites, but killed everyone else. However, Saul and his men kept the best of the sheep and oxen and the fattest of the lambs—everything, in fact, that appealed to them. They destroyed only what was worthless or of poor quality.

—1 Samuel 15:7–9 (TLB)

Our heavenly Father *always* knows what's best for us. When we forget that, we begin to get ourselves into trouble. That is what happened to King Saul in this passage of scripture.

First, Saul took King Agag alive. Remember that God told Saul not to spare anyone. Next, Saul and his army kept "the best of the sheep and cattle, the fat calves and lambs—everything that was good." God had told Saul to destroy everything that belonged to the Amalekites.

Scripture makes it clear that this was not just an "Oops, I forgot" moment. This verse tells us that Saul and his army were *unwilling* to obey. They chose to rebel.

Are you *willing* to obey God? If you are unwilling to obey God, then you demonstrate that you do not love Him and you are not living in Him. First John 2:5 tells us, "But those who obey God's word truly show how completely they love him. That is how we know we are living in him" (NLT).

God has access to information that we do not have access to. In this case, Saul's failure to destroy King Agag and his people led to a race of people, the Agagites, who hated the Jews. Haman, in particular, sought to exterminate all Jews (Esther 9:24). O the rippling impact of our individual acts of obedience and disobedience.

May we obey our Father's voice today and always.

JANUARY 24

Too Big for His Britches

And Samuel told him, "When you didn't think much of yourself, God made you king of Israel. And he sent you on an errand and told you, 'Go and completely destroy the sinners, the Amalekites, until they are all dead.' Then why didn't you obey the Lord? Why did you rush for the loot and do exactly what God said not to?"

—1 Samuel 15:17–19 (TLB)

Proverbs 16:18 tells us, "Pride goes before destruction, and haughtiness before a fall" (NLT). This was certainly true in King Saul's case.

Sometimes when God does great things for us, we forget that He did them and we begin to think we're something extra special. We begin to get too big for our britches. And when we are too big for our britches, we tend to go our own way, forgetting to depend on and obey the One who made us. Have you ever done that?

In my own life, academic things always came easy to me. I had a tendency to look down on those who struggled in school, forgetting the One who had given me the gift of academic excellence. Then one day, the loving two-by-four of God smacked me upside the head, showing me how disobedient I had become and that I was nothing without Him. My being diagnosed with a brain tumor has served as a beautiful constant reminder that I am not the one in charge, and that the One who is extra special is my heavenly Father.

James 1:17 tells us, "Every good and perfect gift is from above, coming down from the Father of the heavenly lights, who does not change like shifting shadows" (NLT).

May we choose to fit into our britches, remembering, "It is He who has made us, and not we ourselves" (Psalm 100:3 NLT).

JANUARY 25

Liar, Liar, Pants on Fire

"But I have obeyed the Lord," Saul insisted. "I did what he told me to; and I brought King Agag but killed everyone else. And it was only when my troops demanded it that I let them keep the best of the sheep and oxen and loot to sacrifice to the Lord."

—1 Samuel 15:20–21 (TLB)

"Did you take the last piece of cake that I was saving for your father?"

"No, Mom. I don't know who took it."

"Well then, why do you have chocolate on the sides of your mouth?"

Have you ever experienced something like that? O what tangled webs we weave!

In this passage of scripture, King Saul was cold busted. He had disobeyed God by bringing back King Agag and by keeping the best of the livestock. God had specifically told him to destroy everything and everyone. Do you see how Saul responded to Samuel when he was caught in the act? He said, "But I *did* obey the Lord." It was a complete lie.

Saul went on to justify his actions by telling Samuel that he kept the best of the plunder in order to sacrifice the animals to the Lord at Gilgal.

Do you ever try to justify your sin, your disobedience? When you do this, you miss out on God's protection. You miss out on the beauty of His perfect plan for you, and you hurt others too.

God only wants us to obey Him so that we can have life—and not just any ol' life. He wants us to have abundant life. Satan lies to us and tells us that our way is better. It's not.

"Lord, we show our trust in you by obeying your laws; our heart's desire is to glorify your name" (Isaiah 26:8 NLT).

JANUARY 26

No Messin' Around

Samuel replied, "Has the Lord as much pleasure in your burnt offerings and sacrifices as in your obedience? Obedience is far better than sacrifice. He is much more interested in your listening to him than in your offering the fat of rams to him. For rebellion is as bad as the sin of witchcraft, and stubbornness is as bad as worshiping idols. And now because you have rejected the word of Jehovah, he has rejected you from being king."

—1 Samuel 15:22–23 (TLB)

When I was growing up, my father had a reputation everywhere we went as being a no-nonsense preacher. He believed in firmly preaching God's truth, not particularly concerned about anyone's feelings, and he let the chips fall where they may. And believe you me, I saw some fallout from that style of preachin' in my day.

One thing people say to me repeatedly about my father is how passionately they feel his love for them because he doesn't mess around. My father's love is an example of God to me. God's love for us is embodied in His truth. His truth is protective, passionate, and loving.

God doesn't mess around either. In this passage of scripture, Samuel doesn't mince words when he talks to King Saul about his disobedience. Samuel compares Saul's rebellion to witchcraft, and his stubbornness to idolatry. To some, this might seem harsh, but our God is to be obeyed with deep reverence and fear (Philippians 2:12). His commands are given only to bring us abundant life (John 10:10).

Psalm 2:11 tells us, "Serve the Lord with reverent fear, and rejoice with trembling" (NLT).

May we rejoice in following our heavenly Father in faithful obedience so that we might have life, and have it in full today and every day.

JANUARY 27

Count Your Blessings

Oh, thank the Lord, for he's so good! His loving-kindness is forever.

—Psalm 118:1 (TLB)

When was the last time you *really* took stock of your blessings? Perhaps you are in a difficult place in life and you find it hard to see the good. Or perhaps you had been counting your blessings just before reading this.

Wherever you find yourself in life, there are always blessings to be counted. No matter how difficult the day or the night, God's love remains.

Isaiah 54:10 promises us, "'For the mountains may move and the hills disappear, but even then my faithful love for you will remain. My covenant of blessing will never be broken,' says the Lord, who has mercy on you" (NLT).

John 1:16 reminds us, "From his abundance we have all received one gracious blessing after another" (NLT).

We are surrounded by blessings. We need only to stop and recognize them, acknowledge them, and praise God for them. Have you counted your blessings today? May you count your many blessings, naming them one by one.

I am sure it will surprise you to discover what the Lord has done.

JANUARY 28

If God Is for Us

In my distress I prayed to the Lord, and he answered me and rescued me. He is for me! How can I be afraid? What can mere man do to me?

—Psalm 118:5–6 (TLB)

King David experienced many times of distress in his life. He faced Goliath, King Saul tried to kill him, he was confronted by his sin with Bathsheba, his child died, his son tried to overthrow him, and so on.

We need not wonder why he said in Psalm 42:3, "Day and night I have only tears for food, while my enemies continually taunt me, saying, 'Where is this God of yours'" (NLT). But the Lord answered David and set him free from his distress.

There have been many times in my life when I was distressed and spent the night crying to God about the issue. Although my circumstance did not instantly change most of those times, God did provide me with a deep, abiding peace and comfort until the answer came. And in each time of distress, He did answer. Each time, His answer was better than I anticipated. My Jesus set me free.

What about you? Have you prayed to the Lord in your distress? Has He answered you and set you free? If so, then you have no reason to fear. You can ask as the psalmist did, "What can mere people do to me?"

JANUARY 29

This Means War

Though all the nations of the world attack me, I will march out behind his banner and destroy them. Yes, they surround and attack me; but with his flag flying above me I will cut them off. They swarm around me like bees; they blaze against me like a roaring flame. Yet beneath his flag I shall destroy them. You did your best to kill me, O my enemy, but the Lord helped me.

—Psalm 118:10–13 (TLB)

Ecclesiastes 3:8b tells us that there is "a time for war and a time for peace" (NLT). In the passage of scripture above, we find David in the midst of battle. Yet before engaging in battle, David sought the Lord. He sought His will and went into battle under the authority of his Lord and Savior.

Proverbs 21:31 tells us, "The horse is prepared for the day of battle, but the victory belongs to the Lord" (NLT).

The battles that you and I face every day are no different in the sense that we must seek the guidance and authority of the Lord before engaging in them. When we act under the authority of God, we can be sure He will rescue us— no matter how threatening our adversary. Ecclesiastes 9:11 reminds us, "The fastest runner doesn't always win the race, and the strongest warrior doesn't always win the battle" (NLT).

Psalm 144:1 says, "Praise the Lord, who is my rock. He trains my hands for war and gives my fingers skill for battle" (NLT).

May we seek the authority of the Lord in every battle we face, knowing that when we follow Him and obey His commands, He will give us victory.

JANUARY 30

When It's Time to Go

God had told Abram, "Leave your own country behind you, and your own people, and go to the land I will guide you to."

—Genesis 12:1 (TLB)

Sometimes God calls us out of our place of comfort and familiarity to embark on something new. It may not make sense to us or others at all, but it is God speaking.

What we are called to do may not even appear possible, but somehow God makes it possible.

Isaiah 43:19 tells us, "For I am about to do something new. See, I have already begun! Do you not see it? I will make a pathway through the wilderness. I will create rivers in the dry wasteland" (NLT).

We may not understand all the reasons why God calls us to our new appointment. During such times, we can take comfort from Isaiah 55:8–9, which reminds us, "'My thoughts are nothing like your thoughts,' says the Lord. 'And my ways are far beyond anything you could imagine. For just as the heavens are higher than the earth, so my ways are higher than your ways and my thoughts higher than your thoughts'" (NLT).

Sometimes it is simply time for us to go. Our task is simply to trust.

May we trust God's plan for us when it is time to go. His way is better than anything we could ever ask for or imagine.

JANUARY 31

Childlike Faith Perfected

O my people, trust him all the time. Pour out your longings before him, for he can help!

—Psalm 62:8 (TLB)

Can you recall a time in your life when someone reached out and caught you?

I recall being a little girl and eagerly running across the street, chasing after my older brother and sister. I didn't bother to look both ways before crossing the street, as I was focused on catching my big brother and sister. By the time I saw the car coming toward me, it was too late. Just as my short life flashed before my eyes, two strong arms grabbed me, pulling me to safety. They were the loving arms of my father, who had been watching the whole incident unfold.

Our heavenly Father is like that.

Isaiah 59:1 tells us, "Listen! The Lord's arm is not too weak to save you, nor is his ear too deaf to hear you call" (NLT).

Psalm 55:22 comforts us with these words: "Give your burdens to the Lord, and he will take care of you. He will not permit the godly to slip and fall" (NLT).

Perhaps your earthly father has failed you in some way. Don't attribute those same flaws to your heavenly Father. Trust in Him at all times. He never disappoints His children.

FEBRUARY 1

Decisions, Decisions

Then, using the most careful workmanship, make a chestpiece to be used as God's oracle; use the same gold, blue, purple, and scarlet threads of fine-twined linen as you did in the ephod.

—Exodus 28:15 (TLB)

Our decisions impact so many lives—not just our own.

In the Old Testament, seeking a decision from God was so important that the high priest wore a special chest piece when approaching the throne of God. The garment was crafted with great skill and care, embodying the significance of hearing from God regarding decisions.

Your life is a summation of choices that you make and of others' choices that impact you. Many decisions we face are profoundly more important than we recognize.

Are you consistently seeking Him with regard to the decisions of your life?

First Chronicles 16:11 tells us, "Search for the Lord and for his strength; continually seek him" (NLT).

May we be always in an attitude of prayer, continually seeking the Father regarding every decision we face in our life.

FEBRUARY 2

Unexpected Opportunities

But as a result, the Messiah will be widely known and honored.

—Luke 21:13 (TLB)

The late Truett Cathy, founder of Chick-fil-A, was well-known for encouraging Christians to make the most of unexpected opportunities to share Christ with others.

One morning, as our family was leaving church, we were met with just such an unexpected opportunity. At the back entrance of the church building, a family was standing and holding a sign that read, "Lost job and in need of food and clothing." As I read the sign and dug through my purse for a few dollars, I felt great compassion for the family. I handed the wife a few dollars and then continued on with my own family to the car as I heard another church member say, "Now, you come back tomorrow and go to the church offices, and they will help you." I saw almost everyone else in the church simply walking past the family, snubbing them.

Proverbs 3:28 says, "If you can help your neighbor now, don't say, 'Come back tomorrow, and then I'll help you'" (NLT).

What also broke my heart once I arrived at our car was the fact that I did not share Christ with the family. God had provided the perfect opportunity, even bringing them to the church door, but I did not share Him. I should have asked my husband to turn the car around so that I could go back and share Christ with the family, instead of only handing them a few dollars, but I didn't. Second Timothy 4:2 says, "Preach the word of God. Be prepared, whether the time is favorable or not. Patiently correct, rebuke, and encourage your people with good teaching" (NLT).

May God have mercy, and may we take advantage of every opportunity to share Christ.

FEBRUARY 3

Knock, Knock. Who's There?

The door to heaven is narrow. Work hard to get in, for the truth is that many will try to enter but when the head of the house has locked the door, it will be too late. Then if you stand outside knocking, and pleading, "Lord, open the door for us," he will reply, "I do not know you."

—Luke 13:25 (TLB)

"Knock, knock." "Who's there?"
"Jim."
"Jim who?"
It is more than a bad knock-knock joke
It is real. And it is no joke at all.

The Holy Bible tells us plainly that if we do not have a living, breathing relationship with our heavenly Father, we will not dwell with Him eternally.

Matthew 7:21 tells us, "Not everyone who calls out to me, 'Lord! Lord!' will enter the Kingdom of Heaven. Only those who actually do the will of my Father in heaven will enter" (NLT). Are you doing the will of your Father in heaven? Do you *know* the will of the Father?

Romans 12:2 tells us, "Don't copy the behavior and customs of this world, but let God transform you into a new person by changing the way you think. Then you will learn to know God's will for you, which is good and pleasing and perfect" (NLT).

May you "seek the Kingdom of God above all else, and live righteously, and he will give you everything you need" (Matthew 6:33 NLT).

FEBRUARY 4

Artificial Light

So watch out that the sunshine isn't blotted out.

—Luke 11:35 (TLB)

A recent annual checkup at my doctor's office revealed that I was severely lacking in vitamin D.

"You're not getting enough sunlight," the doctor said. "There's just no substitute for it," she continued.

I hadn't realized how much of a toll this lack of real light was taking on my body.

It is the same with our spirit. There is no substitute for the real light of Jesus Christ in our life. Anything else is just a cheap substitute that will tax our spirit to the very core, leading us down a broad destructive path.

So how do we know we have the *real* light of Jesus?

In Luke 11:36, Jesus gives us the answer. He says, "If you are filled with light, with no dark corners, then your whole life will be radiant, as though a floodlight were filling you with light" (NLT).

May your whole life radiate the light of Christ like a floodlight, so that everyone may see Him in you.

FEBRUARY 5

Foolproof GPS

In everything you do, put God first, and he will direct you and crown your efforts with success.

—Proverbs 3:6 (TLB)

Our family took a driving vacation to Hershey, Pennsylvania. After one particular stop on the trip, the GPS sent us on a detour that was clearly off the intended path. After double-checking the route on our map, we were able to get back on the right course.

It was a good lesson in the fallibility of global positioning systems.

But our God is infallible. When we seek Him in everything we do, He will show us which path to take—and He will never make a mistake.

Are you in need of His direction for your life?

Psalm 32:8 reminds us, "The Lord says, 'I will guide you along the best pathway for your life. I will advise you and watch over you'" (NLT).

May you follow the map of God all the days of your life.

FEBRUARY 6

The Best Care Package

Let him have all your worries and cares, for he is always thinking about you and watching everything that concerns you.

—1 Peter 5:7 (TLB)

I remember fondly the care packages of zucchini bread and other edible goodies my mother would send to me from over two thousand miles away in Canada when I was in college. It warmed my heart to receive those gifts. They reminded me of all the things I loved about being home—and all the things I loved about my mother.

God sends us care packages from our heavenly home, too. Have you received one lately? Perhaps you should look around to see all of the ways in which God shows His love and care for you. He knows all of your favorite things, all of the things that make you feel special and loved.

And that's not all. He also sends angels to care for us (Hebrews 1:14). He sends His Spirit to teach us everything (John 14:26). He cares about the anguish of our soul (Psalm 31:7), and preserves our life by His care (Job 10:12).

The best care package we've ever received came in the form of a baby born in the little town of Bethlehem one blessed night—Jesus.

May you recognize how complete and incomprehensible the Savior's care is for you, and may you share this bountiful blessing with someone else today.

FEBRUARY 7

The Sky Is Falling

Immediately after the persecution of those days the sun will be darkened, and the moon will not give light, and the stars will seem to fall from the heavens, and the powers overshadowing the earth will be convulsed.

—Matthew 24:29 (TLB)

Do you remember the story of Chicken Little?

Chicken Little warned everyone that the sky was falling. It wasn't. An acorn had simply fallen on his head.

But one day the sky will fall.

The Holy Bible tells us that when Jesus returns, the stars will fall from the sky and the powers in the heavens will be shaken. The sign that the Son of Man is coming will appear in the heavens, and then the Son of Man will come on the clouds with power and great glory (Matthew 24:30).

Have you told someone about the goodness of God this day, this week?

Matthew 24:31 tells us that He will send out His angels with the mighty blast of a trumpet and that they will gather His chosen ones from the farthest ends of heaven and earth.

Would you be ready if the stars began to fall from their places in the sky? May we all make ready should the sky begin to fall today.

FEBRUARY 8

Family Ties

Jesus asked, "Who is my mother? Who are my brothers?" Then he pointed to his disciples and said, "Look, these are my mother and brothers."

—Matthew 12:48–49 (NLT)

The family is very important to God. In Proverbs 8:31, we are told, "And how happy I was with the world he created; how I rejoiced with the human family" (NLT)!

Many are the ties that bind a family together, making it a formidable force when united. Equally many are the conflicts and forces that can tear a family apart. Yet even when divided by conflict, a family's members are still one through blood.

It is also through blood, the life-giving blood of Jesus, that we become members of God's family. Christians, God's family, are a formidable force when united.

As many are the forces threatening our Christian family unity, we must encourage one another and build each other up (1 Thessalonians 5:11).

Galatians 6:10 tells us, "Therefore, whenever we have the opportunity, we should do good to everyone—especially to those in the family of faith."

Blessed be the ties that bind the family of God together through Jesus Christ our Lord.

FEBRUARY 9

Dream a Little Dream

Until God's time finally came—how God tested his patience!

—Psalm 105:19 (TLB)

Do you have unfulfilled dreams planted deep within your heart?

Psalm 37:4 tells us, "Take delight in the Lord, and he will give you your heart's desires" (NLT).

God knows our hearts, the deepest recesses of them, every nook and cranny. His timing is perfect in all things, as it was for Joseph in Genesis 37–45.

We often fail to know and fully understand God's plan for us, but we don't really need to know or understand it. Our job is to take delight in the Lord. When we do, our actions will follow. When our actions follow, we will see the goodness of the Lord in the fulfillment of our dreams.

Sometimes our dreams are completely self-centered, reflecting our lack of commitment to Christ and the sin within our hearts. We must choose to submit our lives to the will of God rather than to our own selfish desires. Once we do, He will fulfill the deepest longings of our heart.

Proverbs 13:19 serves as a warning and reminder that not everyone will see their dreams fulfilled: "It is pleasant to see dreams come true, but fools refuse to turn from evil to attain them" (NLT).

May the love of God enrapture your heart, defining your dreams today and every day that follows.

FEBRUARY 10

En Garde

Keep your eyes open for spiritual danger; stand true to the Lord; act like men; be strong.

—1 Corinthians 16:13 (TLB)

The world we live in is a battleground. There are spiritual forces at war around us constantly. The Holy Bible tells us in Ephesians 6:12, "For we are not fighting against flesh-and-blood enemies, but against evil rulers and authorities of the unseen world, against mighty powers in this dark world, and against evil spirits in the heavenly places."

If we dwell on the evil deeds going on around us, we tend to become discouraged. But the Holy Bible reminds us to take heart, as God has overcome this evil world (John 16:33).

We will face hardship. In 2 Timothy 2:3, Paul says, "Endure suffering along with me, as a good soldier of Christ Jesus" (NLT). And 2 Timothy 2:12 tells us, "If we endure hardship, we will reign with him. If we deny him, he will deny us" (NLT).

The beauty of this battle is that we are not in it alone.

Psalm 144:1 tells us, "Praise the Lord, who is my rock. He trains my hands for war and gives my fingers skill for battle" (NLT).

In this war, we know who wins. God does.

First John 5:4 promises us, "For every child of God defeats this evil world, and we achieve this victory through our faith" (NLT).

FEBRUARY 11

Sweet Peace

For Christ himself is our way of peace. He has made peace between us Jews and you Gentiles by making us all one family, breaking down the wall of contempt that used to separate us.

—Ephesians 2:14 (TLB)

Have you ever been in a situation that left you stressed, nervous, and anxious— feeling as though there could be no peace?

Job felt that way. In Job 3:26, he tells us, "I have no peace, no quietness. I have no rest; only trouble comes" (NLT). But that is not where Job's story ends. God restores Job, and blesses him more in the second half of his life than in the first (Job 42).

Philippians 4:6–7 tells us, "Don't worry about anything; instead, pray about everything. Tell God what you need, and thank him for all he has done. Then you will experience God's peace, which exceeds anything we can understand. His peace will guard your hearts and minds as you live in Christ Jesus" (NLT).

No matter how stressful our circumstances, if we will trust and obey Christ, keeping our mind fixed on Him, we will find peace.

Isaiah 26:3 tells us, "You will keep in perfect peace all who trust in you, all whose thoughts are fixed on you" (NLT)!

May your thoughts be fixed on Him now and always.

FEBRUARY 12

The Point of No Return

There is no use trying to bring you back to the Lord again if you have once understood the Good News and tasted for yourself the good things of heaven and shared in the Holy Spirit, and know how good the Word of God is, and felt the mighty powers of the world to come, and then have turned against God. You cannot bring yourself to repent again if you have nailed the Son of God to the cross again by rejecting him, holding him up to mocking and to public shame.

—Hebrews 6:4–6 (TLB)

It is a popular concept in some pulpits today to neglect preaching about the eternal fires of hell and the consequences of sin, although the New Living Translation of the Holy Bible mentions hell eighteen times. Time and again I hear pastors saying, "It's never too late to accept Christ." There is even a popular Christian song with the lyrics, "It's never too late to get back up again."

My friend, the Holy Bible tells us that one day it will be too late. There is a point of no return. One day the Bridegroom will return for His bride, and if we have not chosen to live for Him, the door to heaven will be shut on us (Matthew 25:1–13).

It seems as though we no longer understand what it means to be a Christian, a follower of Christ. Jesus told us in Matthew 7:21, "Not all who sound religious are really godly people. They may refer to me as 'Lord,' but still won't get to heaven. For the decisive question is whether they obey my Father in heaven" (TLB). It is not an easy road, and there is a cost—a high cost—for serving Christ. We must give up our selfish ways and allow God to have His way in our lives.

Have you truly done that today? May you let God have His way with you today.

FEBRUARY 13

The Love of My Life

Yet day by day the Lord also pours out his steadfast love upon me, and through the night I sing his songs and pray to God who gives me life.

—Psalm 42:8 (TLB)

Who is the love of your life? Is it a spouse, a child, a parent, or someone else?

Jesus longs to be the love of your life today and every day, and He doesn't play second fiddle to anyone else.

Exodus 34:14 tells us, "For you must worship no other gods, but only Jehovah, for he is a God who claims absolute loyalty and exclusive devotion" (TLB).

Isaiah 54:5 says, "For your Creator will be your husband; the Lord of Heaven's Armies is his name! He is your Redeemer, the Holy One of Israel, the God of all the earth" (NLT).

Have you placed someone else in God's rightful position? Do you care more about what that person thinks of you than what God thinks of you?

In Matthew 22:37, Jesus is speaking: "And he said to him, 'You shall love the Lord your God with all your heart and with all your soul and with all your mind'" (NLT).

Is Jesus the love of your life today?

May you give Him first place in your life each and every day that you have breath.

FEBRUARY 14

Be Mine

My health fails; my spirits droop, yet God remains! He is the strength of my heart; he is mine forever!

—Psalm 73:26 (TLB)

We may have many loves, but there is only one true love in all the world. That one true love is God.

God is the very definition of love.

First John 4:8 tells us, "But anyone who does not love does not know God, for God is love" (NLT).

When we have accepted Christ into our heart as Savior, He is ours forevermore, our *true* soul mate—and we are His.

The prophet Ezekiel, speaking of God's love for His chosen people, paints a beautiful word picture of our heavenly Father's love for us: "And when I passed by again, I saw that you were old enough for love. So I wrapped my cloak around you to cover your nakedness and declared my marriage vows. I made a covenant with you, says the Sovereign Lord, and you became mine" (Ezekiel 16:8 NLT).

Have you forgotten whom you belong to today?

May we remember that we are His and He is ours for every day of our lives.

FEBRUARY 15

Everlasting Love

For long ago the Lord had said to Israel: "I have loved you, O my people, with an everlasting love; with loving-kindness I have drawn you to me."

—Jeremiah 31:3 (TLB)

God's love for you knows no end. It endures through every circumstance, as 1 Corinthians 13:7 recounts: "Love never gives up, never loses faith, is always hopeful, and endures through every circumstance" (NLT).

Psalm 103:11 tells us, "For his unfailing love toward those who fear him is as great as the height of the heavens above the earth" (NLT)

In addition, Romans 8:38 says, "And I am convinced that nothing can ever separate us from God's love. Neither death nor life, neither angels nor demons, neither our fears for today nor our worries about tomorrow—not even the powers of hell can separate us from God's love" (NLT).

I know of no other love in all the world that comes close to comparing with God's love as described by Paul. It is so vast that we fail to fully comprehend it.

As Ephesians 3:19 reminds us, "May you experience the love of Christ, though it is too great to understand fully. Then you will be made complete with all the fullness of life and power that comes from God" (NLT).

I pray that you will not keep this love to yourself, but that you will share it with someone you encounter today, allowing God's Holy Spirit to flow through you.

FEBRUARY 16

Everlasting Life

Point out anything you find in me that makes you sad, and lead me along the path of everlasting life.

—Psalm 139:24 (TLB)

The true pathway of life is hard to find. There are many in this world who would lead us away from the path of everlasting life.

But the Holy Bible makes very plain the way to everlasting life.

Proverbs 10:17 says, "People who accept discipline are on the pathway to life, but those who ignore correction will go astray" (NLT).

John 17:3 tells us, "And this is the way to have eternal life—to know you, the only true God, and Jesus Christ, the one you sent to earth" (NLT).

When we get to know the person of Jesus Christ, the one true and living God, that knowledge will lead us into a walk that is in obedience to His divine commands because He is the very definition of love, as evidenced in His every dealing with us.

Second Corinthians 6:6 reminds us of the evidence of relationship with Christ: "We prove ourselves by our purity, our understanding, our patience, our kindness, by the Holy Spirit within us, and by our sincere love" (NLT).

May there be no mistaking that you are on the path that leads to everlasting life, and may you show someone else that way today.

FEBRUARY 17

Your Sin Will Find You Out

But if you don't do as you have said, then you will have sinned against the Lord, and you may be sure that your sin will catch up with you.

—NUMBERS 32:23 (TLB)

Have you ever been bothered by the fact that sinful people seem to "get away with" sinning far too often?

Proverbs 23:17 reminds us, "Don't envy sinners, but always continue to fear the Lord" (NLT).

God sees all and knows all. There are no secret sins that are veiled from Him.

Job 34:21 says, "For God watches how people live; he sees everything they do" (NLT).

Psalm 90:8 tells us, "You spread out our sins before you—our secret sins—and you see them all" (NLT).

When I was a little girl, I was often disturbed when others seemed not to get caught when doing wrong, whereas I was always called out for the tiniest infraction of the rules. Gratitude replaced the frustration as I grew, knowing that God was teaching me His way, the pathway of righteousness, obedience, and blessing.

"Teach me your ways, O Lord, that I may live according to your truth! Grant me purity of heart, so that I may honor you" (Psalm 86:11 NLT).

FEBRUARY 18

Shake It Off

Any city or home that doesn't welcome you—shake off the dust of that place from your feet as you leave.

—Matthew 10:14 (TLB)

Do you hold on to those who have rejected you?

If you have shared Christ's message with someone who refuses to accept Him and His message, then do as the Holy Bible tells you to do and shake that person off, provided it is not your spouse or your child.

The Holy Bible also tells us how we should deal with someone who professes to be a Christian yet is still walking in sin, unrepentant of it.

First Corinthians 5:11 instructs us, "I meant that you are not to associate with anyone who claims to be a believer yet indulges in sexual sin, or is greedy, or worships idols, or is abusive, or is a drunkard, or cheats people. Don't even eat with such people" (NLT).

Often, those who would become Christians see no difference at all between the way Christians and non-Christians live. In fact, some Christians live more wayward and disobedient lives than those who do not profess Christ. God wants us to be holy, distinct, and set apart for His purposes—living a life of light that brings glory and honor to Him. Such a life is attractive to others. They want what they see in us, like a moth drawn to a flame, when we walk in the light of God's truth.

May we live a life worthy of God's call so that we may spend our time sharing Christ with those who are eager to hear about Him.

The fields are white for the harvest. May we all do some pickin' today.

FEBRUARY 19

I Can See Clearly Now

Instantly (it was as though scales fell from his eyes) Paul could see and was immediately baptized. Then he ate and was strengthened.

—ACTS 9:18–19A (TLB)

After years of not being able to read or see clearly at all, my octogenarian mother had surgery to remove cataracts from her eyes. It was life-changing for her, as now the primarily immobile woman could read books, see dust bunnies, and recognize family members seated across the room. Her disposition and outlook changed, too. There was a renewed life and hope about her as she found purpose and began to drink up books and work puzzles once again.

She previously had no idea just how blind she had really become.

Years of sin and the world's evil influence can sometimes cause cataracts to grow on our spiritual eyes as well, altering our perspective and causing us to lose the proper focus in life.

Are you in need of spiritual cataract surgery?

John 9:39 says, "Then Jesus told him, 'I entered this world to render judgment—to give sight to the blind and to show those who think they see that they are blind'" (NLT).

Do you see clearly now, or are you spiritually blind?

May Jesus Christ remove the scales from your eyes today.

"I once was lost, but now am found. Was blind, but now I see."

FEBRUARY 20

First Things First

He was in Greece three months and was preparing to sail for Syria when he discovered a plot by the Jews against his life, so he decided to go north to Macedonia first.

—Exodus 20:3 (TLB)

It is the first commandment: we are to have no other gods but Him. God, the one true and living God, is to be the first, the last, the only one. When we have that right, all of the other priorities in our life will find their proper place.

Are you putting God first in your life?

In Matthew 6:33 Jesus tells us, "Seek the Kingdom of God above all else, and live righteously, and he will give you everything you need" (NLT).

There is no need to apologize to others because we have given God His proper place in our lives. Choosing to do so doesn't make everyday tasks in our life harder either. It is just the opposite

Don't let the world rob you of God, telling you that you just can't put Him first.

When God is first in every area of your life, He multiplies your time, energy, resources, and blessings.

FEBRUARY 21

Hurry Up and Wait

Don't be impatient. Wait for the Lord, and he will come and save you! Be brave, stouthearted, and courageous. Yes, wait and he will help you.

—Psalm 27:14 (TLB)

Every day our world seems to turn just a little bit faster. Have you noticed that?

Patience is a very rare commodity, and decisions are made at lightning speed. If we have to wait more than a minute for anything, we tend to think it is just too long, and we wonder what is wrong.

My friend, that is the world's way, but it is not God's way. God's timing is perfect in all things, and He often asks us to wait.

Jacob waited seven years for Rachel. The Israelites waited forty years to enter the Promised Land. Abraham waited one hundred years for Isaac. The Jews waited generations for the promised Messiah. And we wait now for His promised return.

Isaiah 40:31 says, "But those who wait on the Lord Shall renew their strength; they shall mount up with wings like eagles, they shall run and not be weary, they shall walk and not faint" (NKJV).

Will you wait for God today?

"Then Abraham waited patiently, and he received what God had promised" (Hebrews 6:15 NLT).

FEBRUARY 22

The Distracted Generation

Every young man who listens to me and obeys my instructions will be given wisdom and good sense.

—Proverbs 2:1–2 (TLB)

We live in a time that is filled to the brim with distractions. There are televisions, cell phones, laptops, tablets, and more. It seems as though everyone has not just one but many of these devices. We need only hop in the car to notice the distracted driver who sticks out like a sore thumb. Her texting has distracted her to the point that she has left thirty car lengths in front of her as she weaves back and forth just to stay in her own lane. She thinks no one notices.

Then there is the person in the office, airport, or grocery store who bumps into you because he is engrossed in his electronic device—lost in his own little world.

Lost. That is the condition of the majority of folks in the world.

Their god of choice is electronic. Electronic devices have captured their heart, their mind, and all of their time. Could it be that these devices have captured their soul too? Electronic devices are not bad in and of themselves, but they must have their proper place—not first place.

Nothing should ever steal our focus from God.

Proverbs 4:25 tells us, "Look straight ahead, and fix your eyes on what lies before you" (NLT).

Are you looking everywhere *but* straight ahead?

May we keep our eyes on Jesus, the champion who initiates and perfects our faith (Hebrews 12:2).

FEBRUARY 23

The Love That Will Not Let You Go

Your goodness and unfailing kindness shall be with me all of my life, and afterwards I will live with you forever in your home.

—Psalm 23:6 (TLB)

I have an acquaintance I'll call Shelly. Shelly can be annoying. Having grown up in a difficult family situation, she is at times very needy. That's because she's faced rejection. She was bounced from foster home to foster home growing up.

In each home, the parents told Shelly that they loved her, but as Shelly's neediness and longing for attention began to wear on the family, they each found reason to have her removed her from their home.

Then Shelly found God, and things changed. God made a permanent home inside Shelly's heart.

Ephesians 3:17 tells us, "Then Christ will make his home in your hearts as you trust in him. Your roots will grow down into God's love and keep you strong" (NLT).

Now Shelly has a permanent home with Jesus, and He won't ever let her go.

First Corinthians 13:7 says, "Love never gives up, never loses faith, is always hopeful, and endures through every circumstance" (NLT).

Real love lasts forever.

"Three things will last forever—faith, hope, and love—and the greatest of these is love" (1 Corinthians 13:13 NLT).

FEBRUARY 24

It's All About Who You Know

He saw to it that justice and help were given the poor and the needy and all went well for him. This is how a man lives close to God.

—JEREMIAH 22:16 (TLB)

People often say when trying to find a job or get certain things accomplished that it's all about who you know.

In life, it *is* all about who you know.

To know God is to honor Him by obeying His Word.

Jeremiah 42:6 says, "Whether we like it or not, we will obey the Lord our God to whom we are sending you with our plea. For if we obey him, everything will turn out well for us" (NLT).

When we know and obey God, following the path of righteousness, God will smooth out the road ahead of us.

Isaiah 26:7 tells us, "But for those who are righteous, the way is not steep and rough. You are a God who does what is right, and you smooth out the path ahead of them" (NLT).

Do you know Him, really know Him, today?

May we walk in obedience to Christ with every choice we make and every action we take, and may we never be fake.

FEBRUARY 25

The Center of Your Life

Don't become rich by extortion and robbery; if your riches increase, don't be proud.

—Psalm 62:10 (TLB)

Who or what is at the center of your life today?

There are many who make their living by stealing or extorting, and they don't even realize it. Some of them are in pulpits, and they call themselves pastors or teachers. Some of them are salespeople who bend and twist the truth just enough to make the sale. Then, they rejoice at the expansion of their bank account—and they repeat the deed over and over again.

Proverbs 10:2 tells us, "Tainted wealth has no lasting value, but right living can save your life" (NLT).

Are earthly treasures at the center of your life today? You can't take them with you.

Proverbs 28:6 says, "Better to be poor and honest than to be dishonest and rich" (NLT).

And Proverbs 23:5 tells us, "In the blink of an eye wealth disappears, for it will sprout wings and fly away like an eagle" (NLT).

May we each repent, relinquishing our hold on sin, making Christ the center of every area of our life today.

FEBRUARY 26

Friends in Low Places

Do this instead—start at the foot; and when your host sees you he will come and say, "Friend, we have a better place than this for you!" Thus you will be honored in front of all the other guests. For everyone who tries to honor himself shall be humbled; and he who humbles himself shall be honored.

—LUKE 14:10–11 (TLB)

Are you a name-dropper? Do you pride yourself on knowing people whom this world considers important?

God doesn't look at others the way the world does. He sees the inside of everyone, evaluating the true intentions of every heart.

Jeremiah 17:10 says, "But I, the Lord, search all hearts and examine secret motives. I give all people their due rewards, according to what their actions deserve" (NLT).

Jesus was a friend to people in low places (Matthew 11:19).

Do you have friends in low places, or are you a respecter of persons, seeing some lives as more valuable than others?

May we all follow the example of Jesus, who humbled Himself, becoming the servant of all, regardless of their worldly status.

FEBRUARY 27

Never Alone

If you love me, obey me; and I will ask the Father and he will give you another Comforter, and he will never leave you.

—JOHN 14:15–16 (TLB)

Jennifer, a happy mother of four children, had a husband who loved her. One day, Jennifer's world came crashing down around her. An eighteen-wheeler driven by an intoxicated driver slammed into the family SUV, killing Jennifer's precious family. Jennifer was the lone survivor.

After years of experiencing survivor's guilt, feeling very alone, and trying unsuccessfully to pick up the pieces of her life, Jennifer handed all of the broken pieces of her life over to God. She said a prayer that went something like this:

Father,

Iknowyouhaveaplanforallthings, though Idon'tunderstandit.

I give you all the hurt I feel, and the broken pieces of my life. I feel so alone. Put me together however you want, and help me to know that I'm not alone.

Amen.

The next day, Jennifer received a call from a friend asking her to volunteer her time at a local nursing home three times a week. She accepted the offer. The pain and loneliness Jennifer once felt have now been replaced with the joy of giving to others who are lonely too. She now feels as though the patients in the nursing home are her special new family.

Psalm 68:6a tells us, "God places the lonely in families; he sets the prisoners free and gives them joy" (NLT).

May you always remember that you are never alone.

FEBRUARY 28

Gracious Forgiveness

And what a difference between man's sin and God's forgiveness! For this one man, Adam, brought death to many through his sin. But this one man, Jesus Christ, brought forgiveness to many through God's mercy.

—Romans 5:15 (TLB)

Do you have a tendency to focus on the negative? I think that to do so sometimes is just human nature. But it's not God's nature

In the verse above, it is clear to see that the good God does far outweighs any bad we could ever do. Can you grasp that? God's forgiveness, His wonderful grace toward us, is much, much greater than our sin.

The realization of this, when it finally sinks in, cannot help but change our every thought, our every approach to the choices we have in this life.

Psalm 33:5 says, "He loves whatever is just and good; the unfailing love of the Lord fills the earth" (NLT).

It is little wonder, then, that Paul said in Philippians 4:8, "And now, dear brothers and sisters, one final thing. Fix your thoughts on what is true, and honorable, and right, and pure, and lovely, and admirable. Think about things that are excellent and worthy of praise" (NLT).

May the goodness of God be the focus throughout your entire life.

FEBRUARY 29

The Legacy We Leave

Honor your father and mother, that you may have a long, good life in the land the Lord your God will give you.

—Exodus 20:12 (TLB)

Everyone has a different family.

Growing up, I had a mother who was filled to the brim with youthful exuberance and joy. She was the one who told me I could do anything and be anything.

My father tempered my mother's youthful exuberance and joy with the practical realities of life. He taught me to work hard and to be responsible.

Together, my mother and father were the two most imperfect perfect parents a child could ever ask for, though such may not have appeared to be the case from the outside. I pray that my life brings honor to them. I recall all of the times they cared for me as a sick rascal, stayed up to explain why there was no need to be afraid of the bogeyman, and checked under the bed for monsters. I am blessed to have gone on long driving vacations during which we talked about such things as where water comes from and how bees make honey. My parents taught me the value of time used wisely and the value of money.

But most important of all, they taught me about God.

No matter what else my parents are remembered for, the legacy they have left me is priceless. It is a legacy of loving God, fearing God, and knowing God—personally.

What legacy will you leave behind?

MARCH 1

Whom Are You Pleasing?

Let me add this, dear brothers: You already know how to please God in your daily living, for you know the commands we gave you from the Lord Jesus himself. Now we beg you—yes, we demand of you in the name of the Lord Jesus—that you live more and more closely to that ideal.

—1 Thessalonians 4:1–2 (TLB)

Are you concerned with what others think about you?

Do you ever change your actions, your direction, based on the opinion of others?

The apostle Peter had that tendency. In Galatians 2, we read the account of Peter caving in to the pressure of the Jews around him to impose the Jewish tradition on new Gentile converts. Paul confronts Peter with this, reminding him that pleasing anyone except Christ is hypocrisy, and leads us astray. When we do this, we in turn end up leading others astray (Galatians 2:13).

Philippians 2:13 tells us, "For God is working in you, giving you the desire and the power to do what pleases him" (NLT).

When we walk with Christ, He gives us both the desire and the power to please Him and only Him.

So, whom are you trying to please? Pray the following prayer:

Dear Heavenly Father,

May I long to please you and only you, completely unconcerned with what others may think of me.

Amen.

MARCH 2

The Sin of Omission

Remember, too, that knowing what is right to do and then not doing it is sin.

—James 4:17 (TLB)

Often we become so complacent in our walk with God that we think as long as we do not intentionally or overtly break the Ten Commandments, we are doing okay.

But we're not doing okay.

God has a higher standard for us. Not only does He desire that we obey His commands, but also He wants us to be in such a close personal relationship with Him that we are mindful of His every prodding upon our heart and our soul, and that we obey the Spirit's prodding.

Are you attentive to the Spirit's nudging in your life? Do you hear His voice?

Isaiah 30:21 says, "Your own ears will hear him. Right behind you a voice will say, 'This is the way you should go,' whether to the right or to the left" (NLT).

When you hear His voice, do you obey it or dismiss it?

May we be mindful of the sin of omission, careful to do the things we know we ought—today and every day.

MARCH 3

His Unmistakable Voice

Anyone refusing to walk through the gate into a sheepfold, who sneaks over the wall, must surely be a thief! For a shepherd comes through the gate. The gatekeeper opens the gate for him, and the sheep hear his voice and come to him; and he calls his own sheep by name and leads them out.

—John 10:1–3 (TLB)

Do you know someone with an unmistakable voice? I'm talking about the kind of voice that you can pick out in a crowd—a voice that is distinguishable from any other.

My mother has that kind of voice. It is a mix of calming teddy bear and Shirley Temple, with just a dash of Bette Davis thrown in. It is a distinctive voice, one that is always a comfort to me when I hear it. When I was a child, my mother was often tasked with helping at the church in the Women's Missionary Union. During those times, I was left in the care of others across the hall in the church nursery. I spent many hours in the church nursery, but as long as I could hear my mother's voice across the hall, I felt comfort. As the sound of her voice drew closer, I knew she was coming for me. The nursery worker would open up the baby gate, and I couldn't wait to run and jump into my mother's arms.

Jesus's voice is unmistakable. There is no voice in all the world as distinctive as His. Do you know that voice? He leads us on right paths, staying close beside us (Psalm 23). He calls us by name. He knows us, and we are His. His voice is peace and comfort like nothing else in all the world, and I just can't wait to run and jump into His arms.

Do you hear Him? He's speaking to you. Shh. Be still and listen for His unmistakable voice.

MARCH 4

Tear Down the Walls

It was faith that brought the walls of Jericho tumbling down after the people of Israel had walked around them seven days as God had commanded them.

—Hebrews 11:30 (TLB)

I remember well the words spoken by President Ronald Reagan in his address from the Brandenburg Gate on June 12, 1987: "Mr. Gorbachev, tear down this wall!" The challenge served as a call to change. It was a call to freedom.

Just as the collapse of the Berlin Wall brought freedom and expansion to Eastern Europeans, the destruction of the walls of Jericho brought freedom and expansion to the Jews.

But there are still walls in our world that need removing, and they are within the Christian faith. We have built denominations on account of reasons big and small that have served to alienate, separate, divide, and imprison us.

Ephesians 4:5–6 tells us, "There is one Lord, one faith, one baptism, one God and Father of all, who is over all, in all, and living through all" (NLT).

We must learn to love our fellow Christian believers as God intended.

First Peter 3:8 says, "Finally, all of you should be of one mind. Sympathize with each other. Love each other as brothers and sisters. Be tenderhearted, and keep a humble attitude" (NLT).

May we tear down the walls, and may we be united with all who fear God, those who know His laws (Psalm 119:79).

MARCH 5

God Hog

We loved you dearly—so dearly that we gave you not only God's message, but our own lives too.

—1 Thessalonians 2:8 (TLB)

Are you a God hog?

A God hog is someone who keeps God all to herself, never sharing the amazing blessings she receives as a result of knowing Him personally.

Oh, I know all the excuses, such as how hard it is to share, how people just aren't interested anymore, how people will think you're an oddball, that people don't understand, that you'll lose your job if you share at work.

But what about the consequences of *not* sharing Christ?

Mark 8:38 tells us, "If anyone is ashamed of me and my message in these adulterous and sinful days, the Son of Man will be ashamed of that person when he returns in the glory of his Father with the holy angels" (NLT).

O that we would have a heart like David, as expressed in Psalm 71:17: "O God, you have taught me from my earliest childhood, and I constantly tell others about the wonderful things you do" (NLT).

May the love of God fill our hearts and lives so much that we cannot help but share Him with others every moment of every day, in everything that we do, every word that we say, and the way in which we conduct our lives.

MARCH 6

Open, Sesame

Yes, I am the Gate. Those who come in by way of the Gate will be saved and will go in and out and find green pastures. The thief's purpose is to steal, kill and destroy. My purpose is to give life in all its fullness.

—John 10:9–10 (NLT)

There are many wolves in the world masquerading as sheep, masquerading as good shepherds. The Holy Bible tells us in Matthew 7:15, "Beware of false prophets who come disguised as harmless sheep but are really vicious wolves" (NLT).

But Jesus doesn't stop there. He wants us to be aware and to know exactly how to tell the sheep from the wolves. Matthew 7:16 tells us, "You can identify them by their fruit, that is, by the way they act. Can you pick grapes from thornbushes, or figs from thistles" (NLT)? Jesus also tells us how to deal with the wolves we meet in the world. We are to be as shrewd as snakes and as harmless as doves (Matthew 10:16).

In the story "Ali Baba and the Forty Thieves," the phrase "Open, sesame" is used to open the mouth of a cave in which vast treasure is hidden.

When we follow after the Good Shepherd, He opens freely all the hidden treasures of His kingdom to us, giving us a rich and satisfying life—better than any treasure the world has ever known. But there is no catchphrase that will open this treasure door. No, the only thing that will open this treasure door is having a personal relationship with the Shepherd, Jesus Christ.

May we look past the wolves, thieves, and robbers of the world to find the Good Shepherd's gate, through which we may come and go freely, finding good pastures. No "open, sesame" required.

MARCH 7

Our Personal Advisor

I will instruct you (says the Lord) and guide you along the best pathway for your life; I will advise you and watch your progress.

—Psalm 32:8 (TLB)

When I was a freshman in college, my advisor selected all my classes for the first semester, and things went very well. I wasn't overloaded, I didn't feel stressed or overburdened while working a part-time job, and I made good grades.

The second semester was a different story. With the success of the first semester in tow, I felt I could go it alone and do things my way. So, while all of my classmates were meeting with their advisors for class selections, I decided I didn't need an advisor.

The results spoke for themselves. Going it alone proved to give me my worst semester in college—in every way.

When we choose to go it alone, without God, the results are the same. We don't know the best pathway to take on our own. But God promises to guide us along the best pathway for our life, and He promises to advise and watch over us.

Have you left the watchful care of your Personal Advisor? He's ready for you to return to Him today.

MARCH 8

A Vested Interest

I am the Good Shepherd. The Good Shepherd lays down his life for the sheep. A hired man will run when he sees a wolf coming and will leave the sheep, for they aren't his and he isn't their shepherd. And so the wolf leaps on them and scatters the flock. The hired man runs because he is hired and has no real concern for the sheep.

—John 10:11–13 (TLB)

If you've ever owned a business, you know that no one cares about your business like you do. You may hire very good people, but they just don't have the same vested interest that you have. If there is a fire, the hired help will go home. You are the one who will need to clean up the smoke damage.

As a parent, I have the same type of vested interest in my children. When I leave them in the care of others, those other people may do a good job, but they do not have the same depth of interest, care, duty, or responsibility that I have as my children's mother.

It is like that with our heavenly Father. He made us. He made all the delicate inner parts of our body, and knit us together in our mother's womb (Psalm 139:13). He loves us farther than the moon and back. There is no one on the earth, on the moon, or on the stars who could possibly love us more or have more invested in our success than our Father, our Savior, or our Jesus.

Christ sacrificed His life for us. How could we ever think of living our life apart from Him?

"Savior, like a shepherd lead us, much we need thy tender care."[1]

---

[1] From "Savior, Like a Shepherd Lead Us," lyrics by Dorothy A. Thrupp, 1836.

MARCH 9

One Flock

I am the Good Shepherd and know my own sheep, and they know me, just as my Father knows me and I know the Father; and I lay down my life for the sheep. I have other sheep, too, in another fold. I must bring them also, and they will heed my voice; and there will be one flock with one Shepherd.

—John 10:14–16 (TLB)

Baptist, Catholic, Methodist, Episcopal, Lutheran, Church of Christ, Bible Fellowship—and the list of Christian denominations goes on. Even within these denominations there are denominations.

But is this really what Jesus had in mind? The verse above tells us that Jesus had in mind one flock with one Shepherd.

Often, Christians quibble over the smallest detail, eager to demonize the actions of others, rather than seeking love in the matter. Romans 14:1 tells us, "Accept other believers who are weak in faith, and don't argue with them about what they think is right or wrong" (NLT).

In John 17, there is a beautiful prayer that Jesus prays to the Father before His betrayal and crucifixion. It is a prayer for all generations, and it perfectly depicts His desire for us.

John 17:22–23 says, "I have given them the glory you gave me, so they may be one as we are one. I am in them and you are in me. May they experience such perfect unity that the world will know that you sent me and that you love them as much as you love me" (NLT).

May all of God's sheep come together in the unity and love that He has purposed for us.

MARCH 10

Complete Control

> THE FATHER LOVES ME BECAUSE I LAY DOWN MY LIFE THAT I MAY HAVE IT BACK AGAIN. NO ONE CAN KILL ME WITHOUT MY CONSENT—I LAY DOWN MY LIFE VOLUNTARILY. FOR I HAVE THE RIGHT AND POWER TO LAY IT DOWN WHEN I WANT TO AND ALSO THE RIGHT AND POWER TO TAKE IT AGAIN. FOR THE FATHER HAS GIVEN ME THIS RIGHT.
>
> —JOHN 10:17–18 (TLB)

Are you a control freak? Maybe you live with that special someone who must do what he wants, when he wants, and how he wants to. He is determined to have complete control, yet he ends up angry and frustrated because things are never quite the way he would like them to be.

There is one who relinquishes control of you and of me, allowing us the free will to choose whether or not we will follow Him. His way is perfect and is best, yet He loves us so much that He will not force His way upon us. If we allow the Holy Spirit to control us, the end result is life—both now and in the world to come.

Romans 8:6 tells us, "So letting your sinful nature control your mind leads to death. But letting the Spirit control your mind leads to life and peace" (NLT).

Who is controlling your life today?

MARCH 11

Gumballs and Giving

It is possible to give away and become richer! It is also possible to hold on too tightly and lose everything. Yes, the liberal man shall be rich! By watering others, he waters himself.

—PROVERBS 11:24–25 (TLB)

I grew up as a preacher's kid in a low-income neighborhood on the north side of Houston, Texas. In our church, there were many very generous people. One man in particular often brought our family groceries from his small grocery store when they passed their sell-by dates and had to be taken off the store shelves yet were still perfectly fine to eat. He brought ice cream, fine meats, and candy—all the finest food treasures.

One day, this generous man brought my brother, my sister, and I three five-pound bags of multicolored gumballs, one bag for each of us. The gumballs sparkled in the bag as if they were gold. I treasured mine, counting them and sorting them by color. While I was in the midst of this activity one afternoon, my older brother's friend, Wiley, asked if he might have a gumball from my prized collection. He was met with a quick retort of, "Jimmy has some. Get some from Jimmy." After I'd said this, I returned to counting and sorting my treasure.

I never forgot the shock and disbelief on the face of my brother's friend because I had been so stingy, hoarding, and greedy. Sadly, God had to take more drastic measures to lovingly teach me the simple lesson of being generous.

What about you? Have you learned to give freely from the storehouse of good things God has blessed you with?

Proverbs 21:26 tells us, "Some people are always greedy for more, but the godly love to give" (NLT)!

May we give freely out of the abundance God has given us today and every day.

MARCH 12

A Foolproof Recipe

So give yourselves humbly to God. Resist the devil and he will flee from you. And when you draw close to God, God will draw close to you. Wash your hands, you sinners, and let your hearts be filled with God alone to make them pure and true to him.

—JAMES 4:7–8 (TLB)

Do you have a special foolproof recipe for something? I do.

The recipe is for chocolate chip cookies, which I have baked since I was a child. The cookies come out perfectly every time as long as I carefully follow the recipe. If I don't, the cookies don't turn out like they should.

Have you ever noticed that life works like that, too?

God has given us a foolproof recipe for following Him and avoiding evil. If we humble ourselves and resist the Devil, the Devil will flee from us. And if we come close to God, He will come close to us!

God makes it that easy for us.

If the recipe God has provided is difficult for us to follow, it is a reflection of the condition of our heart. The difficulty is a result of the fact that our loyalty is divided between God and the world. When this happens, things don't turn out right, as they should.

May we follow God's foolproof recipe for our lives so that we may have a life that is full of light and joy (Proverbs 13:9).

MARCH 13

The Belching Fool

The tongue of the wise makes knowledge appealing, but the mouth of a fool belches out foolishness.

—Proverbs 15:2 (NLT)

Picture the scene with me. You are attending a formal dinner, a black tie occasion. The room is quiet save for the delicate clinking of silverware. The conversation is muted.

Then, breaking the silence and the mood, someone belches loudly, mouth open, at the table next to yours. Chances are pretty high that the maître d' and the other people seated at the table neither is pleased nor finds it funny.

When we speak apart from the wisdom and knowledge of God, our words tend to become utter nonsense; we belch forth foolishness.

Proverbs 12:23 tells us, "The wise don't make a show of their knowledge, but fools broadcast their foolishness" (NLT).

Proverbs 14:3 says, "A fool's proud talk becomes a rod that beats him, but the words of the wise keep them safe" (NLT).

"So be careful how you live. Don't live like fools, but like those who are wise" (Ephesians 5:15 NLT).

MARCH 14

Home Alone

Then afterwards he went up into the hills to pray. Night fell, and out on the lake the disciples were in trouble. For the wind had risen and they were fighting heavy seas.

—Matthew 14:23–24 (TLB)

Spending time alone is often viewed in a negative light, but the Holy Bible teaches us that being alone is not always a bad thing.

Jesus often retreated to pray, as Matthew 14:23 tells us: "After sending them home, he went up into the hills by himself to pray. Night fell while he was there alone" (NLT).

And Jesus taught us in Matthew 6:6 to go away by ourselves to pray: "But when you pray, go away by yourself, shut the door behind you, and pray to your Father in private. Then your Father, who sees everything, will reward you."

These are times when it is good to be home alone.

But we must remember that if God is our Savior, we are never truly alone. As John 14:16 tells us, "And I will ask the Father, and he will give you another Advocate, who will never leave you" (NLT).

May you spend your home-alone time in prayer to the Father, so that He may see and reward you.

MARCH 15

Healing Words

Some people like to make cutting remarks, but the words of the wise soothe and heal.

—Proverbs 12:18 (TLB)

Have you ever been in a difficult situation and experienced the loving, encouraging words of someone wise? Such wonderful people often never realize the immeasurable beauty of their words or how those words heal us.

Proverbs 16:24 says, "Kind words are like honey—sweet to the soul and healthy for the body" (NLT).

It is equally beautiful to hear words of wise counsel. Proverbs 25:11 tells us, "Timely advice is lovely, like golden apples in a silver basket."

Are you a fountain of healing words?

When our lives are overflowing with the Spirit of the living God, His love, kindness, and wisdom can't help but pour out of us all the time.

Are His healing words pouring out of you?

"And may the Lord make your love for one another and for all people grow and overflow, just as our love for you overflows" (1 Thessalonians 3:12 NLT).

MARCH 16

Going into the Closet

But when you pray, go away by yourself, all alone, and shut the door behind you and pray to your Father secretly, and your Father, who knows your secrets, will reward you.

—Matthew 6:6 (TLB)

Our times of prayer and communion with God are precious. He calls us to come away with Him, to spend special time with Him in quiet private conversation, just us and God.

When I think of the awesomeness of this opportunity, I am reminded of Psalm 8:4, which says, "What are mere mortals that you should think about them, human beings that you should care for them?"

Our prayers to the Father should never be for show. They should never be for the benefit of any ears other than God's.

Spending time with God in prayer is also an important part of guarding against temptation.

Jesus tells us in Matthew 26:41, "Keep watch and pray, so that you will not give in to temptation. For the spirit is willing, but the body is weak" (NLT)!

And He wants us to be persistent in prayer, as Matthew 7:7 reminds us: "Keep on asking, and you will receive what you ask for. Keep on seeking, and you will find. Keep on knocking, and the door will be opened to you" (NLT).

May you realize the joy of private personal communion with the Father every day for the rest of your life.

MARCH 17

Wearing Green

Even in old age they will still produce fruit and be vital and green.

—Psalm 92:14 (TLB)

What color are you wearing today?

I don't mean your clothing. No, I'm talking about the part of you that everyone sees apart from your clothing. It is your righteousness or your unrighteousness.

Isaiah 61:10 tells us, "I am overwhelmed with joy in the Lord my God! For he has dressed me with the clothing of salvation and draped me in a robe of righteousness. I am like a bridegroom dressed for his wedding or a bride with her jewels" (NLT).

Psalm 92:12–13 says, "But the godly will flourish like palm trees and grow strong like the cedars of Lebanon. For they are transplanted to the Lord's own house. They flourish in the courts of our God" (NLT).

What beautiful promises we have from our loving heavenly Father. How could we not surround ourselves with all that is good, all that is God?

May we become enraptured with the person of Jesus Christ through constant prayer and the reading of His Word, so that we may be encouraged by His promises and His truth, both now and forevermore.

MARCH 18

My Everything

He is a father to the fatherless; he gives justice to the widows, for he is holy.

—Psalm 68:5 (TLB)

If Jesus Christ is your Savior, then you lack no good thing. In this fallen world we live in, sometimes it is difficult to get our minds around this truth.

Psalm 34:10 tells us, "Even strong young lions sometimes go hungry, but those who trust in the Lord will lack no good thing" (NLT).

God is everything we need, whenever we need it. He is our Father, as today's verse reminds us. He is our husband (Isaiah 54:5). He is our healer (Exodus 15:26). He is our refuge and strength (Psalm 46:1). He is our comforter (John 14:16). He is our defender (Proverbs 22:23). Our heavenly Father is all of this and more.

Have you experienced God meeting any of these needs in your own life?

O that we would only come to fully realize this truth in our lives today, and know all that the Father can be to each and every one of us.

MARCH 19

Real Stress Relief

In my distress and anguish your commandments comfort me.

—Psalm 119:143 (TLB)

Are you feeling stressed today?

David knew pressure and stress all too well. Much like David, we face stresses in life, some of which are not of our own making and some of which are. In either case, the burden we carry is often overwhelming to the point that we become physically ill.

Do you see the flaw in this prescription? The burdens that we carry are things that *we* shouldn't be carrying at all.

God's Word tells us in Matthew 11:28–30, "Then Jesus said, 'Come to me, all of you who are weary and carry heavy burdens, and I will give you rest. Take my yoke upon you. Let me teach you, because I am humble and gentle at heart, and you will find rest for your souls. For my yoke is easy to bear, and the burden I give you is light'" (NLT).

Psalm 55:22 says, "Give your burdens to the Lord, and he will take care of you. He will not permit the godly to slip and fall" (NLT).

If you're feeling stressed today, remember that real relief is just a conscious choice away—the choice of giving it to God.

MARCH 20

Have a Little Talk with Jesus

And when you draw close to God, God will draw close to you. Wash your hands, you sinners, and let your hearts be filled with God alone to make them pure and true to him.

—James 4:8 (TLB)

It is impossible for us to resist the temptations in this world without spending time with our Savior, our God, our Jesus. We cannot distance ourselves from Him while living in this evil world and expect to have any kind of relationship with Him.

Do you draw close to God daily? It is the only way to be pure and to have a real relationship with Him.

Are you putting the things of the world ahead of your relationship with Christ?

Luke 12:21 tells us, "Yes, a person is a fool to store up earthly wealth but not have a rich relationship with God" (NLT).

We can't expect to have a relationship with anyone we don't know or spend time with. Have you had a little talk with Jesus today?

MARCH 21

A Gentle and Quiet Spirit

Be beautiful inside, in your hearts, with the lasting charm of a gentle and quiet spirit that is so precious to God.

—1 Peter 3:4 (TLB)

There is a beautiful woman I know. Her inward beauty is so striking that I do not even notice her outward appearance. She is gentle, quiet, and restrained, and when she speaks, her words are full of wisdom. Everything about her exudes God to others and is a beautiful picture of God's complete love for us. She is clothed in His love.

Colossians 3:12 says, "Since God chose you to be the holy people he loves, you must clothe yourselves with tenderhearted mercy, kindness, humility, gentleness, and patience" (NLT).

Isaiah 32:17 tells us, "And this righteousness will bring peace. Yes, it will bring quietness and confidence forever" (NLT).

Do you have a gentle and quiet spirit? It is precious to God, and is a reflection of His life, His purpose being fulfilled in you.

May you clothe yourself in all that is God so that others may see, may know, and may desire a relationship with our loving heavenly Father.

MARCH 22

God's Yardstick

Oh, don't worry, I wouldn't dare say that I am as wonderful as these other men who tell you how good they are! Their trouble is that they are only comparing themselves with each other and measuring themselves against their own little ideas. What stupidity!

—2 Corinthians 10:12 (TLB)

Whom do you use as your standard of comparison? Do you use the world as your standard?

Using the world as our yardstick is only natural, but therein lies the problem. God is divine, and so is His standard for us.

Romans 8:9 tells us, "But you are not controlled by your sinful nature. You are controlled by the Spirit if you have the Spirit of God living in you. (And remember that those who do not have the Spirit of Christ living in them do not belong to him at all)" (NLT).

Choosing to live by the Holy Spirit's power is a choice, an act of the will. It is an act of faith. We cannot attain God's standard apart from the sacrifice of Jesus and the indwelling of the Holy Spirit.

Romans 8:3 says, "The law of Moses was unable to save us because of the weakness of our sinful nature. So God did what the law could not do. He sent his own Son in a body like the bodies we sinners have. And in that body God declared an end to sin's control over us by giving his Son as a sacrifice for our sins" (NLT).

May we put an end to using anything in the world as our standard, and may God's Word be our standard of measurement.

MARCH 23

If Tomorrow Never Comes

For the soul of every living thing is in the hand of God, and the breath of all mankind.

—Job 12:10 (TLB)

What if today was your last day on earth? Would knowing that cause you to do anything differently?

We should live every day that God has blessed us with as though it is our very last, for we know not when that day will come.

James 4:14 tells us, "How do you know what your life will be like tomorrow? Your life is like the morning fog—it's here a little while, then it's gone" (NLT).

It may not be death that ends our life on this earth. There is a day coming when our Lord and Savior will return to take us home.

First Thessalonians 5:2 says, "For you know quite well that the day of the Lord's return will come unexpectedly, like a thief in the night" (NLT).

Do you know someone who needs to know the Savior? The Holy Bible tells us that today is the day of salvation. One day it *will* be too late for us to receive Him as Savior and Lord.

Second Corinthians 6:2 reminds us, "For God says, 'At just the right time, I heard you. On the day of salvation, I helped you.' Indeed, the 'right time' is now. Today is the day of salvation" (NLT).

May we never forget to make the most of the time we are given and to take every opportunity we have to do what is right.

MARCH 24

I Would Never Do That

Dear brothers, if a Christian is overcome by some sin, you who are godly should gently and humbly help him back onto the right path, remembering that next time it might be one of you who is in the wrong.

—Galatians 6:1 (TLB)

Do you ever feel as though there are certain sins you are immune to or just don't struggle with?

I have felt this way myself, only to fall prey to the very sin I was sure I had mastered. The truth is that apart from Christ, we can do nothing (John 15:5).

The Holy Bible tells us in 1 Corinthians 10:12, "If you think you are standing strong, be careful not to fall" (NLT).

Proverbs 16:18 says, "Pride goes before destruction, and haughtiness before a fall" (NLT).

God's Word also reminds us that when we have broken one of God's laws, it is as if we have broken them all. As James 2:10 reminds us, "For the person who keeps all of the laws except one is as guilty as a person who has broken all of God's laws."

What is the solution? The Holy Bible gives us that, too.

In Proverbs 22:4 we find, "True humility and fear of the Lord lead to riches, honor, and long life" (NLT).

May we remain in Christ, our strength and the source of all good things.

MARCH 25

Love Found a Way

Jesus told him, "I am the Way—yes, and the Truth and the Life. No one can get to the Father except by means of me."

—John 14:6 (TLB)

There is a popular notion in today's society that there are many ways to God, but there is a problem with that popular notion, namely that it's not true.

This verse of scripture tells us plainly that there is only one way to the Father, and that way is through Jesus Christ, His Son.

Knowing Him is the only way to have eternal life.

John 17:3 says, "And this is the way to have eternal life—to know you, the only true God, and Jesus Christ, the one you sent to earth" (NLT).

So, have you told the misguided ones? Have you given them His message?

This message is truth. Truth, by its very nature, is confrontational. It is direct. But don't let that stop you from sharing it.

God found a way to show us His love through His Son, Jesus Christ. And He shows us this same love in ways big and small each and every day.

May we not rest until we have shared His truth with someone today.

MARCH 26

Conflicted by Conflict

A dry crust eaten in peace is better than steak every day along with argument and strife.

—Proverbs 17:1 (TLB)

I don't know about you, but I am not someone who wakes up in the morning looking forward to conflict. The Holy Bible tells us that we are to be seekers of peace, not conflict.

Romans 12:18 says, "Do all that you can to live in peace with everyone" (NLT).

But what about those times of unavoidable conflict? How do we handle those times?

Proverbs 15:1 tells us, "A gentle answer deflects anger, but harsh words make tempers flare" (NLT).

Sometimes it is simply the manner in which we deliver information that is conflict-causing in nature that makes all the difference.

Jesus Himself was no stranger to conflict. John 10:22–42 tells of one such instance. Jesus is asked by the religious leaders to tell them who He really is. Jesus gives them His answer, yet they want to stone Him. Each time Jesus speaks, His words communicate truth and seek to point others in the right direction. He leaves the end result in the Father's hands.

Our words should communicate truth and point others in the right direction as well. Does this mean that others will always listen and see things our way? Perhaps not. They may want to stone us, too.

But the results are in the Father's hands.

MARCH 27

The Only Work God Wants

Jesus told them, "This is the will of God, that you believe in the one he has sent."

—John 6:29 (TLB)

We know that faith without works is dead, as James 2:26 tells us. "Just as the body is dead without breath, so also faith is dead without good works" (NLT).

But what is the work that God wants, the work that He requires?

This passage of scripture in the book of John tells us exactly what God wants. He makes it very plain and uncomplicated for us. The only work God wants from you and from me is for us to believe in Jesus.

Is this an easy task, or is it especially burdensome?

The tasks that God sets before us are never burdensome.

In Matthew 11:28–30, we read, "Then Jesus said, 'Come to me, all of you who are weary and carry heavy burdens, and I will give you rest. Take my yoke upon you. Let me teach you, because I am humble and gentle at heart, and you will find rest for your souls. For my yoke is easy to bear, and the burden I give you is light'" (NLT).

Are you doing the work God wants you to do—believing in Jesus?

If you truly believe in Him, it will change every single thing that you say and do—now and forever.

MARCH 28

It's Not Natural

Yet these false teachers carelessly go right on living their evil, immoral lives, degrading their bodies and laughing at those in authority over them, even scoffing at the Glorious Ones.

—Jude 1:8 (TLB)

The life that we live when Christ rules and reigns within us is not the natural life we see lived out by the majority of the world.

Life with Christ is supernatural.

The natural life is life lived in rebellion against God and the things of His Spirit. This life ends in death, both natural death and spiritual death.

In Galatians 6:8, we read, "Those who live only to satisfy their own sinful nature will harvest decay and death from that sinful nature. But those who live to please the Spirit will harvest everlasting life from the Spirit" (NLT).

The supernatural life lived with Christ, with His divine nature dwelling within us, is constantly miraculous.

Second Peter 1:4 reads, "And because of his glory and excellence, he has given us great and precious promises. These are the promises that enable you to share his divine nature and escape the world's corruption caused by human desires" (NLT).

May His divine nature consume every evil that may come against you today and every day.

MARCH 29

Caution: Hazard Ahead

Save some by snatching them as from the very flames of hell itself. And as for others, help them to find the Lord by being kind to them, but be careful that you yourselves aren't pulled along into their sins. Hate every trace of their sin while being merciful to them as sinners.

—JUDE 1:23 (TLB)

Do you know someone who is struggling in sin?

The Holy Bible tells us in Galatians 6:1, "Dear brothers and sisters, if another believer is overcome by some sin, you who are godly should gently and humbly help that person back onto the right path. And be careful not to fall into the same temptation yourself" (NLT).

Helping others back onto the right path can be hazardous. We often make excuses for our failure to help others for fear they will find us to be judgmental. Or we may be too self-important to help others escape the pitfalls of sin.

Galatians 6:3 reminds us, "If you think you are too important to help someone, you are only fooling yourself. You are not that important" (NLT). When we are gentle and humble in our approach, we need only leave the results of our actions to God.

The greater concern in snatching others from the stronghold of sin should be falling into the same sin ourselves. But this should not keep us from helping to restore our wandering brothers and sisters.

James 5:19–20 tells us, "My dear brothers and sisters, if someone among you wanders away from the truth and is brought back, you can be sure that whoever brings the sinner back from wandering will save that person from death and bring about the forgiveness of many sins" (NLT).

MARCH 30

Preparing the Way

And you, my little son, shall be called the prophet of the glorious God, for you will prepare the way for the Messiah.

—Luke 1:76 (TLB)

John the Baptist prepared the way for our Lord Jesus Christ and the message He delivered first to the Jew and then to the Gentile. When Jesus spoke and ministered to others, they often called to mind the preparatory message they first heard from John.

John 1:6–7 tells us, "God sent a man, John the Baptist, to tell about the light so that everyone might believe because of his testimony" (NLT).

One day, Jesus will return (Acts 1:11). You and I are to prepare the way for our Savior's return. We do this by the way that we live each and every day.

The Word of God tells us that in that day when our Lord returns, the accuser, Satan, will be defeated.

Revelation 12:11 says, "And they have defeated him by the blood of the lamb and by their testimony. And they did not love their lives so much that they were afraid to die" (NLT).

Are you preparing the way for our Savior's return, or do you love your life too much to lose it for Him?

May we never forget John 12:25, which reads, "Those who love their life in this world will lose it. Those who care nothing for their life in this world will keep it for eternity" (NLT).

MARCH 31

Bombs Away

Have you visited the treasuries of the snow, or seen where hail is made and stored? For I have reserved it for the time when I will need it in war.

—Job 38:22–23 (TLB)

God's Word tells us that there is a time for war and a time for peace (Ecclesiastes 3:8).

My friend, we are in a time of war today. Satan's army is attacking.

Ephesians 6:12 reminds us, "For we are not fighting against flesh-and-blood enemies, but against evil rulers and authorities of the unseen world, against mighty powers in this dark world, and against evil spirits in the heavenly places" (NLT).

So how do we fight back against such a foe?

God has given us a mighty weapon that no evil can match. That weapon is prayer.

First Chronicles 5:20 tells us what the tribes east of the Jordan did when they sought victory in battle: "They cried out to God during the battle, and he answered their prayer because they trusted in him. So the Hagrites and all their allies were defeated" (NLT).

James 5:16b reminds us, "The earnest prayer of a righteous person has great power and produces wonderful results" (NLT).

It is time we dropped to our knees to let loose this mightiest of weapons against the evil surrounding us.

Bombs away, let us pray.

APRIL 1

The Greatest Story Ever Told

And he said, "Yes, it was written long ago that the Messiah must suffer and die and rise again from the dead on the third day; and that this message of salvation should be taken from Jerusalem to all the nations: There is forgiveness of sins for all who turn to me. You have seen these prophecies come true."

—Luke 24:46–48 (TLB)

It is the greatest story ever told.

Once upon a time, the Son of God came to earth, became a man, lived a sinless life, and showed the world a love that was beyond their comprehension. It was a love greater than anything they had ever seen before. This love was so amazing and so misunderstood that the evil people in the world sought to destroy it.

And they thought they succeeded. But they were wrong.

The Messiah, the Savior of the World, suffered and died, and on the third day He rose from the dead.

Why did He do it? This scripture tells us the reason why.

It is the simple and beautiful message of the cross: "There is forgiveness of sins for all who repent."

This scripture also tells us that the message will be proclaimed to all the nations.

Have you done your part? Have you told the story?

APRIL 2

Resurrected Understanding

Then he said, "When I was with you before, don't you remember my telling you that everything written about me by Moses and the prophets and in the Psalms must all come true?" Then he opened their minds to understand at last these many Scriptures!

—Luke 24:44–45 (TLB)

There are times when I have read the scriptures and felt as though the meaning was veiled, that I didn't have a full and complete understanding of the words written on the page.

Have you ever experienced that?

Just as Jesus opened the eyes of the blind (Matthew 9:30), in this passage of scripture, He opened the minds of the disciples to understand the scriptures. He gave them an understanding of Old Testament prophecy. He gave them a resurrected understanding.

Job 28:28 tells us, "And this is what he says to all humanity: 'The fear of the Lord is true wisdom; to forsake evil is real understanding'" (NLT).

In Mark 4:25, Jesus tells us, "To those who listen to my teaching, more understanding will be given. But for those who are not listening, even what little understanding they have will be taken away from them" (NLT).

"May the Lord lead your hearts into a full understanding and expression of the love of God and the patient endurance that comes from Christ" (2 Thessalonians 3:5 NLT).

APRIL 3

Seeing the Real, Risen Jesus

Within the hour they were on their way back to Jerusalem, where the eleven disciples and the other followers of Jesus greeted them with these words, "The Lord has really risen! He appeared to Peter!"

—Luke 24:33–34 (TLB)

Peter saw Him. The women at the tomb saw Him. They saw the real, risen Jesus. He did exactly what He said He would do, as He always does.

Does that surprise you?

The disciples and others were surprised that Jesus did what He said He would do, but that is the very essence of who Jesus is—He is the way, the truth, and the life, and no one can come to the Father except through Him (John 14:6).

If we truly believe in Jesus, that belief will change everything about us, our lives, and the way we live them It will change the way we see others as well.

We often have a tendency to make Jesus *one of us*—rejecting His divine nature and power.

John 6:40 tells us, "For it is my Father's will that all who see his Son and believe in him should have eternal life. I will raise them up at the last day" (NLT).

Do you see Him? Do you see the real, risen Jesus?

David prayed in Psalm 119:18, "Open my eyes to see the wonderful truths in your instructions" (NLT).

May we pray, as David did, and may God open our eyes so that we might see and recognize the real, risen Jesus living among us today.

APRIL 4

The Cornerstone

The stone rejected by the builders has now become the capstone of the arch! This is the Lord's doing, and it is marvelous to see! This is the day the Lord has made. We will rejoice and be glad in it.

—Psalm 118:22–24 (TLB)

God sees things differently than humanity sees them.

David was a shepherd boy. Not even Samuel, sent to anoint the next king of Israel, saw in David what God saw in him.

And consider Christ, our Savior. He was despised and rejected, yet He became the cornerstone, the foundation of all that is true. He is the capstone, the completion of the hope we have in God Almighty.

We find this important truth repeated throughout scripture, in Genesis 49:24, Isaiah 28:16, Matthew 21:42, Mark 12:10–11, Luke 20:17, Acts 4:11, Ephesians 2:20, and 1 Peter 2:7. This truth is central to our faith. Those who reject Christ are rejected by Him.

First Corinthians 26–28 tells us the following:

Remember, dear brothers and sisters, that few of you were wise in the world's eyes or powerful or wealthy when God called you. Instead, God chose things the world considers foolish in order to shame those who think they are wise. And he chose things that are powerless to shame those who are powerful. God chose things despised by the world, things counted as nothing at all, and used them to bring to nothing what the world considers important. (NLT)

Let us praise our God and Father, and Jesus Christ our cornerstone, for He is our foundation and completion. He has made this wonderful day to bring about all He has purposed to be.

APRIL 5

Misplaced

The women were terrified and bowed low before them. Then the men asked, "Why are you looking in a tomb for someone who is alive?"

—Luke 24:5 (TLB)

I have trouble finding things from time to time. Do you?

Most often, I believe I have misplaced the item. Yet when I find it, it is usually right where it should be—right where I should have looked in the first place.

In this passage of scripture, Jesus is right where He should be, too. His body hasn't been misplaced. He is in the land of the living—right where the women should have looked in the first place. He is doing the will of the One who sent Him.

What about you? Are you where you should be today?

Are you doing the will of the One who sent you, or are you still looking for Christ, thinking you've misplaced Him somehow?

If you look for Him, you will find Him. He is never misplaced. He is always right where He should be—where you should have looked in the first place.

Perhaps you are the one who is misplaced.

May you be found where you should be—doing the will of the Father—when He looks for you today.

APRIL 6

Just Believe

Then they remembered and rushed back to Jerusalem to tell his eleven disciples—and everyone else—what had happened. (The women who went to the tomb were Mary Magdalene and Joanna and Mary the mother of James, and several others.) But the story sounded like a fairy tale to the men—they didn't believe it.

—Luke 24:8–11 (TLB)

The women at the tomb had heard the Old Testament prophecy of the resurrection (Psalm 16:10). Jesus had told them Himself that it would happen (Mark 8:31; Luke 18:33). And now the women at the tomb came face-to-face with the reality of the risen Lord. These women didn't just walk back to tell the disciples—they rushed. They had to tell someone that Jesus was alive!

And He is still alive today. He has ascended to heaven (Luke 24:51), and His power is just as real today as it was then.

Do you believe it, or are you like the disciples who didn't believe and considered the women's story to be nonsense?

The things God does are always supernatural, always good, always extraordinary. And He longs to show Himself to you.

Do you see Him? Do you believe?

May you believe that the supernatural power of Christ is living and working in and around you every moment of every day.

APRIL 7

Earnest and Disciplined Prayer

The end of the world is coming soon. Therefore be earnest, thoughtful men of prayer.

—1 Peter 4:7 (TLB)

Are you earnest and disciplined in your prayer life? What does it mean to be earnest and disciplined in prayer?

Earnest prayer is that which is borne out of the heart's conviction. It is prayer with longing and urgency.

James 5:16 tells us, "Confess your sins to each other and pray for each other so that you may be healed. The earnest prayer of a righteous person has great power and produces wonderful results" (NLT).

Disciplined prayer is that which we regularly do in obedience to our Lord and Savior, Jesus Christ. It is consistent and persistent. There is no end to its zeal, its passion.

The example of Jesus's discipline in prayer is repeated throughout scripture for us to follow, as Luke 5:16 reminds us: "But Jesus often withdrew to the wilderness for prayer" (NLT).

Do you need answers? If so, then you also need an earnest and disciplined prayer life.

Remember that you should never give up (Luke 18:1) and never stop praying (1 Thessalonians 5:17).

APRIL 8

Our Father's Bank and Trust

Some may deny these things, but they are the sound, wholesome teachings of the Lord Jesus Christ and are the foundation for a godly life. Anyone who says anything different is both proud and stupid. He is quibbling over the meaning of Christ's words and stirring up arguments ending in jealousy and anger, which only lead to name-calling, accusations, and evil suspicions. These arguers—their minds warped by sin—don't know how to tell the truth; to them the Good News is just a means of making money. Keep away from them.

—1 Timothy 6:3–5 (TLB)

Have you ever met someone trying to sell you something who made a point of telling you that she was a Christian? She used her proclamation of Christianity as if to say, "Now you *have* to buy from me, as I would *never* steer you wrong."

This is an example of the contradictory teaching that is referred to in 1 Timothy 6. It is ungodly behavior, and it is evidence of a completely self-centered life. It disgraces the name of Jesus Christ and causes most folks I know to run the other way as fast as they can.

True wealth, true riches, can only be found in a close personal relationship with Jesus Christ. Everything else is just money. Have you deposited your life with Christ?

He owns the cattle on a thousand hills (Psalm 50:10), He meets all our needs according to His riches in glory (Philippians 4:19), and He withholds no good thing from those who do what is right (Psalm 84:11). No one can receive anything unless God gives it from heaven (John 3:27). Everything He does is wonderful (Mark 7:37).

Our Father's bank and trust will never fail and will never need a bailout. May we invest everything we have and are in Him.

APRIL 9

What's in Your Wallet?

Do you want to be truly rich? You already are if you are happy and good. After all, we didn't bring any money with us when we came into the world, and we can't carry away a single penny when we die. So we should be well satisfied without money if we have enough food and clothing. But people who long to be rich soon begin to do all kinds of wrong things to get money, things that hurt them and make them evil-minded and finally send them to hell itself.

—1 Timothy 6:6–9 (TLB)

You can tell a lot about a person by examining how he spends his money. Open up his checkbook and what do you find there?

Malachi 3:10 tells us exactly what our spending should look like. It reads, "'Bring all the tithes into the storehouse so there will be enough food in my Temple. If you do,' says the Lord of Heaven's Armies, 'I will open the windows of heaven for you. I will pour out a blessing so great you won't have enough room to take it in! Try it! Put me to the test'" (NLT)!

If we tithe on our net pay rather than on our gross pay, then we aren't bringing all the tithes into God's storehouse. And if we receive a cash gift neglecting its tithe, again we have failed to be the cheerful giver that God desires (2 Corinthians 9:7).

God wants us to put Him to the test with regard to our spending in order to strengthen our faith, spare us many griefs, and fill us with His abundant blessing. The money in our wallet is His. James 1:7 tells us, "Whatever is good and perfect is a gift coming down to us from God our Father, who created all the lights in the heavens. He never changes or casts a shifting shadow" (NLT).

So, what's in your wallet? Have you examined your spending lately? Perhaps it's time you turned your wallet, your checkbook, over to the best money manager in the business, Jesus Christ.

APRIL 10

The Pursuit of What Matters

O Timothy, you are God's man. Run from all these evil things, and work instead at what is right and good, learning to trust him and love others and to be patient and gentle. Fight on for God. Hold tightly to the eternal life that God has given you and that you have confessed with such a ringing confession before many witnesses.

—1 Timothy 6:11–12 (TLB)

The things that the world has to offer can be intoxicating. The problem with intoxication is that it doesn't last. It is temporary. When we finally awaken from our stupor, we find that we have missed out on what really matters— those things that last, those things that are eternal.

Matthew 6:33 reminds us what matters: "Seek the Kingdom of God above all else, and live righteously, and he will give you everything you need" (NLT).

When you look at your life, what do you see there? Do you see a life that is pursuing God, or do you see a life that is pursuing money, things, and all that the world has to offer?

Second Corinthians 4:18b reminds us, "For the things we see now will soon be gone, but the things we cannot see will last forever" (NLT).

May we awaken from our worldly stupor to find the person of Jesus Christ and all that He has to offer us today.

APRIL 11

Here Today, Gone Tomorrow

Tell those who are rich not to be proud and not to trust in their money, which will soon be gone, but their pride and trust should be in the living God who always richly gives us all we need for our enjoyment.

—1 Timothy 6:17 (TLB)

Do you find a sense of security in having a certain balance in your bank account? There was a time when I did. Then one day it was all taken away—all my blood, sweat, and tears money.

I had grown up with very little in the way of worldly goods, so having a substantial rainy-day fund socked safely away in the bank made me feel safe and secure. But do you see the flaw in my thought process, the sin consuming my heart? I had substituted faith in Christ for faith in finances—a very poor substitute. Our God is a jealous God (Exodus 34:14), and when we put anything or anyone in His rightful position, He loves us enough to take it away, revealing how vastly superior He is to any idol we might have. And we know that idols will completely disa pear (Isaiah 2:18).

In Matthew 6:19–20, Jesus tells us, "Don't store up treasures here on earth, where moths eat them and rust destroys them, and where thieves break in and steal. Store your treasures in heaven, where moths and rust cannot destroy, and thieves do not break in and steal" (NLT).

Financial safety nets break, but the safety and security of God's love never breaks. Proverbs 23:5 tells us, "In the blink of an eye wealth disappears, for it will sprout wings and fly away like an eagle" (NLT).

May we remember always that which is eternal so that nothing may take God's rightful place in our lives. "Dear children, keep away from anything that might take God's place in your hearts" (1 John 5:21 NLT).

APRIL 12

Real Living

Tell them to use their money to do good. They should be rich in good works and should give happily to those in need, always being ready to share with others whatever God has given them. By doing this they will be storing up real treasure for themselves in heaven—it is the only safe investment for eternity! And they will be living a fruitful Christian life down here as well.

—1 Timothy 6:18–19 (TLB)

In the 1970s, Coca-Cola claimed to be the real thing. People flocked to the stores to buy it. These days, if we have a nice home, a nice car, nice clothes, lavish vacations, and fancy food, we tend to call that *really living*. The world tends to define real living in material terms.

But the world has it wrong.

God defines the life that is truly life. It is not found in worldly wealth or material possessions. It can only be found in a close personal relationship with Jesus Christ. That relationship manifests itself in the richness of good deeds, a generous spirit, and a willingness to share what we have with others.

In Luke 12:21, Jesus tells us, "Yes, a person is a fool to store up earthly wealth but not have a rich relationship with God" (NLT).

Colossians 3:3 says, "For you died to this life, and your real life is hidden with Christ in God" (NLT).

That's where real life is, with Christ.

May we forsake the counterfeit in order to take hold of that which is truly life today and every day.

APRIL 13

Spring-Cleaning

He made no distinction between them and us, for he cleansed their lives through faith, just as he did ours.

—Acts 15:9 (TLB)

Once more it is the time of year we affectionately refer to as *spring-cleaning*. Time to break out the mop and the duster, and to open the windows and doors. Don't forget that special cleanser. It works wonders.

That cleanser? It's called faith.

Faith cleans deep strongholds of sin like nothing else. It loosens the scaly grip of self-reliance, softening stubborn hardened-heart stains. Faith penetrates even the unrepentant corners of our heart, cleaning out the wickedness and revealing the beauty of a humble heart completely devoted to and dependent upon Him.

Are you ready for some spring-cleaning? It starts with a dose of confession and repentance.

First John 1:9 says, "But if we confess our sins to him, he is faithful and just to forgive us our sins and to cleanse us from all wickedness" (NLT).

Acts 20:21 says, "I have had one message for Jews and Greeks alike—the necessity of repenting from sin and turning to God, and of having faith in our Lord Jesus" (NLT).

May we allow Christ to cleanse our hearts once and for all, filling us with an immovable and unshakable faith in Him.

APRIL 14

Real Love

We know what real love is from Christ's example in dying for us. And so we also ought to lay down our lives for our Christian brothers.

—1 John 3:16 (TLB)

There are many different types of love. There are four Greek terms that we interpret as *love*: *eros*, which is erotic love; *phileo*, which is brotherly love; *storge*, which is parental love; and *agape*, which is unconditional love. Three of these are used in the Holy Bible, *phileo*, *storge*, *agape*, as is one compound form of love: *philostorgos*—a devoted love.

Storge is parental love. We find the negative form of this word, *astorgos*, in Romans 1:31 and 2 Timothy 3:3.

We find the compound form of *lov* in the Greek *philostorgos*, in Romans 12:10, as Paul is describing the type of devotion we should have toward each other as followers of Christ.

Phileo is brotherly affection. This is the term used by Peter in his dialogue with Jesus in John 21:15. In the same passage of scripture, Jesus, conversely, uses the Greek *agape*.

Agape is unconditional love. It is the embodiment of God Himself. It is a sacrificial love. It is the kind of love that God has for us. This is real love.

First John 4:10 says, "This is real love—not that we loved God, but that he loved us and sent his Son as a sacrifice to take away our sins" (NLT).

Won't you share His real love with someone today?

APRIL 15

Walkin' the Walk

If you carefully obey all the commandments I give you, loving the Lord your God, walking in all his ways, and clinging to him, then the Lord will drive out all the nations in your land, no matter how much greater and stronger than you they might be.

—Deuteronomy 11:22–23 (TLB)

If we claim to be Christians, our life is no longer our own. We belong to God.

First John 3:10 tells us, "So now we can tell who are children of God and who are children of the devil. Anyone who does not live righteously and does not love other believers does not belong to God" (NLT).

Being a real follower of Christ means something. It means saying no to the world's way and saying yes to God. We must be obedient to His Word, the Holy Bible.

The world is watching you and me. Do they see a difference?

They should see a very distinct difference in our lives each and every day.

Are you walkin' the walk, or are you just talkin' the talk when it's convenient for you?

My friend, there is no such thing as a part-time Christian. Walking in obedience to Christ is a conscious daily choice. In Luke 9:23, Jesus puts it this way: "If any of you wants to be my follower, you must turn from your selfish ways, take up your cross daily, and follow me" (NLT).

Be who you claim to be today and every day.

APRIL 16

Loving the Judas in Your Life

Love your enemies! Do good to them! Lend to them! And don't be concerned about the fact that they won't repay. Then your reward from heaven will be very great, and you will truly be acting as sons of God: for he is kind to the unthankful and to those who are very wicked.

—Luke 6:35 (TLB)

Do you find it difficult to be kind to evil people? I do. Yet this passage of scripture tells us that is exactly what God wants us to do. What about those people who claim to be Christian, yet the life they live is anything *but* Christian?

I am reminded of Christ's example with regard to Judas Iscariot—one of the Twelve. Judas was keeper of the money for Jesus and His disciples. But Judas was known to dip into the till whenever he cared to. He was a traitor, betraying Christ to be crucified on a cross. Jesus knew that Judas was a wicked man. John 6:70–71 tells us, "Then Jesus said, 'I chose the twelve of you, but one is a devil.' He was speaking of Judas, son of Simon Iscariot, one of the Twelve, who would later betray him" (NLT).

I have often wondered just how Jesus could stand to be with Judas, a man He knew to be a devil. In any event, the love that Christ showed to Judas left him without excuse. There was no reason whatsoever for Judas to reject Christ, yet he did.

Perhaps you have a Judas in your life. You've prayed repeatedly for the situation to change, for the person's heart to change, or for the person to be removed from your immediate sphere of influence, your circle. Consider that God may have placed this Judas in your life in order that she may be without excuse. Love this person as Christ loved Judas.

And never stop praying. The person may yet come to Him.

APRIL 17

The Real You

Once you were less than nothing; now you are God's own. Once you knew very little of God's kindness; now your very lives have been changed by it.

—1 Peter 2:10 (TLB)

Who are you?

First Corinthians 6:17 tells us, "But the person who is joined to the Lord is one spirit with him" (NLT).

Are you one spirit with Christ? If so, your life, your behavior, will reflect this oneness.

Romans 6:6 tells us what this oneness looks like in our lives. It says, "We know that our old sinful selves were crucified with Christ so that sin might lose its power in our lives. We are no longer slaves to sin."

Are you still a slave to sin?

Philippians 3:18 tells us, "For I have told you often before, and I say it again with tears in my eyes, that there are many whose conduct shows they are really enemies of the cross of Christ" (NLT).

It is how you live every moment of every day—whether anyone is looking or not—that proves the real you.

Third John 1:11 says, "Dear friend, don't let this bad example influence you. Follow only what is good. Remember that those who do good prove that they are God's children, and those who do evil prove that they do not know God" (NLT).

I pray that your life will prove that the real you belongs to God.

APRIL 18

Because I'm Happy

When a man is gloomy, everything seems to go wrong; when he is cheerful, everything seems right!

—Proverbs 15:15 (TLB)

Do you have a happy heart?

When the Holy Spirit is controlling our life, we have more than happiness. There is a deep, true, and abiding joy—regardless of our circumstance.

What does it mean for life to be a continual feast?

God's Word is a continual feast, as is our life with Him. The fruit provided during the feast with God is greater than any meal we could ever enjoy on earth.

Galatians 5:22–23 tells us, "But the Holy Spirit produces this kind of fruit in our lives: love, joy, peace, patience, kindness, goodness, faithfulness, gentleness, and self-control. There is no law against these things" (NLT)!

I can't imagine any greater feast than the fruit described here. Can you?

May your heart be filled with the happiness and joy that only a close personal relationship with God can bring, and may you experience this happiness, this joy, every moment of every day.

APRIL 19

Of Humpty Dumpty and Great Falls

He heals the brokenhearted, binding up their wounds.

—Psalm 147:3 (TLB)

Have you ever taken a tumble in your life? I'm not talking about a little trip and fall but of an *all the king's horses* kind of event—one of those falls people rarely recover from.

There is a nursery rhyme in which one such character takes a tumble he never recovers from. His name is Humpty Dumpty. Do you remember the story?

Humpty Dumpty had such a great fall from his wall that all the king's horses and all the king's men failed in their attempt to put him back together again.

But that's where Humpty Dumpty's story differs from yours and mine. You see, for the King of Kings and the Lord of Lords, there is no broken life that He can't mend, no broken heart that is out of His reach.

Not only does He put us back together again when we humble ourselves and repent of our sin, but also when He fixes us, He makes us better than we ever were before.

Isaiah 59:1 reminds us, "Listen! The Lord's arm is not too weak to save you, nor is his ear too deaf to hear you call" (NLT).

May He always catch you when you fall.

APRIL 20

Reconciled to God

For God wanted all of himself to be in his Son. It was through what his Son did that God cleared a path for everything to come to him—all things in heaven and on earth—for Christ's death on the cross has made peace with God for all by his blood.

—Colossians 1:19–20 (TLB)

What does it mean to be reconciled to God, to make peace with Him?

When Jesus Christ died on the cross, God made His peace with you. He made His peace with me too, and with everything and everyone in all the world.

We often have difficulty simply making peace with those in our own home. Yet through the shedding of Christ's blood, God made peace with us all.

Why would God do this? He has more love for us than we can possibly get our minds around.

Second Corinthians 5:18 tells us, "And all of this is a gift from God, who brought us back to himself through Christ. And God has given us this task of reconciling people to him" (NLT).

May we follow the sacrificial example of our God and Savior, being reconciled not only to God but also to each other.

"May God give you more and more mercy, peace, and love" (Jude 1:2 NLT).

APRIL 21

Gladly, the Cross-Eyed Bear

Then he said to all, "Anyone who wants to follow me must put aside his own desires and conveniences and carry his cross with him every day and keep close to me!"

—Luke 9:23 (TLB)

There is a story that has been told throughout the ages of a young girl who misunderstood the line "Gladly, the cross I'll bear" in the beloved hymn "Keep Thou My Way" by Fannie Crosby and Theodore E. Perkins. The girl thought that the song was about a cross-eyed bear named Gladly.

The story is cute, but what does it really mean to take up our cross daily to follow Christ?

It means we must choose to obey God every single day and in every situation that we face. It is an act of the will. But we don't have to go it alone. The Holy Spirit helps us in our times of weakness.

Romans 8:26 tells us, "And the Holy Spirit helps us in our weakness. For example, we don't know what God wants us to pray for. But the Holy Spirit prays for us with groanings that cannot be expressed in words" (NLT).

When we pray and ask the Father for help, He will even put up roadblocks for us to help us avoid temptation, to make a way of escape for us. We must not bulldoze God's roadblock, His way for us to escape.

First Corinthians 10:13 says, "The temptations in your life are no different from what others experience. And God is faithful. He will not allow the temptation to be more than you can stand. When you are tempted, he will show you a way out so that you can endure" (NLT).

May God grant us the will to gladly bear the cross each day.

APRIL 22

Living in the Light

But if we are living in the light of God's presence, just as Christ does, then we have wonderful fellowship and joy with each other, and the blood of Jesus his Son cleanses us from every sin.

—1 John 1:7 (TLB)

When we are living in the light of Christ, we desire all things light, all things pure, all things transparent, all things known by the One who knows us.

God's light becomes our guide. Though it may be for only one step at a time, this light is more than enough.

Yet, Isaiah warns us of walking in our own light and treating that light as though it were the light of God.

Isaiah 50:11 says, "But watch out, you who live in your own light and warm yourselves by your own fires. This is the reward you will receive from me: You will soon fall down in great torment" (NLT).

Are you walking in the true light, God's light? Are you allowing this light to fill you, to guide you?

The light of Christ can produce nothing impure.

As Ephesians 5:9 tells us, "For this light within you produces only what is good and right and true" (NLT).

May we walk in the light, as He is in the light, so that we may have fellowship with each other, and so that the blood of Jesus Christ will cleanse us from all sin (1 John 1:7).

APRIL 23

Owe No Human Being

Pay all your debts except the debt of love for others—never finish paying that! For if you love them, you will be obeying all of God's laws, fulfilling all his requirements.

—Romans 13:8 (TLB)

Keeping up with the Joneses is not a biblical principle. It is covetous behavior.

The Holy Bible tells us in Exodus 20:17, "You must not covet your neighbor's house. You must not covet your neighbor's wife, male or female servant, ox or donkey, or anything else that belongs to your neighbor" (NLT).

As Christians, we are to love others and treat them the way we want to be treated.

I am often disturbed to hear of Christians who simply choose not to pay their debts or who fail to pay their bills in a timely manner.

Romans 13:7 says, "Give to everyone what you owe them: Pay your taxes and government fees to those who collect them, and give respect and honor to those who are in authority" (NLT).

May we honor God in every aspect of our lives, down to each penny that we spend.

APRIL 24

On Eagle's Wings

But they that wait upon the Lord shall renew their strength. They shall mount up with wings like eagles; they shall run and not be weary; they shall walk and not faint.

—Isaiah 40:31 (TLB)

I once had a job where my employer had a difficult time allowing me to do the work that had been assigned to me. This particular boss exhibited the same behavior toward everyone reporting to him. Each time I became excited about accomplishing the goals I was assigned, my wings were clipped and I fell to the ground. When I finally inquired of this boss as to why I was never allowed to fly, I was told the reason was fear—fear that I might fail.

That is the world's way. It is fearful, stifling. It clips the bird's wings just as it begins to take flight. It reins in the stallion that is longing to run in the open field.

That is not God's way.

God's way provides wind beneath the eagle's wings so that it may soar beyond the clouds. His way is not stifling, nor is it fearful. He allows the stallion to run at full speed through the open meadow, finding new strength with every rotation of his withers.

God's way defines true freedom, although only by becoming slaves in obedience to God do we truly become free (1 Peter 2:16).

APRIL 25

Perfecting Imperfection

But you are to be perfect, even as your Father in heaven is perfect.

—Matthew 5:48 (TLB)

Recently I passed a car bearing a bumper sticker for a local church. The slogan read, "No perfect people allowed." Although I know that no one except Christ is perfect, the statement struck me as arrogant, as though the church members were taking pride in their sinfulness. That church is not a place I would have any desire to attend.

As God's children, we cannot choose to continually dwell in sin.

Romans 6:1–2 tells us, "Well then, should we keep on sinning so that God can show us more and more of his wonderful grace? Of course not! Since we have died to sin, how can we continue to live in it" (NLT)?

God's grace covers our sin, and when His Holy Spirit dwells within us, sin is no longer in charge.

Romans 8:6 tells us, "So letting your sinful nature control your mind leads to death. But letting the Spirit control your mind leads to life and peace" (NLT).

Having Christ as our Savior changes our *want to*. We no longer want to sin; we want to please Christ.

"I don't mean to say that I have already achieved these things or that I have already reached perfection. But I press on to possess that perfection for which Christ Jesus first possessed me" (Philippians 3:12 NLT).

APRIL 26

Simon the Sorcerer

But Peter replied, "Your money perish with you for thinking God's gift can be bought!"

—Acts 8:20 (TLB)

Simon the sorcerer had accepted Jesus Christ as his Savior. He saw Peter and John laying hands on the new converts and watched as those converts received the Holy Spirit's power. Simon wanted to be able to do that too. He offered Peter and John money to buy this power.

But the gifts of God cannot be bought with money. These gifts have already been purchased with the blood of Jesus Christ.

Our churches are filled with people like Simon the sorcerer who think that if they give more money to the building fund or to missions, they too can receive the Holy Spirit's power.

It doesn't work that way.

We need only to ask our heavenly Father for the gifts of the Holy Spirit.

Luke 11:13 tells us, "So if you sinful people know how to give good gifts to your children, how much more will your heavenly Father give the Holy Spirit to those who ask him" (NLT)?

May we seek first His kingdom and His righteousness, so that all these things may be added unto us (Matthew 6:33).

APRIL 27

A Mighty God

After this presentation to the elders, Moses and Aaron went to see Pharaoh. They told him, "We bring you a message from Jehovah, the God of Israel. He says, 'Let my people go, for they must make a holy pilgrimage out into the wilderness, for a religious feast, to worship me there.'"

—Exodus 5:1 (TLB)

We serve a mighty God who is worthy to be honored and praised. God personally met with Moses in the burning bush. It was a holy meeting, a divine appointment. After much struggle with God, Moses had chosen to obey Him, with the help of his brother, Aaron, as a spokesman.

Our mighty God has given you a task as well.

Have you struggled with God and yourself only to let Satan win? Perhaps it is not too late. Your obedience to Him is a celebration of your relationship. It is your own personal festival honoring the faith and commitment you have made to serving Him.

I have no idea what task God has given to you, but I do know that it is important.

Pharaoh did not know the God the Israelites served (Exodus 5:2), but because of Moses's and Aaron's obedience, he was about to know the mighty power of the one true and living God.

Do you know that power?

May you follow in obedience after Him today so that others might know the mighty God we serve.

APRIL 28

Be, Don't Seem

Do you remember how the Lord led you through the wilderness for all those forty years, humbling you and testing you to find out how you would respond, and whether or not you would really obey him?

—Deuteronomy 8:2 (TLB)

Just who are you?

Are you a real Christian, someone who has repented of sin? Are you someone whose heart's desire is to follow after Christ, to walk in purity and in obedience to Him?

Or are you someone who said a prayer once, seeing it as your onetime ticket into heaven? Do you still live and do as you please? Do you treat God like a genie in a bottle, praying only when you want something?

Our churches are full of people who do not know Christ. Why?

It is because many in positions of church leadership are more concerned with numbers than need. They are more concerned with dollars than discipleship. In these churches, there is no true growth, only revolving doors of membership. Our character, our integrity, is infinitely important, and it teaches others— whether that is our intention or not.

Jesus said in Matthew 28:19–20, "Therefore, go and make disciples of all the nations, baptizing them in the name of the Father and the Son and the Holy Spirit. Teach these new disciples to obey all the commands I have given you. And be sure of this: I am with you always, even to the end of the age" (NLT).

May we truly be who we say we are, not simply giving the appearance of something, someone, we are not.

APRIL 29

A Mighty Deliverance

And now I have heard the groanings of the people of Israel, in slavery now to the Egyptians, and I remember my promise. "Therefore tell the descendants of Israel that I will use my mighty power and perform great miracles to deliver them from slavery and make them free. And I will accept them as my people and be their God. And they shall know that I am Jehovah their God who has rescued them from the Egyptians."

—Exodus 6:5–7 (TLB)

God promised deliverance to His people. He heard their prayers, and now He was going to deliver them. The manner in which God was going to bring this deliverance would cause all nations to recognize Him as the one true and living God—I AM.

There was to be no denying it, and there was no denying Him, Yahweh, the Lord. He is El-Shaddai, God Almighty.

It was time for the world to stand up and take notice. No longer would God be silent before them With a mighty hand and outstretched arm, He would show forth His power.

That same power is alive and well today. God's power is available to deliver each and every one of us from sin and destruction.

Do you need the deliverance of God today?

May we never forget His mighty power, ready to save us when we call upon our El-Shaddai.

APRIL 30

His Powerful Hand

The Egyptians will find out that I am indeed God when I show them my power and force them to let my people go.

—Exodus 7:5 (TLB)

There is no hand more powerful than the hand of God.

Exodus 15:6 tells us, "Your right hand, O Lord, is glorious in power. Your right hand, O Lord, smashes the enemy" (NLT).

That same hand that smashes the enemy is mighty to save the righteous.

Psalm 138:7 says, "Though I am surrounded by troubles, you will protect me from the anger of my enemies. You reach out your hand, and the power of your right hand saves me" (NLT).

God showed His power both to save and to destroy when He rescued the Israelites from slavery in Egypt. His might was demonstrated through ten miraculous plagues before the pharaoh, yet the pharaoh still hardened his heart against God.

Whether we are for God or against Him, we will be sure to know His power. And one day we will see His power as it has never been seen before. Mark 14:62 records, "Jesus said, 'I am. And you will see the Son of Man seated in the place of power at God's right hand and coming on the clouds of heaven'" (NLT).

May you be on the right side of His powerful hand on that day.

MAY 1

Purity and Praise

The purity of silver and gold can be tested in a crucible, but a man is tested by his reaction to men's praise.

—Proverbs 27:21 (TLB)

Are you a humble person, or do you allow the slightest compliment or accolade to go straight to your head, distorting every ounce of reality?

Second Corinthians 6:6 says, "We prove ourselves by our purity, our understanding, our patience, our kindness, by the Holy Spirit within us, and by our sincere love" (NLT).

We ought to be the same person whether we receive praise or not. If praise changes things, then we must examine who we really are before God. After all, He is the only one truly worthy of praise.

Have you passed this test?

"He alone is your God, the only one who is worthy of your praise, the one who has done these mighty miracles that you have seen with your own eyes" (Deuteronomy 10:21 NLT).

MAY 2

The Consequences of Rebellion

So Moses and Aaron requested another audience with Pharaoh and told him: "Jehovah, the God of the Hebrews, asks, 'How long will you refuse to submit to me? Let my people go so they can worship me. If you refuse, tomorrow I will cover the entire nation with a thick layer of locusts so that you won't even be able to see the ground, and they will finish destroying everything that escaped the hail.'"

—Exodus 10:3–4 (TLB)

I remember a time as a teenager when I asked my father's permission to go somewhere with a friend. My father said no. I responded, "Yes, sir," and then I turned to tell my friend, who was waiting for me on the front porch. In our house, when Daddy said no, it meant no. There was no questioning, groveling, or attempting to manipulate that would succeed at anything other than punishment for questioning his authority. Not having grown up in that kind of household, my friend said, "Go ask again!"

Quicker than a flash, and before I had the chance to warn my friend to watch out, my father, having heard her, rounded the corner to say, "Young lady, in this house, no means no. It's called submission to authority. We don't tolerate rebellion in this house."

God doesn't tolerate rebellion in His house, either.

If we continue in rebellion against Him, we best watch out, too. Proverbs 17:11 warns, "Evil people are eager for rebellion, but they will be severely punished." On the contrary, John 8:51 says, "I tell you the truth, anyone who obeys my teaching will never die" (NLT)!

May we live in obedience to Christ so that we may avoid the consequences of rebellion.

MAY 3

The Power of His Favor

"Tell all the men and women of Israel to ask their Egyptian neighbors for gold and silver jewelry." (For God caused the Egyptians to be very favorable to the people of Israel, and Moses was a very great man in the land of Egypt and was revered by Pharaoh's officials and the Egyptian people alike.)

—Exodus 11:2–3 (TLB)

God's favor is powerful. He can cause others to look favorably upon us in a moment's notice in order to bring about blessing and the beauty of His divine plan.

Have you experienced it?

There have been countless times when others have accepted me, hired me, or given me gifts that could only have been the result of God's inconceivable favor. The Greek transliteration of the word *favor* here is *charis*, the Hebrew *chen*, being interpreted as "grace" or "blessing."

In Exodus 33:13, Moses asked God for His continued favor. Moses said, "If it is true that you look favorably on me, let me know your ways so I may understand you more fully and continue to enjoy your favor. And remember that this nation is your very own people" (NLT).

We do not know the ways of God, as His ways are higher than our ways, and His thoughts are higher than our thoughts (Isaiah 55:9). And though we know He has no favorites (Romans 2:11), He has shown His *favor* to all of us in the death, burial, and resurrection of His Son, Jesus Christ.

That is powerful.

"For his anger lasts only a moment, but his favor lasts a lifetime! Weeping may last through the night, but joy comes with the morning" (Psalm 30:5 NLT).

MAY 4

Make Disciples

Therefore go and make disciples in all the nations, baptizing them into the name of the Father and of the Son and of the Holy Spirit, and then teach these new disciples to obey all the commands I have given you; and be sure of this—that I am with you always, even to the end of the world.

—Matthew 28:19–20 (TLB)

When was the last time you heard the plan of salvation shared in your church? If your answer indicates that you have done so recently, then thank your heavenly Father for providing your flock with a loving earthly shepherd.

If you can't remember the last time you heard the plan of salvation, I would venture to say that you are among the vast majority of church members today.

It is sad to see local churches embracing the way of the world rather than the ways of God. My friend, this ought not be.

The church must be about the Father's business, which involves teaching what it really means to be a follower of Christ. Jesus spent countless hours instructing His disciples. We must pattern ourselves after Him, instructing others about Christ.

Second Timothy 4:2 reminds us, "Preach the word of God. Be prepared, whether the time is favorable or not. Patiently correct, rebuke, and encourage your people with good teaching" (NLT).

May we remember our charge as recorded in Ephesians 4:11–12: "Now these are the gifts Christ gave to the church: the apostles, the prophets, the evangelists, and the pastors and teachers. Their responsibility is to equip God's people to do his work and build up the church, the body of Christ" (NLT).

MAY 5

Clean Up Your Act

In everything you do, stay away from complaining and arguing so that no one can speak a word of blame against you. You are to live clean, innocent lives as children of God in a dark world full of people who are crooked and stubborn. Shine out among them like beacon lights.

—Philippians 2:14–15 (TLB)

Do you need to clean up your act? Do you have bad habits?

Are your bad habits things that are common in today's world but uncommon in God's world?

My friend, if the Holy Bible tells us that something is wrong, it is wrong. It makes no difference how many people in the world find the behavior acceptable, and it does not matter their power or position. God's power and position is always superior.

There are many wonderful benefits to living a clean, pure life.

Second Timothy 2:21 tells us, "If you keep yourself pure, you will be a special utensil for honorable use. Your life will be clean, and you will be ready for the Master to use you for every good work" (NLT).

Do you want to be ready for the Master to use you for every good work?

Let us we pray and ask that the Father will help us to clean up our act so that we might be a special utensil for His honorable use.

MAY 6

Our High Priest

Moses alone shall come near to the Lord; and remember, none of the ordinary people are permitted to come up into the mountain at all.

—Exodus 24:2 (TLB)

Why was it that only Moses could come near to the Lord? What made him so special? After all, he was a murderer, and he wasn't a good speaker either. So, why were none of the other people allowed to climb up the mountain with him?

The answer does not indicate something we can see with worldly eyes.

The reason Moses was the only one allowed to come close to the Lord was because he had been called by God to serve as Israel's high priest. Only the high priest could enter into the holy of holies, and this mountain, Sinai, was holy ground.

In the verses that follow, God enters into covenant with His people, the Israelites. Moses, acting again as their high priest, leads them in worship and offering sacrifices to God as they affi rm the Book of the Covenant together aloud. It is a beautiful picture of God preparing Israel and the world for the coming sacrifice of His Son, Jesus, to be our everlasting High Priest. He has made a new covenant, and it is for all of us. Romans 11:27 says, "And this is my covenant with them, that I will take away their sins" (NLT).

Second Corinthians 3:6 tells us, "He has enabled us to be ministers of his new covenant. This is a covenant not of written laws, but of the Spirit. The old written covenant ends in death; but under the new covenant, the Spirit gives life" (NLT).

May you impart the life-giving new covenant of His Spirit to someone who needs Him today.

MAY 7

Run Away

Run from anything that gives you the evil thoughts that young men often have, but stay close to anything that makes you want to do right. Have faith and love, and enjoy the companionship of those who love the Lord and have pure hearts.

—2 Timothy 2:22 (TLB)

Overcoming temptation and sin involves effort, conscious choice, and the help of the Holy Spirit.

We must run away from sin.

James 4:7 tells us, "So humble yourselves before God. Resist the devil, and he will flee from you" (NLT).

We must become master over sin.

Genesis 4:7 says, "You will be accepted if you do what is right. But if you refuse to do what is right, then watch out! Sin is crouching at the door, eager to control you. But you must subdue it and be its master" (NLT).

And we must pray and ask for God's help in overcoming temptation.

In Matthew 26:41, Jesus exhorts us, "Keep watch and pray, so that you will not give in to temptation. For the spirit is willing, but the body is weak" (NLT)!

We can't do it alone. Apart from Him, we can do nothing (John 15:5).

May we encourage one another to run away from sin and temptation each and every day, so that we may finish well the race set before us.

MAY 8

Intensely God

Then Moses, Aaron, Nadab, Abihu, and seventy of the elders of Israel went up into the mountain. And they saw the God of Israel; under his feet there seemed to be a pavement of brilliant sapphire stones, as clear as the heavens.

—Exodus 24:9–10 (TLB)

Can you picture it? They saw God. Talk about your mountaintop experience.

Previously in Exodus, only Moses, Israel's high priest, was allowed to enter the most holy place, Mount Sinai. But now that the covenant has been made and has been sealed, the elders are invited up the mountain to see the Lord God of Israel.

The Holy Bible tells us that under God's feet "there seemed to be a surface of brilliant blue lapis lazuli, as clear as the sky itself." Lapis lazuli is known for its magnificently intense blue color. If you are a chemist, then you know that this intensity comes from the presence of the S_3 radical anion in the crystal. An electron excitement of the highest doubly filled molecular orbital into the lowest singular molecular orbital creates this intense color.

I don't know about you, but when the S_3 radical anion (Father, Son, and Holy Spirit) entered my life, His doubly filled molecular orbital created an intensity of color that my life had never known before.

And this intense color is just what lies under His feet.

May we know Him, may we see Him all around us, and may the intensity of all that He is fill our lives so completely that others are drawn to the beauty of all that He is.

MAY 9

Joy in the Everyday

And let us not get tired of doing what is right, for after a while we will reap a harvest of blessing if we don't get discouraged and give up.

—Galatians 6:9 (TLB)

There is no shortcut to faithful obedience to Christ. And faithful obedience to Christ isn't always accompanied by applause, fanfare, or a ticker-tape parade. No, the Christian life doesn't come wrapped in a pretty little package with a bow either, but it is the stuff that dreams—real, lasting, eternal dreams—are made of.

Obedience and faithfulness do not always seem exciting either. They are acts that may seem mundane and monotonous to those who do not have a personal relationship with Jesus Christ. Yet to the Christian, the life of faithfulness and obedience to Christ epitomizes the pinnacle of joy and freedom. It is freedom from sin and eternal punishment. It is freedom to love others in a way only a follower of Christ can. And at the root of faithfulness and obedience to Christ is a deep, abiding joy.

Psalm 16:11 tells us, "You will show me the path of life; In Your presence is fullness of joy; At Your right hand are pleasures forevermore" (NLT).

Are you struggling with faithfulness and obedience in the everyday? May you not grow weary of doing good, knowing the truth that in due season you will reap if you do not lose heart.

MAY 10

Making the Grade

Come to me and I will give you rest—all of you who work so hard beneath a heavy yoke. Wear my yoke—for it fits perfectly—and let me teach you; for I am gentle and humble, and you shall find rest for your souls; for I give you only light burdens.

—Matthew 11:28 (TLB)

Do you ever feel pressured to make better grades? Or maybe you feel pressured to perform better in some other area of life.

God always wants us to give Him our best (Proverbs 3:9). If we are not doing that, then some adjustments need to be made and we need to refocus our priorities. But once we have done this, we need to remember to leave the results up to God.

This passage of scripture reminds us that God also wants to be our teacher. Keep in mind that He's the best teacher you'll ever have. He is never too strict or harsh, nor is He too lenient. His tests? Many are open book—taken straight from the Bible. Best of all, He makes Himself available for tutoring twenty- four hours a day, seven days a week. All we have to do is call upon His name.

Do you need to be reminded to let God have control today?

He wants us to lay all of our burdens—including worry about what grades we'll receive—at His feet, and He wants us to find rest. He never gives us too much homework. The burden He gives us is never too much to bear. His yoke is easy, and His burden is light.

Give God everything that you have and are and allow Him to make the grade. He never fails.

MAY 11

Nanny-Nanny Boo-Boo

Do not rejoice against me, O my enemy, for though I fall, I will rise again! When I sit in darkness, the Lord himself will be my Light.

—Micah 7:8 (TLB)

It's human nature to gloat. Even as a toddler on the playground, I heard the menacing chant of "nanny-nanny boo-boo" when my foot missed the ball it was intending to kick, or when Susie got to home base in hide-and-go-seek before being tagged. And don't forget the tongue-wagging!

As grown-ups, we have our own "nanny-nanny boo-boos," like an insincere "bless your heart" or an "I told you so."

But God doesn't want us to gloat. Gloating is retaliatory, and it is arrogant. Such things are sinful.

First Peter 3:9 says, "Don't repay evil for evil. Don't retaliate with insults when people insult you. Instead, pay them back with a blessing. That is what God has called you to do, and he will grant you his blessing."

Jesus provided the perfect example for us to follow, as 1 Peter 2:23 reminds us: "He did not retaliate when he was insulted, nor threaten revenge when he suffered. He left his case in the hands of God, who always judges fairly" (NLT).

May you resist the urge to gloat over anyone, leaving your situation always in the hands of God, who always judges fairly.

MAY 12

Communion with God

Yet, even though the elders saw God, he did not destroy them; and they had a meal together before the Lord.

—Exodus 24:11 (TLB)

This passage of scripture is truly remarkable. Moses, Aaron, Nadab, Abihu, and the seventy elders of Israel saw God. They gazed upon Him. Not only that, but also they ate and drank a covenant meal in His presence.

I simply cannot get my human mind to fully understand it.

It was long believed that it was impossible to see God and live to tell about it (see Genesis 32:30; Exodus 32:20; Judges 6: 2–23). Yet here we find true fellowship, real communion, a sealing of the covenant relationship that God made with His people, Israel.

It is an amazing picture of His love for Israel, and a foretelling of the new covenant, sharing this same love with all the world.

Not only does God show forth His love for us by sending His one and only Son, Jesus, but also He humbles Himself to commune with us. A perfect God came down from His throne to experience holy communion with sinful humankind. There is coming another great time of holy communion with our God. It is the wedding feast of the Lamb. Your invitation has been sent. The reception is everlasting. Have you responded?

In Revelation 19:9, we read, "And the angel said to me, 'Write this: Blessed are those who are invited to the wedding feast of the Lamb.' And he added, 'These are true words that come from God'" (NLT).

Will you be there?

MAY 13

Ten Treasured Commandments

And the Lord said to Moses, "Come up to me into the mountain, and remain until I give you the laws and commandments I have written on tablets of stone, so that you can teach the people from them."

—Exodus 24:12 (TLB)

The Ten Commandments are beautiful. They are a demonstration of God's loving care and protective nature toward all that is His.

One of the things I love most about this verse of scripture is God's simply calling to Moses to come up to Him on the mountain. And God asks Moses to stay there while He provides the tablets of stone that Moses will use to teach the people.

It reminds me of a special time before my first child was born. My mother wanted me to come up for a visit and stay for a while so that she could give some special beautiful treasures to me. These treasures were all sorts of books and other assorted goodies she thought would be valuable in teaching my future children. Having used them with me, she knew them to be especially valuable.

And they have been.

God's Ten Commandments are beyond valuable. They are to be followed, treasured.

Psalm 19:8 tells us, "The commandments of the Lord are right, bringing joy to the heart. The commands of the Lord are clear, giving insight for living." And Psalm 119:93 says, "I will never forget your commandments, for by them you give me life" (NLT).

May we find joy in the life-giving treasured commands of our loving heavenly Father today and always.

MAY 14

The Majesty and Glory of Our God

Then Moses went up the mountain and disappeared into the cloud at the top. And the glory of the Lord rested upon Mount Sinai, and the cloud covered it six days; the seventh day he called to Moses from the cloud.

—Exodus 24:15–16 (TLB)

Like winter's first snow blanketing the dying grass before spring's revival, so the cloud shrouded Mount Sinai in God's glory for six days before revealing all the majesty that is our Lord. On the seventh day, when God called to Moses from inside the cloud, Moses disappeared into the cloud as he climbed higher up the mountain to commune with our Lord. To the people below, God's presence on the summit looked like a consuming fire.

Isaiah 29:6 says, "I, the Lord of Heaven's Armies, will act for you with thunder and earthquake and great noise, with whirlwind and storm and consuming fire" (NLT). It is an awesome, powerful love God has for us that acts with such passion, and calls to Moses from within the cloud to dwell with Him for forty days and nights. The number forty is significant, as it indicates a period of testing and trial, for example, forty days and nights of rain for Noah and the ark, forty years of wandering for Israel, forty days of testing for Jesus in the wilderness, forty days the spies investigated the Promised Land, and forty days Jonah warned Nineveh to repent.

I find it beautiful that at the end of each of these periods of forty, the majesty and glory of our God is revealed as never before.

First Chronicles 29:11 sums it up best when it says, "Yours, O Lord, is the greatness, the power, the glory, the victory, and the majesty. Everything in the heavens and on earth is yours, O Lord, and this is your kingdom. We adore you as the one who is over all things" (NLT).

MAY 15

Branded by God

During those celebration days each year you must explain to your children why you are celebrating—it is a celebration of what the Lord did for you when you left Egypt. This annual memorial week will brand you as his own unique people, just as though he had branded his mark of ownership upon your hands or your forehead.

—Exodus 13:8–9 (TLB)

Are you branded by God? Is there a visual sign in your life celebrating all that He has done for you?

A young man I knew as a child, Coy, had run away from God for most of his life. His parents loved God and prayed constantly for his salvation. They asked my father to pray too, and to speak with their son about Christ. Coy said he still was not ready to serve Christ—there were too many things he still wanted to do *his* way. That night, my father received a call about midnight from Coy's mother. Coy had been in an accident on his motorcycle. His skull was crushed and there were massive internal injuries. He was not expected to make it through the night.

Coy survived that night, and he still lives today. But he was never the same— not because he became a paraplegic or because he could barely see or speak. Coy was never the same because he met God that night. And every day that has followed, Coy has celebrated passionately all that the Lord has done for him. With a strong hand, God rescued Coy from himself. When you see Coy, you can clearly see the branding of God upon his life.

Do others see clearly the mark of God upon your life?

May we celebrate all that the Lord has done for us, so that others may be branded by Him too.

MAY 16

A Hurried Meal

Eat it with your traveling clothes on, prepared for a long journey, wearing your walking shoes and carrying your walking sticks in your hands; eat it hurriedly. This observance shall be called the Lord's Passover.

—Exodus 12:11 (TLB)

As young children, my brother, my sister, and I were often slow to finish our dinner—piddling and playing with the food on our plates. Our mother would tell us stories of her days in the United States Air Force when eating quickly and urgently was a requirement. There was no chewing each bite thirty-two times, and definitely no piddling around. It was all about survival.

For the Israelites, it was all about survival, too. God wanted families to remember the Lord's Passover and teach their children the importance of following His commands completely. There are often things He knows that we do not.

Much like the obedience taught in the military, God's lessons in obedience are designed as loving safeguards for us, protecting us from ourselves. God's rules are never meant to limit or inhibit our joy. They are meant for just the opposite. When we follow God's rules, we have fullness of joy.

Psalm 119:2 tells us, "Joyful are those who obey his laws and search for him with all their hearts" (NLT).

May all generations remember the hurried meal eaten in remembrance of the Lord's Passover.

MAY 17

A New Beginning

From now on, this month will be the first and most important of the entire year. Annually, on the tenth day of this month (announce this to all the people of Israel) each family shall get a lamb (or, if a family is small, let it share the lamb with another small family in the neighborhood; whether to share in this way depends on the size of the families).

—Exodus 12:2–4 (TLB)

It was a new beginning. The old days of slavery had passed away, and a newfound freedom was beginning. This was the beautiful freedom that only obedience to God could bring, and it was cause for celebration! The new beginning would be marked by the Lord's Passover and would change much, including the Hebrew calendar.

But change can be difficult sometimes, even when it is change for the better. When we try to see with human, earthly eyes that which can only be seen with spiritual eyes that trust, we get ourselves into trouble. Hebrews 11:27 tells us, "It was by faith that Moses left the land of Egypt, not fearing the king's anger. He kept right on going because he kept his eyes on the one who is invisible" (NLT).

Moses trusted God. Do you trust God with the new beginnings in your life?

Isaiah 43:19 says, "For I am about to do something new. See, I have already begun! Do you not see it? I will make a pathway through the wilderness. I will create rivers in the dry wasteland" (NLT).

May we keep our eyes focused on the one who is invisible so that we may make the most of each new beginning.

MAY 18

The Protection of Our God

For I will pass through the land of Egypt tonight and kill all the oldest sons and firstborn male animals in all the land of Egypt, and execute judgment upon all the gods of Egypt—for I am Jehovah. The blood you have placed on the doorposts will be proof that you obey me, and when I see the blood I will pass over you and I will not destroy your firstborn children when I smite the land of Egypt.

—Exodus 12:12–13 (TLB)

God longs to protect us.

Psalm 31:19 tells us, "How great is the goodness you have stored up for those who fear you. You lavish it on those who come to you for protection, blessing them before the watching world" (NLT).

God longed to protect the Israelites, too.

Judgment was about to fall upon the Egyptians because of their idolatry and because of Pharaoh's hard heart. As long as the Israelites followed in obedience after the command of God, they would escape the coming death.

When we act in obedience to Him, He hides us beneath the shelter of His mighty wings (Psalm 91:4).

It was only by the shedding of the blood of the lamb that the Israelites were protected from death. And it is only through the shedding of the blood of the Lamb of God that we are saved from eternal death.

Are you marked by the blood of the Lamb?

May you follow in obedience after Christ today and every day so that you may dwell within the loving protection of our God.

MAY 19

I Remember

And when you come into the land that the Lord will give you, just as he promised, and when you are celebrating the Passover, and your children ask, "What does all this mean? What is this ceremony about?" you will reply, "It is the celebration of Jehovah's passing over us, for he passed over the homes of the people of Israel, though he killed the Egyptians; he passed over our houses and did not come in to destroy us." And all the people bowed their heads and worshiped.

—Exodus 12:25–27 (TLB)

"I remember . . ."

My mother and father said those words many times before recounting some miraculous event when I was a child. They were wonderful stories of God's provision, His rescue, and His salvation. Many of these stories I retell to my own children and others, adding personal miracles, and I hope and pray they will continue to pass them down. The stories are full of priceless lessons. It is important that we remember. Psalm 111:4 tells us, "He causes us to remember his wonderful works. How gracious and merciful is our Lord" (NLT)!

It was important for the Israelite children to know the stories of God's love, His mercy, and His deliverance, and that this was the same God who was still more than able to provide for every possible need they could ever have. He had proven Himself in immeasurably mighty miracles.

Do you remember?

May you pass down each and every miracle from generation to generation, so that others may know and worship our mighty God.

"I remember the days of old. I ponder all your great works and think about what you have done" (Psalm 143:5 NLT).

MAY 20

My Legendary Jesus

Everything has been entrusted to me by my Father. Only the Father knows the Son, and the Father is known only by the Son and by those to whom the Son reveals him.

—Matthew 11:27 (TLB)

Have you ever lost someone truly extraordinary, someone with a legendary personality with whom you were intimately acquainted?

I have been blessed to know two such people in my lifetime, and I often smile when I hear others describe them. You see, their descriptions do not at all match the people I knew. They weren't even close. These people were not intimately acquainted with, nor did they *really know*, my extraordinary loved ones.

The same is often true when I hear others describing my Jesus. They get Him all wrong. It's because they are not intimately acquainted with Him.

Do you ever feel that way?

Jesus's was and is a personality larger than life itself. He is the stuff legends are made of, but He's no legend. He's real, and I know Him.

Do you *really know* Him?

First John 2:3 tells us how we can be sure we know Christ. It says, "And we can be sure that we know him if we obey his commandments" (NLT).

May we all become more intimately acquainted with the One who was, and is, and is to come.

MAY 21

Friend of God

You are like an unfaithful wife who loves her husband's enemies. Don't you realize that making friends with God's enemies—the evil pleasures of this world—makes you an enemy of God? I say it again, that if your aim is to enjoy the evil pleasure of the unsaved world, you cannot also be a friend of God.

—JAMES 4:4 (TLB)

What does it mean to be friends with the world?

Quite simply, being friends with the world means that we are allowing ourselves to be controlled by fleshly desires rather than by God's Spirit.

First John 2:16 tells us, "For the world offers only a craving for physical pleasure, a craving for everything we see, and pride in our achievements and possessions. These are not from the Father, but are from this world" (NLT).

These things are death to the spirit that God has given us. James 4:4 tells us clearly that we can't have it both ways. We can't be friends with both God and the world. Too many Christians are trying to have it both ways, and it just doesn't work.

Which side are you on today?

Are you satisfying the craving for the Spirit, or are you satisfying the cravings of the flesh?

One is temporary, and the other is eternal.

May you choose to be a friend of God, satisfying the deepest longings of His Spirit, so that you may know a joy much greater than the world could ever give.

MAY 22

Don't Bite

But if you are always biting and devouring one another, watch out! Beware of destroying one another.

—GALATIANS 5:15 (NLT)

It's not nice to bite.

When I worked with two-year-olds in day care back in my youth, we had a "no biting" rule. It seemed there was always one little rascal with a biting problem. These rascal kids longed to have their way, and when they didn't get it, the teeth came out.

Do you have a biting problem? When you fail to get your way, do the teeth come out?

Remember, if you devour everyone around you in order to get your way, you will end up miserable and alone—with all the worldly toys, but none of the eternal ones.

Is that really what you want?

Next time you feel like biting, remember Philippians 2:3, which says, "Don't be selfish; don't try to impress others. Be humble, thinking of others as better than yourselves" (NLT).

And may you leave your biting ways behind.

MAY 23

The Hard Way or the Easy Way?

Which do you choose? Shall I come with punishment and scolding, or shall I come with quiet love and gentleness?

—1 Corinthians 4:21 (TLB)

Are you the type who learns things the hard way or the easy way?

Having an older brother and sister who tended to test the boundary lines of discipline on the home front, I never wanted to learn things the hard way. I had a desire to please those in authority over me and go the easy route.

But going the easy route doesn't necessarily mean that one's heart is bent on pleasing God. Consider the brother of the prodigal son in Luke 15. The true condition of the brother's heart was revealed upon his prodigal brother's return. The elder brother refused to join in the celebration of his wandering brother's return to the fold and seeing the error of his ways.

The elder son was more concerned with keeping up appearances than having love and compassion for his younger brother.

In your desire to please, just who is it you are pleasing?

Are you fooling yourself into believing you are really seeking God, when all the while your rebellious heart is simply keeping up appearances?

May we truly learn God's way of obedience from the heart. May we take His yoke upon us and learn from Him, for His yoke is easy to bear and the burden He gives us is light (Matthew 11:28–30).

MAY 24

True Beauty Within

Be beautiful inside, in your hearts, with the lasting charm of a gentle and quiet spirit that is so precious to God.

—1 Peter 3:4 (TLB)

The allure of outward appearances can be extremely deceptive, pulling us away from all that we know to be true. It can shift our hearts and minds away from spiritual truth to worldly lies within a moment.

We must remain grafted into the vine, and make a conscious choice every day to say no to the desires of the flesh.

When we look at outward appearances, we miss out on what God's Spirit is doing. Samuel would have never chosen David to succeed Saul as king had he been looking at the outward appearance.

First Samuel 16:7 tells us, "But the Lord said to Samuel, 'Don't judge by his appearance or height, for I have rejected him. The Lord doesn't see things the way you see them People judge by outward appearance, but the Lord looks at the heart'" (NLT).

May we all have reverence for God, may our gentleness be evident to all, and may His Spirit within radiate to everyone around us.

"Charm is deceptive, and beauty does not last; but a woman who fears the Lord will be greatly praised" (Proverbs 31:30 NLT).

MAY 25

Crouching Tiger, Hidden Dragon

You will be accepted if you do what is right. But if you refuse to do what is right, then watch out! Sin is crouching at the door, eager to control you. But you must subdue it and be its master.

—Genesis 4:7 (NLT)

God said these words to Cain, warning him of the danger to come, warning of sin's devastating power, but Cain failed to listen. Cain allowed sin to control him, and he did the unthinkable—killing his own brother.

Have you allowed sin to control you? Have you done the unthinkable?

First Peter 5:8 warns us, "Stay alert! Watch out for your great enemy, the devil. He prowls around like a roaring lion, looking for someone to devour" (NLT).

Satan, the dragon referred to in the book of Revelation, hides in wait for those whose hearts are not completely ruled by the Holy Spirit. He is the Author of Lies and the Great Deceiver, but one day he will be defeated.

Revelation 12:7–9 tells us the following:

Then there was war in heaven. Michael and his angels fought against the dragon and his angels. And the dragon lost the battle, and he and his angels were forced out of heaven. This great dragon—the ancient serpent called the devil, or Satan, the one deceiving the whole world—was thrown down to the earth with all his angels. (NLT)

May we stay alert, pray, and ask the Father to guard our hearts and minds against any and all temptation, so that we may subdue sin and be its master each and every day.

MAY 26

Get Back Up Again

During the night, with the Midianites camped in the valley just below, the Lord said to Gideon, "Get up! Take your troops and attack the Midianites, for I will cause you to defeat them!"

—Judges 7:9 (TLB)

There are times in life when our mistakes can seem like a banner waved by the enemy to stop us dead in our tracks. We see the defeat as something permanent, and we give up hope.

May we never settle there, for our God is so much greater than any obstacle we may encounter.

Psalm 94:19 tells us, "When doubts filled my mind, your comfort gave me renewed hope and cheer" (NLT).

And Psalm 78:7 reminds us, "So each generation should set its hope anew on God, not forgetting his glorious miracles and obeying his commands" (NLT).

Are you discouraged? Do you feel as though all hope is gone?

Take heart, my friend. What is impossible for people is possible with God (Luke 18:27).

In 2 Corinthians 4:16 we find encouragement: "That is why we never give up. Though our bodies are dying, our spirits are being renewed every day" (NLT).

May He fill your life with good things, and may your youth be renewed like the eagle's (Psalm 103:5).

MAY 27

Got to Tell Somebody

But life is worth nothing unless I use it for doing the work assigned me by the Lord Jesus—the work of telling others the Good News about God's mighty kindness and love.

—Acts 20:24 (TLB)

We are all commanded to go and make disciples. In Matthew 28:19–20, Jesus tells us, "Therefore, go and make disciples of all the nations, baptizing them in the name of the Father and the Son and the Holy Spirit. Teach these new disciples to obey all the commands I have given you. And be sure of this: I am with you always, even to the end of the age" (NLT).

There is a beautiful promise in this scripture. It is that we are not alone. Jesus is with us always, even to the end of the age

When we recount all of the incredible blessings that are ours simply from knowing God, we cannot help but tell others of Him!

Isaiah 52:7 says, "How beautiful on the mountains are the feet of the messenger who brings good news, the good news of peace and salvation, the news that the God of Israel reigns" (NLT)!

Do you have beautiful feet that are sharing the good news?

May we finish the work God has given us to do, sharing the good news that Jesus saves.

MAY 28

Keep On Keeping On

So if you are suffering according to God's will, keep on doing what is right and trust yourself to the God who made you, for he will never fail you.

—1 Peter 4:19 (TLB)

Do you ever get discouraged when you are doing right and wondering how much longer you will have to endure?

Galatians 6:9 reminds us that God's timing is perfect and that we can endure. It says, "So let's not get tired of doing what is good. At just the right time we will reap a harvest of blessing if we don't give up."

The Holy Bible also reminds us not to make judgments about others before Christ's return. We don't always see the secrets and private motives of others. First Corinthians 4:5 says, "So don't make judgments about anyone ahead of time—before the Lord returns. For he will bring our darkest secrets to light and will reveal our private motives. Then God will give to each one whatever praise is due" (NLT).

Our job is to be available and to walk in obedience to God. If we do that, we can count on Him to take care of the rest.

Psalm 37:18 says, "Day by day the Lord takes care of the innocent, and they will receive an inheritance that lasts forever" (NLT).

MAY 29

Blinded by the Light

I was blinded by the intense light and had to be led into Damascus by my companions.

—Acts 22:11 (TLB)

Saul of Tarsus, aka Paul the apostle, was blinded by the light on the road to Damascus. It pleased God to use this man, the son of a Jewish mother and Roman father, to spread the good news to Jew and Gentile alike. He was uniquely qualified to carry out the tasks God had set before him.

You are uniquely qualified, too.

When you walk in obedience to Christ, making yourself available to Him at all times, the light of your life shines so bright that it cannot be hidden.

Matthew 5:14–16 tells us, "You are the light of the world—like a city on a hilltop that cannot be hidden. No one lights a lamp and then puts it under a basket. Instead, a lamp is placed on a stand, where it gives light to everyone in the house. In the same way, let your good deeds shine out for all to see, so that everyone will praise your heavenly Father" (NLT).

But many in the world have been blinded to this light, as 2 Corinthians 4:4 says: "Satan, who is the god of this world, has blinded the minds of those who don't believe. They are unable to see the glorious light of the Good News. They don't understand this message about the glory of Christ, who is the exact likeness of God" (NLT).

May we never give up and never get discouraged "for the light makes everything visible. This is why it is said, 'Awake, O sleeper, rise up from the dead, and Christ will give you light'" (Ephesians 5:14 NLT).

MAY 30

Caught in the Splendor

I will meditate about your glory, splendor, majesty, and miracles.

—Psalm 145:5 (TLB)

It is good to dwell on the goodness and the splendor of God, and call to mind all of the glorious miracles He has done for us.

Psalm 103:2 reminds us, "Let all that I am praise the Lord; may I never forget the good things he does for me" (NLT).

Meditating on the majesty of God, being caught up in the splendor of all that He is, allows us to regain the proper spiritual perspective and shed the worldliness that distracts and drags us away from His holy purposes.

Do you need to be reminded today of God's splendor?

Deuteronomy 33:26 says, "There is no one like the God of Israel. He rides across the heavens to help you, across the skies in majestic splendor."

Have you experienced the majesty of God riding across the heavens to help you? Perhaps you just need to call the events to mind.

First Chronicles 16:29 tells us, "Give to the Lord the glory he deserves! Bring your offering and come into his presence. Worship the Lord in all his holy splendor" (NLT).

May you be caught up in the splendor of all that is our Master, our Savior, our Jesus, today and every day.

MAY 31

Just Like Daddy

Yes, dear friends, we are already God's children, right now, and we can't even imagine what it is going to be like later on. But we do know this, that when he comes we will be like him, as a result of seeing him as he really is.

—1 John 3:2 (TLB)

At a recent family gathering, several adults were commenting about how my nieces and nephews were considerably like their fathers. My sister-in-law asked if I was seeing similar traits in my two children. I responded that I was seeing a great deal of their father—their heavenly Father—in them and that it made me very happy.

Are you becoming more and more like Daddy?

In order to become just like Him, we must spend time with Him. Are you doing that?

To be like Him, we must also do the things that He would have us do. Are you doing that, too?

Colossians 3:10 tells us, "Put on your new nature, and be renewed as you learn to know your Creator and become like him" (NLT).

May we spend time with our beloved Father, doing the things that please Him so that we may be just like Him.

JUNE 1

Silence the Horn

Don't praise yourself; let others do it!

—Proverbs 27:2 (TLB)

Were you taught not to toot your own horn? I was.

I heard this from my parents and my grandparents, and from many teachers in school, too. They would say, "Don't be a bragger" or "You shouldn't think too highly of yourself" (NLT).

The Holy Bible confirms this teaching in Romans 12:3, which reads, "For I say, through the grace given to me, to everyone who is among you, not to think of himself more highly than he ought to think, but to think soberly, as God has dealt to each one a measure of faith (NKJV)."

When we are tempted to toot to others about our own accomplishments, we must remember that God sees all things (Proverbs 24:12). He will give to us according to our due (Jeremiah 17:10).

The Holy Bible tells us that Moses was more humble than any other man (Numbers 12:3). God wants us to be humble, too. It is much easier for God to lead, guide, and direct a humble man or woman than someone who is boastful.

And don't forget, "Pride goes before destruction, and haughtiness before a fall" (Proverbs 16:18 NLT).

Next time you are tempted to brag about your accomplishments, remember that apart from Christ, we can do nothing (John 15:5).

JUNE 2

The Faithful Few

It is the same today. Not all the Jews have turned away from God; there are a few being saved as a result of God's kindness in choosing them.

—Romans 11:5 (TLB)

Are you one of God's faithful few?

What does it look like to be one of God's faithful?

Jesus tells us in Matthew 24:25, "A faithful, sensible servant is one to whom the master can give the responsibility of managing his other household servants and feeding them" (NLT).

There are many examples of God's faithful servants in the Holy Bible. Paul mentions Epaphras as a faithful servant in Colossians 1:7, and Ephesians 3:5 tells us about Moses's faithfulness when it says, "Moses was certainly faithful in God's house as a servant. His work was an illustration of the truths God would reveal later" (NLT).

Have you been God's faithful servant? If not, you can start today. And remember that God rewards His faithful.

Luke 19:17 reads, "'Well done!' the king exclaimed. 'You are a good servant. You have been faithful with the little I entrusted to you, so you will be governor of ten cities as your reward'" (NLT).

"But be sure to fear the Lord and faithfully serve him. Think of all the wonderful things he has done for you" (1 Samuel 12:24 NLT).

JUNE 3

Lord Willin' and the Creek Don't Rise

Don't brag about your plans for tomorrow—wait and see what happens.

—Proverbs 27:1 (TLB)

When I was young, I had a tendency to plan every detail of my life. It didn't take long to figure out that life just doesn't allow for the detail and depth of planning I was counting on. Creeks *do* rise on occasion, and sometimes we are unable to cross them.

Some folks have a tendency to be planners, which is not necessarily a bad thing. It's when our planning supersedes the plans of the Almighty that is the problem.

James 4:13–16 tells us the following:

Look here, you who say, "Today or tomorrow we are going to a certain town and will stay there a year. We will do business there and make a profit." How do you know what your life will be like tomorrow? Your life is like the morning fog—it's here a little while, then it's gone. What you ought to say is, "If the Lord wants us to, we will live and do this or that." Otherwise you are boasting about your own pretentious plans, and all such boasting is evil. (NLT)

God has plans for us. When we become adamant about our own pretentious plans, we miss out on God's best for us.

Jeremiah 29:11 tells us, "'For I know the plans I have for you,' says the Lord. 'They are plans for good and not for disaster, to give you a future and a hope'" (NLT).

Our days are in His hands. May we commit each one of those days to Him.

JUNE 4

Speak Up

You should defend those who cannot help themselves.

—Proverbs 31:8 (TLB)

Vanessa had been treated poorly by her manager for years. She mentioned some things to the powers that be from time to time, but nothing was ever done about the problem. The abuse was common knowledge to everyone around Vanessa, yet no one ever spoke up about it.

One day, a new manager joined the company. This manager witnessed the abuse and knew he had to speak up for Vanessa. Her spirit was being crushed like a bug day after day.

The new manager went to Human Resources with the stories of abuse. Vanessa's manager was fired after a full investigation. Vanessa was then given her manager's job. She had always been more qualified. And the company began to thrive as never before.

Speaking up pays off. Why? Because it is the right thing to do. It is what God wants us to do. And God rewards us for doing what is right (Isaiah 58:11).

Isaiah 1:17 tells us, "Learn to do good. Seek justice. Help the oppressed. Defend the cause of orphans. Fight for the rights of widows" (NLT).

May we speak up for those who need our voice today and every day.

JUNE 5

God Is True

True, some of them were unfaithful, but just because they broke their promises to God, does that mean God will break his promises? Of course not! Though everyone else in the world is a liar, God is not. Do you remember what the book of Psalms says about this? That God's words will always prove true and right, no matter who questions them.

—Romans 3:3–4 (TLB)

God is true. His Word is true. He never lies. He never fails. When we accept Him as our Savior, we are saved by His grace, but that does not mean we have no responsibility. We must still obey Him.

There are many in our pulpits today who preach just the opposite, but they need to read the Holy Bible they claim to believe.

Romans 3:5–8 tells us the following:

"But," some might say, "our sinfulness serves a good purpose, for it helps people see how righteous God is. Isn't it unfair, then, for him to punish us?" (This is merely a human point of view.) Of course not! If God were not entirely fair, how would he be qualified to judge the world? "But," someone might still argue, "how can God condemn me as a sinner if my dishonesty highlights his truthfulness and brings him more glory?" And some people even slander us by claiming that we say, "The more we sin, the better it is!" Those who say such things deserve to be condemned. (NLT)

Someone who continues in willful disobedience to God, claiming that God's grace will cover his sin, does not know Him as Savior.

Jesus tells us in Matthew 7:21, "Not everyone who calls out to me, 'Lord! Lord!' will enter the Kingdom of Heaven. Only those who actually do the will of my Father in heaven will enter."

May His goodness and His truth draw us all into a right relationship with Him.

JUNE 6

That's Paradise

And Jesus replied, "Today you will be with me in Paradise. This is a solemn promise."

—Luke 23:43 (TLB)

Paradise is where the story of the Holy Bible begins—the Garden of Eden. Adam and Eve are there, but more importantly, God is there. He even walks and talks with them in the cool of the evening (Genesis 3:8).

Paradise is where the story of the Holy Bible ends, too. Those who have done the will of God will be there. And more importantly, God will be there.

Revelation 2:7 tells us, "Anyone with ears to hear must listen to the Spirit and understand what he is saying to the churches. To everyone who is victorious I will give fruit from the tree of life in the paradise of God" (NLT).

Jesus promised the thief on the cross that he will be with Him in paradise because the thief believed in Him. The thief believed that Jesus was the Son of God.

What more is required of us than simply to believe? Nothing. Why? Because true believing is active, and obedience is the evidence of it.

Romans 10:10 says, "For it is by believing in your heart that you are made right with God, and it is by openly declaring your faith that you are saved" (NLT).

That's paradise.

JUNE 7

Roadblock Ahead

But remember this—the wrong desires that come into your life aren't anything new and different. Many others have faced exactly the same problems before you. And no temptation is irresistible. You can trust God to keep the temptation from becoming so strong that you can't stand up against it, for he has promised this and will do what he says. He will show you how to escape temptation's power so that you can bear up patiently against it.

—1 Corinthians 10:13 (TLB)

Recent heavy rains in our city prompted city officials to put up roadblocks to protect citizens from flooded roadways. The news re orted one evening that,

sadly, someone had driven around a roadblock only to meet their demise when the floodwaters engulfed their car and they were unable to get out.

Some might say, "Who would be foolish enough to drive around a roadblock? Surely they saw the high water ahead!" Yet you and I do it every day.

God sets up roadblocks for us to protect us from the temptations to sin that lie ahead. He gives us commandments and other rules to live by in order to protect us. Yet just like the driver going around the roadblock, we bulldoze, drive around, and move God's protective roadblocks out of the way so that we can sin. And like that driver, if we don't turn around, we will eventually meet our demise.

Ecclesiastes 8:5–6, in talking about obedience to the king says, "Those who obey him will not be punished. Those who are wise will find a time and a way to do what is right, for there is a time and a way for everything, even when a person is in trouble" (NLT).

May we be mindful of God's protective roadblocks all around us and rest in safety.

JUNE 8

Wake Up

Do you think the work of harvesting will not begin until the summer ends four months from now? Look around you! Vast fields of human souls are ripening all around us, and are ready now for reaping.

—John 4:35 (TLB)

When suggesting in a recent adult Bible fellowship class that we gather on the weekend to visit folks in our community door-to-door, I was met with an overwhelming lack of interest.

Having grown up with a pastor father who constantly visited the people of any and every community we lived in, I was surprised by this. After all, the Holy Bible tells us in Matthew 28:19–20, "Therefore, go and make disciples of all the nations, baptizing them in the name of the Father and the Son and the Holy Spirit. Teach these new disciples to obey all the commands I have given you. And be sure of this: I am with you always, even to the end of the age" (NLT).

If we don't wake up and tell those around us of God's love for them, then who will?

Romans 10:14 tells us, "But how can they call on him to save them unless they believe in him? And how can they believe in him if they have never heard about him? And how can they hear about him unless someone tells them" (NLT)?

May we awaken from our slumber and quickly carry out the tasks given to us by the One who sent us, as the night is coming when no one will work (John 9:4).

JUNE 9

Rejected Silver

"O Lord God," I said, "I can't do that! I'm far too young! I'm only a youth!"

—Jeremiah 1:6 (TLB)

Jeremiah was a reluctant prophet, yet God had put His words in Jeremiah's mouth and promised to protect him (Jeremiah 1:7–9). God still places His words in people's mouths today, and He protects them as they proclaim His unpopular truth.

In the book of Jeremiah, we find that both Israel and Judah are living in staunch rebellion against God, much as we find our world today.

In Jeremiah 6, God uses Jeremiah to give Judah a final warning with regard to their constant hard-hearted rebellion, and He proclaims Jeremiah a tester of metals, that is, a tester of the quality of the people.

The result of this quality test is found in Jeremiah 6:28–30, which says, "They are the worst kind of rebel, full of slander. They are as hard as bronze and iron, and they lead others into corruption. The bellows fiercely fan the flames to burn out the corruption. But it does not purify them, for the wickedness remains. I will label them 'Rejected Silver,' for I, the Lord, am discarding them" (NLT).

I don't know about you, but I do not want to be discarded by God.

May we repent of our slander and corruption, and may God soften our hearts and quicken our feet to serve Him every day of our lives.

JUNE 10

Faith vs. Sight

We know these things are true by believing, not by seeing.

—2 Corinthians 5:7 (TLB)

Do you live by faith or by sight? Following is a little test:

Sight says, "Leaving the home I know and love to become a missionary can't be God's will for my life. It would be too much change for my family. It just isn't reasonable."

Faith says, "Then he said to the crowd, 'If any of you wants to be my follower, you must turn from your selfish ways, take up your cross daily, and follow me'" (Luke 9:23 NLT).

Sight says, "I can't be the teacher that you've called me to be, Lord. My family needs a lawyer's salary to survive and make ends meet. It's only practical."

Faith says, "And this same God who takes care of me will supply all your needs from his glorious riches, which have been given to us in Christ Jesus" (Philippians 4:19 NLT).

Let me ask the question again: Do you live by faith or by sight?

May we live by faith and be the seeds described in Luke 8:15: "And the seeds that fell on the good soil represent honest, good-hearted people who hear God's word, cling to it, and patiently produce a huge harvest" (NLT).

JUNE 11

Real Treasure

If your profits are in heaven, your heart will be there too.

—Matthew 6:21 (TLB)

Do you treasure earthly things?

Many people are driven to spend the majority of their lives working to get a bigger house, a better car, nicer clothes, and a bigger bank account, to go on lavish vacations and so forth.

Working and being able to afford these things is not wrong. In the scripture above, it is the motivation of our heart that God is speaking to. God knows that we need things, and His Word tells us that He will provide for all of those needs.

Matthew 6:31–33 tells us, "So don't worry about these things, saying, 'What will we eat? What will we drink? What will we wear?' These things dominate the thoughts of unbelievers, but your heavenly Father already knows all your needs. Seek the Kingdom of God above all else, and live righteously, and he will give you everything you need" (NLT).

In Matthew 6:19–20, Jesus says, "Don't store up treasures here on earth, where moths eat them and rust destroys them, and where thieves break in and steal. Store your treasures in heaven, where moths and rust cannot destroy, and thieves do not break in and steal" (NLT).

Real treasure can only be found in knowing, *really knowing*, the person of Jesus Christ.

JUNE 12

Drawn to Repentance

Don't you realize how patient he is being with you? Or don't you care? Can't you see that he has been waiting all this time without punishing you, to give you time to turn from your sin? His kindness is meant to lead you to repentance.

—Romans 2:4 (TLB)

Do you ever stop to think about how kind and good God is and has been to you?

When we stop, even for a moment, to consider all of the goodness of God, His blessings, and His mercy, sacrifice, and love, how can we possibly be so hard-hearted as to *not* repent of our sin?

Real repentance is much more than feeling sorrow for being *caught* in sin. The Holy Bible tells us what real repentance is.

Second Corinthians 7:10 tells us, "For the kind of sorrow God wants us to experience leads us away from sin and results in salvation. There's no regret for that kind of sorrow. But worldly sorrow, which lacks repentance, results in spiritual death" (NLT).

Have you been drawn to repent of a particular sin that has a strong hold on your life? Remember what God's Word says in Proverbs 15:22: "An evil man is held captive by his own sins; they are ropes that catch and hold him" (NLT).

First John 5:18 promises us, "We know that God's children do not make a practice of sinning, for God's Son holds them securely, and the evil one cannot touch them" (NLT).

May the goodness and kindness of God lead us to repentance now and always.

JUNE 13

Secret Admirers

But Jesus told him, "Anyone who lets himself be distracted from the work I plan for him is not fit for the Kingdom of God."

—LUKE 9:62 (TLB)

Are you a true follower of Christ or simply a secret admirer?

Secret admirers are those people who admire everything about Christ and the things He has done but who are not willing to take that next step of committing to follow Him. In certain circumstances, these people do not even want others to know that they admire Him. Hence, they are *secret* admirers.

Satan would be in the category of secret admirer, too.

The Holy Bible tells us that much is required of us in order to be followers of Christ, and that we are to count the cost, giving great consideration to the decision.

In Luke 14:28–29, Jesus tells us, "But don't begin until you count the cost. For who would begin construction of a building without first calculating the cost to see if there is enough money to finish it? Otherwise, you might complete only the foundation before running out of money, and then everyone would laugh at you" (NLT).

He also tells us that the reward far outweighs the cost.

First Peter 3:14 tells us, "But even if you suffer for doing what is right, God will reward you for it. So don't worry or be afraid of their threats" (NLT).

May we refuse to be secret admirers, and may we proclaim the salvation of our faithful Savior now and forevermore.

JUNE 14

Sugar, Spice, and Everything Nice

Kind words are like honey—enjoyable and healthful.

—Proverbs 16:24 (TLB)

We all enjoy hearing kind words—especially when they are true and sincere. God's Words are always true. They are also always sincere.

Psalm 33:4 tells us, "For the word of the Lord holds true, and we can trust everything he does" (NLT).

Proverbs 10:32 says, "The lips of the godly speak helpful words, but the mouth of the wicked speaks perverse words" (NLT).

And Proverbs 30:5 says, "Every word of God proves true. He is a shield to all who come to him for protection" (NLT).

What about your words? Are they kind, truthful, sincere?

First Peter 2:1 reminds us, "So get rid of all evil behavior. Be done with all deceit, hypocrisy, jealousy, and all unkind speech" (NLT).

We must remember that our speech, whether kind or unkind, truthful or false, sincere or insincere, is a reflection of the condition of our heart. "For out of the abundance of the heart, the mouth speaks" (Matthew 12:34 NKJV).

JUNE 15

His Prized Possession

And it was a happy day for him when he gave us our new lives through the truth of his Word, and we became, as it were, the first children in his new family.

—JAMES 1:18 (TLB)

Do you know you are God's prized possession?

Out of all that God has created on this earth, we are His favorites.

It's nice to be God's favorites. He has given us everything and infinitely more than that. When we consider all that He has done for us, His requirements of us seem so small.

He requires that we believe in His Son, Jesus. We read in John 11:25, "Jesus told her, 'I am the resurrection and the life. Anyone who believes in me will live, even after dying'" (NLT).

He requires that we re ent of sin. As Acts 20:21 tells us, "I have had one message for Jews and Greeks alike—the necessity of repenting from sin and turning to God, and of having faith in our Lord Jesus" (NLT).

And we must have faith. Hebrews 11:6 says, "And it is impossible to please God without faith. Anyone who wants to come to him must believe that God exists and that he rewards those who sincerely seek him" (NLT).

May we live in the complete fullness of the knowledge that we are beloved, prized, and adored by the Creator of the Universe, and may we strive to please Him more each day.

JUNE 16

The Time We Are Given

So be careful how you act; these are difficult days. Don't be fools; be wise: make the most of every opportunity you have for doing good.

—Ephesians 5:15–16 (TLB)

The time we are given on this earth is limited. Our life, our time, is in His hands (Psalm 31:15).

James 4:14 says, "How do you know what your life will be like tomorrow? Your life is like the morning fog—it's here a little while, then it's gone" (NLT).

We should always be available to be used by God, yet some people wait on the sidelines, never doing anything because they are still waiting for God to tell them what to do.

The problem with that is that they fail to recognize the many opportunities God has placed all around them to serve Him.

Colossians 4:5 says, "Live wisely among those who are not believers, and make the most of every opportunity" (NLT).

Are your eyes open to the many opportunities God has laid before you? Is your heart prepared?

Psalm 90:12 tells us, "Teach us to realize the brevity of life, so that we may grow in wisdom" (NLT).

We must work, because the time is coming when our many opportunities will end (John 9:4).

JUNE 17

Safe in God's Treasure Pouch

Even when you are chased by those who seek to kill you, your life is safe in the care of the Lord your God, secure in his treasure pouch! But the lives of your enemies will disappear like stones shot from a sling!

—1 Samuel 25:29 (NLT)

These words were spoken by Abigail to David as she sought to appease his anger toward her foolish husband, Nabal.

It was true for David. God had held him safe and secure in His treasure pouch while the likes of King Saul tried on more than one occasion to kill him.

The same is true for you and me. Psalm 63:8 reminds us of God's protection: "I cling to you; your strong right hand holds me securely" (NLT).

Do remember the story of Peter and Jesus in the midst of the storm, recorded in Matthew 14:22–33? Jesus came to rescue the disciples in the midst of the storm, walking on the water. But they were afraid, thinking He was a ghost. Matthew 14:28–31 tells us what happened next:

Then Peter called to him, "Lord, if it's really you, tell me to come to you, walking on the water." "Yes, come," Jesus said. So Peter went over the side of the boat and walked on the water toward Jesus. But when he saw the strong wind and the waves, he was terrified and began to sink. "Save me, Lord!" he shouted. Jesus immediately reached out and grabbed him. "You have so little faith," Jesus said. "Why did you doubt me?" (NLT)

Peter had been safe in the treasure pouch of Jesus all along.

May we never fail to believe that all God's children are safe in His treasure pouch—now and forevermore.

JUNE 18

Distracted Driving

But Martha was the jittery type and was worrying over the big dinner she was preparing. She came to Jesus and said, "Sir, doesn't it seem unfair to you that my sister just sits here while I do all the work? Tell her to come and help me."

—LUKE 10:40 (TLB)

We live in a distracted generation.

From freeway texting to people so engrossed in their electronic devices that they can't walk without bumping into others, almost everywhere you turn, you see distractions and the distracted.

We are distracted from our true, God-given purpose too, just like Martha. God's plans are so far beyond and better than any and every distraction that could ever steal us away.

We all know that distracted driving leads to crashes. That is true not only in cars, but also in life God wants us to focus all of our attention on Him, and He wants us to obey Him. When we do that, we don't crash, even when difficulties and distractions are all around us.

Joshua 1:7 reminds us, "Be strong and very courageous. Be careful to obey all the instructions Moses gave you. Do not deviate from them, turning either to the right or to the left. Then you will be successful in everything you do" (NLT).

May you focus all of your attention on the road God has set before you, so that you may be successful in all you do.

JUNE 19

Tradition vs. Truth

The traditional fasts and times of mourning you have kept in July, August, October, and January are ended. They will be changed to joyous festivals if you love truth and peace!

—Zechariah 8:19 (TLB)

Are you living your life based on tradition or real biblical truth?

I recently had a conversation with someone who was quoting a passage that doesn't exist in the Holy Bible. It was, "The lion will lay with the lamb." We've probably all heard the quotation, but its source isn't scripture. The scripture says in Isaiah 11:6, "In that day the wolf and the lamb will live together; the leopard will lie down with the baby goat. The calf and the yearling will be safe with the lion, and a little child will lead them all" (NLT).

I've also heard a great many people say that suicide sends one's soul straight to hell. Yet this is not a biblical notion either. There are six biblical examples of suicide: Abimelech (Judges 9:54), Saul (1 Samuel 31:4), Saul's armor-bearer (1 Samuel 31:4–6), Ahithophel (2 Samuel 17:23), Zimri (1 Kings 16:18), and Judas (Matthew 27:5). Of these examples, Judas is the only one we are certain did not go to heaven.

How well do you know God's holy Word? Are you living by tradition and hearsay, or are you living by the truth of God's Word? Are you getting your truth from the lips of others, or are you reading your Holy Bible each and every day to learn the truth for yourself?

May we fill our lives up with so much of God's truth that we have no room for tradition.

JUNE 20

May I Take It Back?

When he saw her, he tore his clothes in anguish. "Alas, my daughter!" he cried out. "You have brought me to the dust. For I have made a vow to the Lord and I cannot take it back."

—JUDGES 11:35 (TLB)

How many times have you wished you never said it, did it, thought it?

There are so many words, deeds, and thoughts we wish we could take back. And though God forgives, we must still face consequences.

The story of Jephthah in Judges 11 is a prime example. Jephthah was a great warrior of Gilead who had been driven to the land of Tob by his half-brothers, who did not want him to share in their inheritance. Jephthah was the son of a prostitute. When the Ammonites began to attack Israel, the elders of Gilead asked him to return. They promised to make Jephthah judge over Israel if he would lead them in victory over the Ammonites.

Jephthah made a vow that if God would give him victory over the Ammonites, he would give to the Lord as a sacrifice whatever came out of his house first to meet him.

Jephthah's daughter came out to meet him first. O how he wished he could take back that vow.

Our actions, our words, can have powerful, widespread impact—both for bad and for good. Proverbs 14:15b says, "The prudent carefully consider their steps" (NLT).

May we consider carefully the impact of everything we say and do, allowing the Holy Spirit to control our lives always.

JUNE 21

The Struggle of Depression

What is faith? It is the confident assurance that something we want is going to happen. It is the certainty that what we hope for is waiting for us, even though we cannot see it up ahead.

—Hebrews 11:1 (TLB)

Do you struggle with depression?

We all have days in which circumstances leave us upset or distraught for a time, but dwelling in a depressed state continually is a reflection of our heart's condition.

Depression exposes a lack of faith, for the two are mutually exclusive. They cannot coexist. The Holy Bible tells us in Hebrews 11:6, "And it is impossible to please God without faith. Anyone who wants to come to him must believe that God exists and that he rewards those who sincerely seek him."

If your heart is breaking, God is there for you.

Psalm 34:18 promises, "The Lord is close to the brokenhearted; he rescues those whose spirits are crushed" (NLT).

God is also the source of all comfort.

Second Corinthians 1:3 tells us, "All praise to God, the Father of our Lord Jesus Christ. God is our merciful Father and the source of all comfort" (NLT).

Do you believe it?

May we never forget His goodness, as 2 Corinthians 1:4 reminds us, "He comforts us in all our troubles so that we can comfort others. When they are troubled, we will be able to give them the same comfort God has given us" (NLT).

JUNE 22

What to Do

And if you leave God's paths and go astray, you will hear a voice behind you say, "No, this is the way; walk here."

—Isaiah 30:21 (TLB)

Have you ever wondered what God wanted you to do or where He wanted you to go? Perhaps that is precisely where you find yourself right now.

The Holy Bible promises us that God will guide us on the paths we should take.

Psalm 32:8 reminds us, "The Lord says, 'I will guide you along the best pathway for your life. I will advise you and watch over you'" (NLT).

God led Abram to leave his homeland of Haran and follow Him in faith when he was seventy-five years old (Genesis 12). Often when God is speaking to us, we fail to listen, but God's voice is often a whisper.

In 1 Kings 19:11–12, God whispered to Elijah.

"Go out and stand before me on the mountain," the Lord told him. And as Elijah stood there, the Lord passed by, and a mighty windstorm hit the mountain. It was such a terrible blast that the rocks were torn loose, but the Lord was not in the wind. After the wind there was an earthquake, but the Lord was not in the earthquake. And after the earthquake there was a fire, but the Lord was not in the fire. And after the fire there was the sound of a gentle whisper. (NLT)

Do you hear Him telling you what to do?

May you seek Him with your whole heart until you find Him (Jeremiah 29:13).

JUNE 23

Hiding from God

That evening they heard the sound of the Lord God walking in the garden; and they hid themselves among the trees.

—Genesis 3:8 (TLB)

Are you hiding from God?

When a dog chews up its owner's favorite sofa, it hides. Why? The dog hides because it knows it was naughty.

Naughtiness is sin. The word sounds cute, but it is still sin.

After Adam and Eve ate from the tree of the knowledge of good and evil, they hid. They hid from God because they had been naughty. They had sinned, and they knew it was wrong.

When we sin, we often hide from God too. We think that if we hide from Him, He won't see our sin. But He does see it.

Job 34:21 tells us, "For God watches how people live; he sees everything they do" (NLT).

Jeremiah 16:17 says, "I am watching them closely, and I see every sin. They cannot hope to hide from me" (NLT).

We are so much more transparent than we realize.

May we come before our heavenly Father in confession and repentance, as 1 John 1:9 reminds us, "But if we confess our sins to him, he is faithful and just to forgive us our sins and to cleanse us from all wickedness" (NLT).

JUNE 24

When We've Had Enough

Then he went on alone into the wilderness, traveling all day, and sat down under a broom bush and prayed that he might die. "I've had enough," he told the Lord. "Take away my life. I've got to die sometime, and it might as well be now."

—1 Kings 19:4 (TLB)

Have you ever felt as though you've had enough?

That is exactly where we find Elijah in this passage of scripture. He had killed all of the prophets of Baal, and the evil queen Jezebel had sent a message saying, "May the gods strike me and even kill me if by this time tomorrow I have not killed you just as you killed them" (1 Kings 19:2b NLT).

Elijah fled for his life to Beersheba to leave his servant, and then he went on alone into the wilderness. He was exhausted and stressed beyond words. But notice God's loving care of Elijah after he poured out his heart.

First Kings 19:5–6 tells us, "Then he lay down and slept under the broom tree. But as he was sleeping, an angel touched him and told him, 'Get up and eat!' He looked around and there beside his head was some bread baked on hot stones and a jar of water! So he ate and drank and lay down again" (NLT). Afterward, Elijah had the strength to travel forty days and nights to Mount Sinai, the mountain of God.

Sometimes when we are overwhelmed with life, a good meal and a rest can help to brighten our perspective, giving us strength to face the journey ahead, much like a child who hasn't had his or her nap or supper but who then slumbers a bit and afterwards has a meal.

May we remember always to be open and honest in our conversations with God. He will meet our every need, even when we've had enough.

JUNE 25

The Propensity to Sin

So if your hand or foot causes you to sin, cut it off and throw it away. Better to enter heaven crippled than to be in hell with both of your hands and feet.

—Matthew 18:8 (TLB)

Recently, I had a conversation with someone I have known for some time. This person was trying to convince me that homosexual people are born as homosexuals.

"You're right," I said. "We are all born into sin."

Romans 5:12 tells us, "When Adam sinned, sin entered the world. Adam's sin brought death, so death spread to everyone, for everyone sinned" (NLT).

When ruled by our flesh, we each have a propensity to commit certain sins. Each of us may have a different sin we struggle with, such as gluttony, drunkenness, lying, adultery, homosexuality, covetousness, or greed. The list could go on and on.

But, it is still sin.

We can't excuse it away or take a pill to fix it. The answer is a real personal relationship with Jesus Christ, God's Son. He is the answer. He is the Great Physician. We must choose to be ruled by God's Spirit rather than our flesh.

First John 3:9 tells us, "Those who have been born into God's family do not make a practice of sinning, because God's life is in them. So they can't keep on sinning, because they are children of God" (NLT).

May the Spirit of the living God dwell in you richly, keeping you from the propensity to sin.

JUNE 26

You Can Lead a Horse to Water

But if you are unwilling to obey the Lord, then decide today whom you will obey. Will it be the gods of your ancestors beyond the Euphrates or the gods of the Amorites here in this land? But as for me and my family, we will serve the Lord.

—Joshua 24:15 (TLB)

There is an old saying that goes, "You can lead a horse to water, but you can't make it drink." The same is true of the choice to follow after Christ. We can lead, guide, direct, educate, and spend an entire life in church, but if a person doesn't make a personal decision to follow Christ with everything they have and everything they are, we can't make them

God gives us the free will to choose.

Romans 6:16 tells us, "Don't you realize that you become the slave of whatever you choose to obey? You can be a slave to sin, which leads to death, or you can choose to obey God, which leads to righteous living" (NLT).

Even though many know this truth, they are still very stubborn, not wanting to give up their own way, much like the horse.

Romans 2:5 warns us about such stubbornness: "But because you are stubborn and refuse to turn from your sin, you are storing up terrible punishment for yourself. For a day of anger is coming, when God's righteous judgment will be revealed" (NLT).

May we escape this terrible punishment, as God has led us to His springs of living water so that we never thirst again.

JUNE 27

Light Up the Sky

For God had made two huge lights, the sun and moon, to shine down upon the earth—the larger one, the sun, to preside over the day and the smaller one, the moon, to preside through the night; he had also made the stars. And God set them in the sky to light the earth, and to preside over the day and night, and to divide the light from the darkness. And God was pleased.

—Genesis 1:16–18 (TLB)

Have you ever lain on your back beneath a clear night sky to admire the stars, surrounded by an orchestra of nature? God's handiwork is always amazing and awe-inspiring.

During a recent trip to Yellowstone National Park, the glory of all that God is—all that He has done—struck me in a new and profound way.

I can say along with David, "When I look at the night sky and see the work of your fingers—the moon and the stars you set in place—what are mere mortals that you should think about them, human beings that you should care for them" (Psalm 8:3–4 NLT)?

Seeing God's handiwork in great surround begs us to worship our Creator rather than His creation (Deuteronomy 4:19).

Daniel 12:3 says it beautifully: "Those who are wise will shine as bright as the sky, and those who lead many to righteousness will shine like the stars forever" (NLT).

O that His wisdom would fill our lives so completely that we shine as bright as the sky, our righteousness like the stars forever.

JUNE 28

Narrow Thinking

The door to heaven is narrow. Work hard to get in, for the truth is that many will try to enter but when the head of the house has locked the door, it will be too late. Then if you stand outside knocking, and pleading, "Lord, open the door for us," he will reply, "I do not know you."

—Luke 13:24 (TLB)

The world is full of those who would ridicule, deride, and condemn the narrow mind. They would have you believe it is a mind that cannot know love, or that it is a critical and judgmental mind, having no place in a modern world.

Even the prophets in Isaiah's day were ridiculed by the rebellious people of Judah. Isaiah 30:10–11 says, "They tell the seers, 'Stop seeing visions!' They tell the prophets, 'Don't tell us what is right. Tell us nice things. Tell us lies. Forget all this gloom. Get off your narrow path. Stop telling us about your "Holy One of Israel."'"

But that's not what God says. God wants us to focus on truth, on Him. Philippians 3:13–14 tells us, "No, dear brothers and sisters, I have not achieved it, but I focus on this one thing: Forgetting the past and looking forward to what lies ahead, I press on to reach the end of the race and receive the heavenly prize for which God, through Christ Jesus, is calling us" (NLT). God wants us to find the narrow gate.

Matthew 7:13 says, "You can enter God's Kingdom only through the narrow gate. The highway to hell is broad, and its gate is wide for the many who choose that way" (NLT).

May we narrow the focus of our mind to find the remarkable person of Jesus Christ.

JUNE 29

The Real Race vs. The Rat Race

You were getting along so well. Who has interfered with you to hold you back from following the truth?

—GALATIANS 5:7 (TLB)

The world is a constant sea of distractions from the real eternal purposes that Jesus Christ has for your life.

There is television, to-do lists, work, play, school, and doctor and dentist appointments, and the list could go on and on. We schedule every moment of every day, tripping over each other as we frantically peck at our electronic devices.

We are surrounded by people, yet some of us rarely take the time to show common courtesy, let alone the real concern Jesus showed to every person He ever came into contact with.

Philippians 2:16 says, "Hold firmly to the word of life; then, on the day of Christ's return, I will be proud that I did not run the race in vain and that my work was not useless" (NLT).

And 1 Corinthians 9:24 reminds us, "Don't you realize that in a race everyone runs, but only one person gets the prize? So run to win" (NLT)!

Are you winning the race? Are you putting your faith completely in Christ, dependent on the Holy Spirit's power to guide you?

May we pray without ceasing (1 Thessalonians 5:17), humbling ourselves and resisting the Devil (James 4:7), so that we may say along with Paul, "I have fought the good fight, I have finished the race, and I have remained faithful" (2 Timothy 4:7 NLT).

JUNE 30

The Passion of the Christ

He put on righteousness as armor and the helmet of salvation on his head. He clothed himself with robes of vengeance and of godly fury.

—Isaiah 59:17 (TLB)

Are you a passionate person?

This verse tells us that Jesus Christ wrapped himself in a cloak of divine passion. A life of God's kind of passion is a life that is full to the brim with controlled emotion. A person who lives a passionate life feels deeply, very deeply. A person who lives a passionate life is aware of and completely sensitive to others.

God is passionate in His love for you and for me (Zechariah 8:2).

God's passion does not follow after the desires and inclinations of our sinful nature. On the contrary, as James 4:5 tells us, "Do you think the Scriptures have no meaning? They say that God is passionate that the spirit he has placed within us should be faithful to him" (NLT).

Are you wearing the body armor of righteousness? Is the helmet of salvation on your head?

May the passion of our divine God fill you with His Holy Spirit to become faithful to Him, through every ounce of your being.

JULY 1

Simply Beautiful

Everything is appropriate in its own time. But though God has planted eternity in the hearts of men, even so, many cannot see the whole scope of God's work from beginning to end.

—Ecclesiastes 3:11 (TLB)

Have you ever stopped to notice that God's handprint on things makes them beautiful?

His handprint on people makes them beautiful, too, simply beautiful. Is there something in your life that is not so beautiful?

When we turn things over to God, depending completely on Him, He will make our life beautiful in His own time. The concept is very simple, yet so often we fail to allow God's Holy Spirit to control our lives, and depend upon ourselves, instead.

Do you desire a beautiful family? Give your family to God. What about your livelihood? Commit your way to Him.

Do you want to have a beautiful life? Give your life completely and totally to God. He will make your life more beautiful than you could ever imagine it to be.

It will be simply beautiful.

JULY 2

Are We There Yet?

And I am sure that God who began the good work within you will keep right on helping you grow in his grace until his task within you is finally finished on that day when Jesus Christ returns.

—Philippians 1:6 (TLB)

When I was a child growing up, our family didn't have much money. Yet every summer our father would take two weeks of vacation and we would drive across the country, visiting family along the way, and explore some unknown destination on an adventure of our father's making.

I remember every trip fondly, although there were times when the air-conditioning broke down in the heat of summer, and times when we became exhausted. "Are we there yet, Father?" I would often ask.

When we became exhausted from those long drives across the country, my father knew just when to stop and buy ice cream cones to soothe the savage beasts my brother, my sister, and I had become. At that moment, I adored my father more than life itself. He read my mind. The cold, refreshing treat gave new life to my weary little body.

Like a child on a cross-country driving vacation, I often ask God, "Are we there yet?"

He lovingly and patiently answers me through His Word. No, we are not there yet. In fact, we will not be there yet until that glorious day when our sweet Jesus returns. He has a lot of work to do in and through our lives, and that can sometimes be exhausting for us.

But don't lose heart. There are ice-cream cones along the way.

JULY 3

Old Glory

But we Christians have no veil over our faces; we can be mirrors that brightly reflect the glory of the Lord. And as the Spirit of the Lord works within us, we become more and more like him.

—2 Corinthians 3:18 (TLB)

There is a glory that has shown itself throughout the ages. It is the glory of God.

Some think this glory is old and out of date, yet they fail to realize that truth never changes.

Second Corinthians 4:4 tells us, "Satan, who is the god of this world, has blinded the minds of those who don't believe They are unable to see the glorious light of the Good News. They don't understand this message about the glory of Christ, who is the exact likeness of God" (NLT)

God's truth is timeless as our heavenly Father is timeless.

Hebrews 13:8 tells us, "Jesus Christ is the same yesterday, today, and forever" (NLT).

James 1:17 says, "Whatever is good and perfect is a gift coming down to us from God our Father, who created all the lights in the heavens. He never changes or casts a shifting shadow" (NLT).

Does your life reflect truth, *real* truth, the truth of God?

May we live life in such a way that we become more and more like Him, reflecting the glory of the Lord to the world around us each and every day.

JULY 4

You're a Grand Ol' Flag

Rich men are conceited, but their real poverty is evident to the poor.

—Proverbs 28:11 (TLB)

At this time of year in the United States, we see the flag waving its true colors brilliantly from houses, storefronts, and light posts, and even on people.

But did you ever think about the fact that who you are and what you believe waves its true colors before the world just as boldly?

It's true.

The Holy Bible tells us in 2 Corinthians 6:4, "In everything we do, we show that we are true ministers of God. We patiently endure troubles and hardships and calamities of every kind" (NLT).

Conversely, Philippians 3:18 says, "For I have told you often before, and I say it again with tears in my eyes, that there are many whose conduct shows they are really enemies of the cross of Christ" (NLT).

What does your life reveal to others?

What flag are you waving to the world around you?

May we remember Matthew 5:16, which tells us, "In the same way, let your good deeds shine out for all to see, so that everyone will praise your heavenly Father" (NLT).

JULY 5

A Firm Foundation

All who listen to my instructions and follow them are wise, like a man who builds his house on solid rock.

—Matthew 7:24 (TLB)

You don't have to be born into a Christian family, or even a stable functional one, to set your life on the firm foundation of Jesus Christ.

Though many would have you believe that your upbringing determines the course of your life, this verse clearly tells us that anyone who listens to Jesus's teaching and follows it is wise, and is setting his life, his personal house, on a firm foundation.

What about you? Is your house on a firm foundation? Are you listening to and following the teachings of Jesus, or are you following the ways of the world?

Psalm 75:3 tells us, "When the earth quakes and its people live in turmoil, I am the one who keeps its foundations firm" (NLT).

When the storms of life surround us and all the world seems to be falling apart, may we always hope, always trust, in the one true and living God, our Savior, Jesus Christ.

He is the foundation that never fails.

JULY 6

Masquerade Party

It will become as evident as yeast in dough. Whatever they have said in the dark shall be heard in the light, and what you have whispered in the inner rooms shall be broadcast from the housetops for all to hear!

—LUKE 12:2–3 (TLB)

Are you ever surprised to learn that the character of someone close to you is not what you thought it was? It can be a startling blow.

It may surprise you and me when someone isn't whom they represent themselves to be, but it doesn't surprise God. He knows each and every heart, and He judges us accordingly.

This passage of scripture reminds us that one day all the masks will come off and we will know the truth about each other.

Sometimes the masks come off before the party has ended.

In Numbers 32:23, Moses warned the Israelites about saying one thing and doing another: "But if you fail to keep your word, then you will have sinned against the Lord, and you may be sure that your sin will find you out" (NLT).

The truth of who we really are, in the depth of our heart and soul, will always reveal itself. It is just a matter of when.

Do you have doubts about the character of someone close to you? Ask God to reveal that person's true nature.

He answers prayer (Hosea 14:8).

JULY 7

Settling Your Estate

And afterwards, when he wanted those rights back again, it was too late, even though he wept bitter tears of repentance. So remember, and be careful.

—Hebrews 12:17 (TLB)

When my mother passed away, one thing became abundantly clear to me as our family began the tedious task of settling her estate: her affairs were in order.

The things that came to light regarding her life were not ugly things; they were beautiful things. We received cards from people she had shown kindness to many years ago, and they never forgot her kindness. One particular note that stood out to me was from a woman whom my mother had bought clothes and other gifts for. The woman, now sixty-six years old, was just a girl when my mother gave to her, yet she remembered the kindness shown for all of those years and wanted us to know.

Matthew 25:40 tells us, "And the King will say, 'I tell you the truth, when you did it to one of the least of these my brothers and sisters, you were doing it to me'" (NLT)!

Are your affairs in order? Have you settled your estate with God? If you died today, what would come to light about your life?

First Timothy 5:25 says, "In the same way, the good deeds of some people are obvious. And the good deeds done in secret will someday come to light" (NLT).

May we live our lives in such a way that our good deeds done in secret will someday come to light.

JULY 8

The Heavenly Father's Care

Therefore, angels are only servants—spirits sent to care for people who will inherit salvation.

—Hebrews 1:14 (NLT)

The world we live in is a crazy, mixed-up place. Yet what a joy it is to know that we don't have to face this crazy, mixed-up place on our own.

In John 14:16, Jesus tells us, "And I will ask the Father, and he will give you another Advocate, who will never leave you" (NLT).

Not only has our heavenly Father given us an Advocate, the Holy Spirit, who will never leave us, but also He has sent us our own personal honor guard of angels to guard us wherever we go.

Psalm 34:7 says, "For the angel of the Lord is a guard; he surrounds and defends all who fear him" (NLT).

Are you in need of the heavenly Father's care?

Psalm 103:13 lovingly reassures us, "The Lord is like a father to his children, tender and compassionate to those who fear him" (NLT).

And Psalm 91:4 says, "He will cover you with his feathers. He will shelter you with his wings. His faithful promises are your armor and protection" (NLT).

May you find comfort in claiming the promises of the heavenly Father's care.

JULY 9

Bringing Up Baby

And when a person is still living on milk it shows he isn't very far along in the Christian life, and doesn't know much about the difference between right and wrong. He is still a baby Christian!

—Hebrews 5:13 (TLB)

You don't expect a baby to run at one week old, do you? Neither does God. In the same manner, you wouldn't expect a healthy twenty-year-old to still drink milk from a baby bottle, would you? Neither does God.

Hebrews 5:14 says, "You will never be able to eat solid spiritual food and understand the deeper things of God's Word until you become better Christians and learn right from wrong by practicing doing right" (TLB).

In the Christian life, as in the physical life, it is important for us to grow and mature. Just as doctors give us information to guide what is expected with regard to our physical growth, the Holy Bible is our guide for healthy spiritual growth. God wants us to be mature and complete in Him. He doesn't want us to miss out on any of His blessings. Are you still drinking milk from the bottle?

Hebrews 6:1 tells us the following:

Let us stop going over the same old ground again and again, always teaching those first lessons about Christ. Let us go on instead to other things and become mature in our understanding, as strong Christians ought to be. Surely we don't need to speak further about the foolishness of trying to be saved by being good, or about the necessity of faith in God. (TLB)

May we mature into the effective Christians God wants us to be.

JULY 10

Making the Bitter Better

Look after each other so that not one of you will fail to find God's best blessings. Watch out that no bitterness takes root among you, for as it springs up it causes deep trouble, hurting many in their spiritual lives.

—Hebrews 12:15 (TLB)

Is there any root of bitterness in your life?

Bitterness can be sneaky and take root when you fail to forgive others or have unrighteous anger in your heart. Bitterness is a deadly poison, robbing you of joy and destroying your relationships.

When you are bitter, you are incapable of loving others fully and completely.

Ephesians 4:31 tells us, "Stop being mean, bad-tempered, and angry. Quarreling, harsh words, and dislike of others should have no place in your lives" (TLB).

We know what causes bitterness, but how do we get rid of it?

Ephesians 4:32 has the answer. It says, "Instead, be kind to each other, tenderhearted, forgiving one another, just as God has forgiven you because you belong to Christ" (TLB).

In order to avoid bitterness, we must practice being kind, we must practice being tenderhearted, and we must make a practice of forgiving one another.

May we follow the practices of Jesus and have loving habits toward others so that we may live better rather than bitter.

JULY 11

Alive

For whatever God says to us is full of living power: it is sharper than the sharpest dagger, cutting swift and deep into our innermost thoughts and desires with all their parts, exposing us for what we really are.

—Hebrews 4:12 (TLB)

Are you alive?

That may sound like a silly question, but I'm not just talking about your physical body. I'm talking about the real you, the part of you that lasts forever—your soul.

What causes us to live a dead life is allowing our sin nature to control the way we comport ourselves.

Colossians 2:13 tells us, "You were dead in sins, and your sinful desires were not yet cut away. Then he gave you a share in the very life of Christ, for he forgave all your sins" (TLB).

Accepting Christ as your Savior and allowing the Holy Spirit to control you gives new life to your body and soul!

That's worth celebrating!

First Thessalonians 5:10 tells us, "He died for us so that we can live with him forever, whether we are dead or alive at the time of his return" (TLB).

May we live in such a way that we consider ourselves dead to the power of sin and alive to God through Jesus Christ (Romans 6:11).

JULY 12

Promises, Promises

And by that same mighty power he has given us all the other rich and wonderful blessings he promised; for instance, the promise to save us from the lust and rottenness all around us, and to give us his own character.

—2 Peter 1:4 (TLB)

Promises, promises.

Are you tired of all the people who have made you promises and then broken them?

Numbers 32:23 tells us, "But if you don't do as you have said, then you will have sinned against the Lord, and you may be sure that your sin will catch up with you" (TLB).

People may break their promises, but God never does. Psalm 119:140 says, "I have thoroughly tested your promises, and that is why I love them so much" (TLB).

The promises in God's Word are amazing. He never fails us. And claiming His promises gives us strength and hope to face any and every trial that could possibly come our way.

Second Samuel 22:31 reminds us, "As for God, his way is perfect;

The word of the Lord is true. He shields all who hide behind him" (TLB).

May we come to know in the depth of our soul that God's promises are enough to sustain us through life's brightest and darkest days.

Second Corinthians 7:1 tells us, "Having such great promises as these, dear friends, let us turn away from everything wrong, whether of body or spirit, and purify ourselves, living in the wholesome fear of God, giving ourselves to him alone" (TLB).

JULY 13

The Beauty of Our God

God's glory-light shines from the beautiful Temple on Mount Zion.

—Psalm 50:2 (TLB)

The beauty of all that God is, all that He touches, is mind-blowing. Look around you. Can you see the beauty of our God?

Open your eyes to see Him, His beauty, and His touch upon the lives of others, making them beautiful.

Psalm 96:6 says, "Honor and majesty surround him; strength and beauty fill his sanctuary."

With strength and beauty filling His sanctuary, is it any wonder that His very presence, His power, His touch, makes all things beautiful?

Isaiah 61:3 tells us, "To all who mourn in Israel, he will give a crown of beauty for ashes, a joyous blessing instead of mourning, festive praise instead of despair. In their righteousness, they will be like great oaks that the Lord has planted for his own glory" (NLT).

There is no mistaking the beauty of God in the world around us. It is an astounding light, a beacon drawing others to Him like a moth to a flame.

May your life and mine exhibit God's unmistakable beauty through every breath that we take and every step that we make, for Jesus' sake, amen.

JULY 14

My Security Blanket

With them on guard you can sleep without fear; you need not be afraid of disaster or the plots of wicked men, for the Lord is with you; he protects you.

—Proverbs 3:24–26 (TLB)

When my children were very young, they each carried around a security blanket, much like Linus from the *Peanuts* gang. The blankets were each a soft thermal fabric with satin trim, given to them by their Grandma Jeek.

The children were very attached to their blankets, even carrying them with them in the car on the way to preschool and kindergarten. The mere thought of separation from their *blankie* brought tears. They hugged their blankies, stroked them, and even spoke to them tenderly.

Yet when each of my children accepted Christ as their personal Savior, the need for the blankie began to subside. For now, there was real security—the security that can only come from a relationship with Jesus Christ. They were developing a new bond with a new blanket of security.

When we trust and obey our loving heavenly Father, we have a security blanket like no other. He leads us beside peaceful streams, guides us along right paths, walks with us through the darkest valley, and pursues us with goodness and unfailing love all the days of our life (Psalm 23).

Psalm 63:8 tells us, "I cling to you; your strong right hand holds me securely" (NLT).

May you come to fully realize and experience the blanket of security you have in Christ today and every day of your life.

JULY 15

Livin' in High Cotton

Oh, what a wonderful God we have! How great are his wisdom and knowledge and riches! How impossible it is for us to understand his decisions and his methods!

—Romans 11:33 (TLB)

I love old Southern sayings. Sayings like "livin' in high cotton" and "enough money to burn a wet mule" used to mean that folks had come into some money.

When we accept Jesus Christ as our Savior, we are livin' in some serious high cotton, too. There is nothing compared to the riches we experience as a child of the King. He owns the cattle on a thousand hills (Psalm 50:10). Everything He has, He shares with us. He holds nothing back.

Psalm 34:10 tells us, "Even strong young lions sometimes go hungry, but those who trust in the Lord will lack no good thing" (NLT).

And Matthew 7:11 says, "So if you sinful people know how to give good gifts to your children, how much more will your heavenly Father give good gifts to those who ask him" (NLT).

Are you living as though you know this to be true?

May we say with David, from Psalm 63:5, "You satisfy me more than the richest feast. I will praise you with songs of joy" (NLT).

And may we know the secret riches, treasures hidden in darkness, so that we may know the Lord, the One who calls us by name (Isaiah 45:3).

JULY 16

Madder than a Wet Hen

When Jesus saw her weeping and the Jewish leaders wailing with her, he was moved with indignation and deeply troubled.

—John 11:33 (TLB)

Do you ever get angry?

While we should not make a practice of being in an angry state of mind, there are good reasons to become angry in life. But we must not allow our anger to lead us into sin.

Psalm 4:4 tells us, "Don't sin by letting anger control you. Think about it overnight and remain silent" (NLT).

In scripture, Jesus became angry on occasion for good reason. He was madder than a wet hen at finding the temple turned into a marketplace. John 2:15 tells us, "Jesus made a whip from some ropes and chased them all out of the Temple. He drove out the sheep and cattle, scattered the money changers' coins over the floor, and turned over their tables" (NLT).

When the hypocrites who had tried to stone Jesus sought to comfort Mary at the tomb after Lazarus's death, the Holy Bible tells us in John 11:38, "Jesus was still angry as he arrived at the tomb, a cave with a stone rolled across its entrance" (NLT).

What about you? And what about me? Do we follow the example of Jesus in scripture regarding anger? Do we call sin what it is, or do we tolerate sin with a laugh and a politically correct smile on our face?

May we act in righteous indignation toward sin, doing what we can to effect positive change every day of our lives.

JULY 17

Catawampus

Watch your step. Stick to the path and be safe.

—Proverbs 4:26 (TLB)

The best-laid plans of mice and men often go awry.[2] Have you ever made plans that went awry?

It seems we often have the best intentions, determined to stay the course on the straight and narrow road, but we somehow end up catawampus.

When we take our eyes off God, we always end up catawampus.

Isaiah 53:6 tells us, "All of us, like sheep, have strayed away. We have left God's paths to follow our own. Yet the Lord laid on him the sins of us all" (NLT).

But our story doesn't have to end there. God gives us abundant hope. When we keep our eyes on Him, He will lead us on the best path for our lives. He will lead us along the straight and narrow road.

Psalm 32:8 gives us this promise: "The Lord says, 'I will guide you along the best pathway for your life. I will advise you and watch over you'" (NLT).

Are you allowing God to guide you along the best pathway for your life? Have you marked out a straight path of trust in and obedience to Him?

There is no better place on earth than the straight and narrow road that leads to heaven.

---

[2] Adapted from a line in "To a Mouse" by Robert Burns: "The best laid schemes o' mice an' men / Gang aft a-gley."

JULY 18

The Measure of a Person

The man who speculates is soon back to where he began—with nothing.

—Ecclesiastes 5:15 (TLB)

The true measure of a person is not found in the possessions she is able to acquire during her lifetime, nor is it found in the size of the bank account she leaves to her heirs.

In Luke 12:15, Jesus warns, "Beware! Guard against every kind of greed. Life is not measured by how much you own" (NLT).

No, the Holy Bible tells us about the true measure of a person's life, his or her real worth.

Acts 20:24 tells us, "But my life is worth nothing to me unless I use it for finishing the work assigned me by the Lord Jesus—the work of telling others the Good News about the wonderful grace of God" (NLT)

That is what life is really all about.

Whether you are a doctor, ditch-digger, teacher, homemaker, fireman, or accountant, or whether you work in any of a number of other professions, your true value is measured by your service to God and to others.

Have you shared the good news of Jesus with others throughout your lifetime?

Does your life exhibit the fruit of His Holy Spirit living and breathing inside of you?

May we spend each and every day in complete devotion and service to our God, for this is the true measure of a person.

JULY 19

Jesus Loves the Little Children

But Jesus said, "Let the little children come to me, and don't prevent them. For of such is the Kingdom of Heaven."

—Matthew 19:14 (TLB)

What is it about children that causes Jesus to love them so much?

Perhaps the answer can be found in Matthew 18:2–4, which says, "Jesus called a little child to him and put the child among them. Then he said, 'I tell you the truth, unless you turn from your sins and become like little children, you will never get into the Kingdom of Heaven. So anyone who becomes as humble as this little child is the greatest in the Kingdom of Heaven'" (NLT).

Do you have a spirit as humble as a little child's?

When we accept Jesus Christ as our Savior, we become His children, and O the care the Father gives His precious children.

First John 3:1 tells us, "See how very much our Father loves us, for he calls us his children, and that is what we are! But the people who belong to this world don't recognize that we are God's children because they don't know him" (NLT).

O the joys of being God's precious child.

"And may you have the power to understand, as all God's people should, how wide, how long, how high, and how deep his love is" (Ephesians 3:18 NLT).

JULY 20

A Crushing Blow

We are pressed on every side by troubles, but not crushed and broken. We are perplexed because we don't know why things happen as they do, but we don't give up and quit.

—2 Corinthians 4:8 (TLB)

Have you ever experienced a crushing blow?

You know the kind I'm talking about, the type that gives you the feeling of being kicked in the gut by someone. It is that "I have to sit down" feeling after the delivery of some shocking or crushing news that you didn't expect.

This ol' fallen world we live in tends to deliver those blows to us now and again. But the verse above reminds us of the difference a real relationship with Christ makes.

He gives us hope that doesn't disappoint. Romans 5:5 goes on to say, "And this hope will not lead to disappointment. For we know how dearly God loves us, because he has given us the Holy Spirit to fill our hearts with his love" (NLT).

Our great power to live victoriously in spite of crushing blows comes from God. It is not of ourselves. Our fragile human nature proves this to be true.

Second Corinthians 4:9 tells us, "We are hunted down, but never abandoned by God. We get knocked down, but we are not destroyed" (NLT). Only through the light of God, the power of God, could this ever be true.

May you grow ever closer to our loving heavenly Father through every crushing blow as He proves His goodness and love to you time and time again.

JULY 21

The Dream in Your Heart

(But remember, it's not because I am wiser than any living person that I know this secret of your dream, for God showed it to me for your benefit.)

—Daniel 2:30 (TLB)

Has God ever granted you the interpretation of a dream?

It is an amazing and beautiful thing to know and understand when God has placed something in our heart. Though it may not always be pleasant, it is always done out of God's great love for us.

In Daniel 2, King Nebuchadnezzar is described as having had such disturbing dreams that he could not go back to sleep. He demanded that someone tell him what he dreamed as well as its meaning.

God wanted King Nebuchadnezzar to know the meaning of the dreams in his heart, so He provided the interpretation through Daniel. This brought glory and honor to God, and it also changed the heart of the king.

Daniel 2:47 tells us of some of the impact on King Nebuchadnezzar's life: "The king said to Daniel, 'Truly, your God is the greatest of gods, the Lord over kings, a revealer of mysteries, for you have been able to reveal this secret'" (NLT).

When God places a dream in your heart, He does so for a reason, and its truth will be revealed in His perfect timing.

JULY 22

That We Are Underlings

I cannot understand how you can bother with mere puny man, to pay any attention to him! And yet you have made him only a little lower than the angels and placed a crown of glory and honor upon his head.

—Psalm 8:4–5 (TLB)

Do you ever try to take on the role of Almighty God?

Do you blame Him for the things that are the result of your own poor decision making?

It amazes me that God is even mindful of us, as we are so small and seemingly insignificant in the grand scheme of God's design.

Yet the Holy Bible tells us how valuable we are to God. Matthew 10:29–31 says, "What is the price of two sparrows—one copper coin? But not a single sparrow can fall to the ground without your Father knowing it. And the very hairs on your head are all numbered. So don't be afraid; you are more valuable to God than a whole flock of sparrows" (NLT).

We are all a part of God's plan, but sometimes in remembering our value to God, we forget our place and try to usurp Him.

When we do this, 1 Corinthians 1:25 can help to keep us in check. It says, "This foolish plan of God is wiser than the wisest of human plans, and God's weakness is stronger than the greatest of human strength" (NLT).

May we walk in complete dependence upon Christ, content in His love for us, and remembering that we are underlings.

JULY 23

Just Show Me the Baby

In everything you do, stay away from complaining and arguing so that no one can speak a word of blame against you. You are to live clean, innocent lives as children of God in a dark world full of people who are crooked and stubborn. Shine out among them like beacon lights.

—Philippians 2:14–15 (TLB)

When I was a young employee, I had a wonderful boss named David Varney who, knowing my need for a challenge, relished giving me difficult tasks to complete.

I never failed to complete the tasks assigned, for which Mr. Varney would reward me by saying, "Well done, PJ."

Yet instead of saying, "Thank you," which would have been the graceful thing to do, I would begin to recount the difficulties and challenges I faced in accomplishing the task. Mr. Varney would then say to me, as a loving father would, "PJ, don't tell me about the labor pains. Just show me the baby."

Unfortunately, my kind boss had to say these words to me on more than one occasion. I still need to hear those words from time to time.

God doesn't want us to be complainers.

Can you imagine Jesus saying to the disciples, "Do you know how hard it was to feed the five thousand? And in that heat?"

Certainly not.

May we follow the beautiful and perfect example of Jesus in gracefully holding our tongue when we are tempted to complain.

JULY 24

Absolute Value

How great he is! His power is absolute! His understanding is unlimited.

—Psalm 147:5 (TLB)

The world around us is a corrupting influence. It lies, telling us that the wrong things are valuable.

Only Christ has real, lasting value. Only a close personal relationship with Him can show us just how far short the world's treasures fall.

In Philippians 3:7–9a (NLT), Paul tells us the following:

I once thought these things were valuable, but now I consider them worthless because of what Christ has done. Yes, everything else is worthless when compared with the infinite value of knowing Christ Jesus my Lord. For his sake I have discarded everything else, counting it all as garbage, so that I could gain Christ and become one with him.

No other investment provides such a return. Worldly investments are fickle. They rise and fall in value. You need only take a look at your financial portfolio to see evidence of this truth.

But our Lord's value is constant. His value is absolute. It never changes. It is immeasurable.

May you realize and invest in the absolute value of Jesus Christ with everything you have and everything you are.

JULY 25

Unsolved Mysteries

Do you know the mind and purposes of God? Will long searching make them known to you? Are you qualified to judge the Almighty?

—Job 11:7 (TLB)

Life is full of mysteries that you and I fail to understand.

Ecclesiastes 11:5 says, "Just as you cannot understand the path of the wind or the mystery of a tiny baby growing in its mother's womb, so you cannot understand the activity of God, who does all things" (NLT).

Yet God does choose to reveal certain of His mysteries to us. In fact, He charged both Paul and Apollos with explaining certain of the mysteries of God (1 Corinthians 4:1).

Is there a mystery you seek the answer to? God is the wonderful revealer of mysteries.

Job 12:22 tells us, "He uncovers mysteries hidden in darkness; he brings light to the deepest gloom" (NLT).

And Jeremiah 33:3 comforts us with this remarkable promise about the future: "Ask me and I will tell you remarkable secrets you do not know about things to come" (NLT).

May we ask our heavenly Father when we are in need of the solution to any of life's great mysteries.

JULY 26

Creatures of Habit

Keep putting into practice all you learned from me and saw me doing, and the God of peace will be with you.

—Philippians 4:9 (TLB)

Human beings are creatures of habit.

Have you ever noticed that when doing something you know will have a negative outcome if you continue it for any length of time, you often continue to do it nevertheless?

Why is that?

It is because the behavior has become habit.

O that we had the heart of David! As he said in Psalm 119:34, "Give me understanding and I will obey your instructions; I will put them into practice with all my heart" (NLT).

So why not fill our lives with all good habits, all things God wants us to do?

When a woman blessed Jesus's mother, Luke 11:28 tells us, "Jesus replied, 'But even more blessed are all who hear the word of God and put it into practice'" (NLT).

May we fill our lives with all good habits, those things that are pleasing to God, so there may be no room in our lives for things that are wrong.

JULY 27

Waste Not, Want Not

"Now gather the scraps," Jesus told his disciples, "so that nothing is wasted."

—John 6:12 (TLB)

Are you a good steward of all that God has entrusted to you, or do you waste the many blessings that have been showered upon you by your Creator to be shared with others?

Jesus walked on the earth just as we do, yet He wasted nothing. He never wasted time even though He did not keep a frantic pace. He never wasted words on those He knew to be unwilling to listen.

And He never wasted miracles, either.

After Jesus fed the five thousand, as recorded in John 6, He asked His disciples to gather up all that was left over so that nothing would be wasted.

The old saying "waste not, want not" may seem trite, but it is true. When we are good stewards of all that God has entrusted to us, then we fail to want for anything in God's good kingdom.

First Corinthians 4:2 tells us, "Now, a person who is put in charge as a manager must be faithful" (NLT).

God has put you and me in charge as managers of much within His kingdom— time, talents, material wealth, our bodies, and so forth.

May we manage these gifts in such a way that we will one day hear our Master say, "Well done, my good and faithful servant" (Matthew 25:21 NLT).

JULY 28

Breathless

Since earliest times men have seen the earth and sky and all God made, and have known of his existence and great eternal power. So they will have no excuse when they stand before God at Judgment Day.

—Romans 1:20 (TLB)

On a recent trip to Poipu Beach on the Hawaiian island of Kauai, I was overwhelmed with the amazing beauty of all that God has created. The breathtaking beauty of the waves crashing against the shore, the black and white swans, the magnificent colors of every tropical flower—it is beyond words.

Everything God does is beyond words, beyond description. Does His work and His creation leave you breathless?

King David wrote in Psalm 65:8, "Those who live at the ends of the earth stand in awe of your wonders. From where the sun rises to where it sets, you inspire shouts of joy" (NLT).

God has painted with perfection every plant, animal, and insect. We have no excuse for not knowing God, for not committing everything we have and are to the One who gave it all to us.

How could we not walk with our awesome and amazing God, the One who leaves us breathless?

May we comprehend but a small piece of all that He is and all that He has done.

JULY 29

Perfect Inspiration

In response to all he has done for us, let us outdo each other in being helpful and kind to each other and in doing good.

—Hebrews 10:24 (TLB)

Have you ever given any thought to what inspires or motivates you?

In Ecclesiastes 4:4, Solomon tells us, "Then I observed that most people are motivated to success because they envy their neighbors. But this, too, is meaningless—like chasing the wind."

Keeping up with the Joneses is not a new conce t, and there is certainly better motivation than envy of our neighbors. There is also a better reason to be inspired than to achieve worldly success.

Hebrews 10:24 says, "Let us think of ways to motivate one another to acts of love and good works" (NLT).

What better inspiration could there possibly be in all the world than the shed blood of God's Son, Jesus?

Does the thought of all that our heavenly Father has done for you inspire you? Does His love motivate you to love others?

Does His love inspire you to do good to others? It should.

May we consider all that God has done, allowing it to purify our conscience from sin and to spur us on to love others and perform good deeds.

JULY 30

I Have Two Fathers

Since we respect our fathers here on earth, though they punish us, should we not all the more cheerfully submit to God's training so that we can begin really to live?

—Hebrews 12:9 (TLB)

I have two fathers—one earthly and one heavenly. I am a member of two families—one earthly and one heavenly.

My earthly father, though not perfect, has provided immeasurable discipline, teaching me the value of obedience. I am a part of his bloodline, and nothing or no one can ever change that.

The heavenly Father has shown me truth and freedom. He has taught me how to be free from the slavery of sin, and He is all things perfect. I am a part of His bloodline, too, having accepted the shed blood of His Son, Jesus Christ, as forgiveness and freedom from sin. Nothing and no one can ever change that.

Not all earthly fathers are good. In John 8:34–38 (NLT), we find Jesus's explanation:

Jesus replied, "I tell you the truth, everyone who sins is a slave of sin. A slave is not a permanent member of the family, but a son is part of the family forever. So if the Son sets you free, you are truly free. Yes, I realize that you are descendants of Abraham. And yet some of you are trying to kill me because there's no room in your hearts for my message. I am telling you what I saw when I was with my Father. But you are following the advice of your father."

Our heavenly Father is always good.

May we submit our spirits each day to the discipline of the Father so that we might find life—abundant and free.

JULY 31

All God Requires

But I will freely do what the Father requires of me so that the world will know that I love the Father. Come, let's be going.

—JOHN 14:31 (TLB)

Do you know what God requires of you?

In Micah 6:8, God tells us what He requires: "No, O people, the Lord has told you what is good, and this is what he requires of you: to do what is right, to love mercy, and to walk humbly with your God" (NLT).

Are you doing what is right? How do we know what is right?

The Holy Bible answers that question for us in Romans 2:13: "For merely listening to the law doesn't make us right with God. It is obeying the law that makes us right in his sight" (NLT).

Under the new covenant, God's law is written on our hearts and in our minds (Hebrews 10:16). Under this covenant, the Spirit gives us life (2 Corinthians 3:6).

Are you doing all that God requires of you? If so, then you know true freedom—the freedom that comes from choosing to be God's slave, each and every day of your life.

May you realize completely all that God requires of you today.

AUGUST 1

Treasure Hunters

The Kingdom of Heaven is like a treasure a man discovered in a field. In his excitement, he sold everything he owned to get enough money to buy the field—and get the treasure, too!

—Matthew 13:44 (TLB)

People love the idea of finding treasure. From books to movies to news reports, we just can't seem to get enough of the stuff.

One member of my family is on the lookout to the point that he carries a metal detector to assist in his search for buried treasure.

With all this hunting for treasure, one would think we would have enough sense to go for the good stuff. No, I'm not talking about gold, diamonds, or other precious gems. I'm referring to the most valuable treasure of all—a personal relationship with Jesus Christ.

Have you found this treasure? If not, are you searching for it?

Deuteronomy 4:29 tells us, "But from there you will search again for the Lord your God. And if you search for him with all your heart and soul, you will find him" (NLT).

He is more valuable than all the riches the world could ever offer you.

In Luke 12:33, Jesus tells us, "Sell your possessions and give to those in need. This will store up treasure for you in heaven! And the purses of heaven never get old or develop holes. Your treasure will be safe; no thief can steal it and no moth can destroy it" (NLT).

Are you hunting for the right treasure? If you look with all your heart and soul, you will find Him.

AUGUST 2

We've Got Spirit, Yes We Do

But when the Father sends the Comforter instead of me—and by the Comforter I mean the Holy Spirit—he will teach you much, as well as remind you of everything I myself have told you.

—JOHN 14:26 (TLB)

"We've got spirit, yes we do! We've got spirit. How 'bout you?"

It is a cheer heard at football and basketball games in high schools and colleges throughout the United States. When it comes to team spirit, there seems to be no shortage.

But what about Team Jesus? Do you have His Holy Spirit?

Romans 15:13 tells us, "I pray that God, the source of hope, will fill you completely with joy and peace because you trust in him. Then you will overflow with confident hope through the power of the Holy Spirit" (NLT).

And Galatians 5:22–23 says, "But the Holy Spirit produces this kind of fruit in our lives: love, joy, peace, patience, kindness, goodness, faithfulness, gentleness, and self-control. There is no law against these things" (NLT)!

Now that is truly something worth getting excited about!

When we believe in Jesus Christ, He identifies us as being His own by giving us His Holy Spirit, whom He promised long ago (Ephesians 1:13 NLT).

I have Jesus, yes I do. I have Jesus. How 'bout you?

AUGUST 3

Confusion Says

God is not one who likes things to be disorderly and upset. He likes harmony, and he finds it in all the other churches.

—1 Corinthians 14:33 (TLB)

Do you ever feel as though you are confused or that your life is out of order?

The Holy Bible often compares us to sheep who wander around in confusion and getting into all sorts of trouble when there is no shepherd.

In Matthew 9:36, we learn of the consideration Jesus has for His confused sheep: "When he saw the crowds, he had compassion on them because they were confused and helpless, like shee without a shepherd" (NLT).

But that doesn't happen when we're walking with God. No, He sets our feet on solid ground, steadies us as we go (Psalm 40:2), and guides us continually (Isaiah 58:11).

God is not the author of confusion.

Confusion says, "I don't know where to go or what to do."

Jesus says, "He will feed his flock like a shepherd. He will carry the lambs in his arms, holding them close to his heart. He will gently lead the mother sheep with their young" (Isaiah 40:11 NLT).

May this loving Shepherd, the God of all peace, guide you continually, protecting you from all confusion.

AUGUST 4

Share and Share Alike

All the believers were of one heart and mind, and no one felt that what he owned was his own; everyone was sharing.

—Acts 4:32 (TLB)

When I was very young, sharing was not my strong suit.

But when I became a Christian, there were many wonderful examples of sharing for me to follow in our local church.

There was an elderly man in our church when I was young named Mr. Stone, who volunteered to mow the lawn and play the organ each week. Another gentleman owned a small grocery store and gave food slightly past its expiration date that was still good to families in need, including ours.

Still others in the church volunteered to clean the church, babysit for those who could not afford to pay a babysitter, and provide taxi service for those without a car.

Second Corinthians 9:8 says, "And God will generously provide all you need. Then you will always have everything you need and plenty left over to share with others" (NLT).

This is God's design for His church, and what a beautiful thing it is. O that we would all learn to truly share and share alike.

AUGUST 5

Truth in Tinkertoys

Our bodies have many parts, but the many parts make up only one body when they are all put together. So it is with the "body" of Christ. Each of us is a part of the one body of Christ. Some of us are Jews, some are Gentiles, some are slaves, and some are free. But the Holy Spirit has fitted us all together into one body. We have been baptized into Christ's body by the one Spirit, and have all been given that same Holy Spirit.

—1 Corinthians 12:12–13 (TLB)

Do you remember Tinkertoys?

As children, my brother, my sister, and I loved them. Sometimes we would each stockpile one particular type of Tinkertoy, such as the rods, spools, or connector clips. But it never took very long to realize that we couldn't really do anything or make anything unless we put all the different pieces together.

It is the same with all the different members in the body of Christ.

Romans 12:6 tells us, "In his grace, God has given us different gifts for doing certain things well. So if God has given you the ability to prophesy, speak out with as much faith as God has given you" (NLT).

Perhaps you're a flag, an endcap, or a coupling. Whichever part you are, you belong to the same set.

And we can't make the airplane without you.

First Corinthians 12:18 says, "But our bodies have many parts, and God has put each part just where he wants it" (NLT).

What a blessing and a joy to know that God has put you right where He wants you.

AUGUST 6

Our Christian Family

And let us not get tired of doing what is right, for after a while we will reap a harvest of blessing if we don't get discouraged and give up. That's why whenever we can we should always be kind to everyone, and especially to our Christian brothers.

—Galatians 6:9–10 (TLB)

Have you ever noticed that we are often the ugliest to the members of our own family?

Unfortunately, the same can often be said about the way we treat our Christian family.

Are you guilty? Me, too.

I could make excuses for myself, saying that I expect more from them because they are Christians! That is true. But it doesn't justify my withholding good things from them, or thinking ill of them, or even treating them poorly. The condition of our heart is reflected in our attitude toward others, and it is as plain as the nose on our face.

Proverbs 3:27 says, "Do not withhold good from those who deserve it when it's in your power to help them" (NLT).

God set the example for us, as Psalm 84:11 promises: "For the Lord God is our sun and our shield. He gives us grace and glory. The Lord will withhold no good thing from those who do what is right" (NLT).

Perhaps it is time we reexamine our treatment of our family.

AUGUST 7

Salvation's Symphony

Let us not neglect our church meetings, as some people do, but encourage and warn each other, especially now that the day of his coming back again is drawing near.

—Hebrews 10:25 (TLB)

People sometimes come up with all manner of excuses not to attend church. We call it a house of hypocrites; we attend sporting events in instead; we sleep late; and so on. But when we do that, we miss out on the beautiful symphony God is creating in His body of believers.

The symphony sometimes starts a bit rough. There are beginners who must learn alongside the more experienced players. Those beginning notes are often painful to hear, but with the right training and practice, the new members begin to harmonize beautifully alongside the masters.

As the orchestra grows and develops, it gains new instruments, and a depth of sound develops that is indescribable by mere words. And this beautiful symphony, like a pied piper of sorts, draws people from miles around, longing to be a part.

Psalm 98:6 tells us, "With trumpets and the sound of the ram's horn. Make a joyful symphony before the Lord, the King" (NLT)!

May we find ways to encourage one another to play the instruments we've been given.

The symphony is just not the same without each one.

AUGUST 8

Caring for the Body

Yes, we are especially glad to have some parts that seem rather odd! And we carefully protect from the eyes of others those parts that should not be seen, while of course the parts that may be seen do not require this special care. So God has put the body together in such a way that extra honor and care are given to those parts that might otherwise seem less important. This makes for happiness among the parts, so that the parts have the same care for each other that they do for themselves.

—1 Corinthians 12:23–25 (TLB)

Have you ever noticed that some parts of your body need more care than others?

These parts require more time and attention, and sometimes they cost more to care for, too. But they're worth it. Go without that extra required something and the whole body notices. So does everyone else around you. I can't imagine what these parts would be like without that extra care. In fact, I know my quality of life would not be nearly the same without this care.

It is the same in the body of Christ. Some of us need more care and attention, but what those members give back to the body is so much greater than the care they require. Sometimes we get lazy and don't want to give that extra care, or sometimes we spare the necessary expense. Before long, that part suffers, and every other part is affected.

Isaiah 40:11 paints a beautiful picture of how God cares for us: "He will feed his flock like a shepherd. He will carry the lambs in his arms, holding them close to his heart. He will gently lead the mother sheep with their young" (NLT).

May we follow this example as we care for every member in the body of Christ.

AUGUST 9

In His Image

Then God said, "Let us make a man—someone like ourselves, to be the master of all life upon the earth and in the skies and in the seas."

—Genesis 1:26 (TLB)

We were made in the image of God. Think about that for a minute. You and I were designed to be a reflection of God, to *be* like Him!

He put us in charge of the fish, the birds, the livestock, the wild animals, and the small animals that scurry along the ground. He entrusted us with His creation—an awesome responsibility.

Psalm 24:1 tells us, "The earth is the Lord's, and everything in it. The world and all its people belong to him" (NLT). Do you long to be like the One in whose image you were created?

O that we would desperately aspire to be like our Maker, our Creator, the one true and living God of the Universe. O that we would care deeply about and for His creation, as He does. And O that we would fully and completely believe in Jesus Christ, the visible image of our invisible God.

Colossians 1:15–16 (NLT) aptly instructs us as follows:

Christ is the visible image of the invisible God. He existed before anything was created and is supreme over all creation, for through him God created everything in the heavenly realms and on earth. He made the things we can see and the things we can't see—such as thrones, kingdoms, rulers, and authorities in the unseen world. Everything was created through him and for him.

Each and every moment of the day, may we reflect the image of the One who created us.

AUGUST 10

The Blessing

Then God blessed them and said, "Be fruitful and multiply. Fill the earth and govern it. Reign over the fish in the sea, the birds in the sky, and all the animals that scurry along the ground."

—Genesis 1:28 (NLT)

Family blessings have been important throughout history—especially the blessing bestowed by the father. A blessing is to sanctify, or set apart, for the receiving of divine favor.

Jacob went so far as to trick his father, Isaac, in order that he might receive the blessing belonging to his older twin brother, Esau (Genesis 27:41).

In Genesis 1:28, our Father, God, blesses all humanity with the bearing of fruit. And we know that the fruit given to us by God's Spirit is love, joy, peace, patience, kindness, goodness, faithfulness, gentleness, and self-control (Galatians 5:22–23). How amazing to know that our heavenly Father has imparted this blessing to us so that we might be fruitful.

Our Father has also set us apart with divine favor to multiply and reign over His creation.

May we say, as with Paul in Ephesians 1:3, "All praise to God, the Father of our Lord Jesus Christ, who has blessed us with every spiritual blessing in the heavenly realms because we are united with Christ" (NLT).

AUGUST 11

The Miraculous

And so he did only a few great miracles there, because of their unbelief.

—Matthew 13:58 (NLT)

Have you ever experienced something unexplainable, something only God could do? I have.

One such miracle involved a friend of mine at Baylor University. We attended a Christian concert at a local church together. Near the end of the concert, a man tapped my friend on the shoulder, asking her if she wanted to accept Christ as Savior. She said yes, and the two began walking to the sanctuary at the front of the church. But when my friend reached the front, the gentleman who had tapped her on the shoulder was nowhere to be found. My friend returned to where we were seated. When the concert ended, we both turned around to thank the man who had tapped her on the shoulder, but the people behind us advised there was never any such man. We both knew this was a *God thing*.

Though the skeptics may explain such things away, we who believe know such things to be the regular activities of God. We can see God so clearly in all that He has created around us. So why is it that so many people reject Him? And why do they choose other gods, rather than the one true and living God?

Psalm 53:1 tells us, "Only fools say in their hearts, 'There is no God.' They are corrupt, and their actions are evil; not one of them does good" (NLT).

May we share Him and share our stories, for there is no excuse for not knowing I AM (Exodus 3:14).

AUGUST 12

True Jews

For you are not real Jews just because you were born of Jewish parents or because you have gone through the Jewish initiation ceremony of circumcision. No, a real Jew is anyone whose heart is right with God. For God is not looking for those who cut their bodies in actual body circumcision, but he is looking for those with changed hearts and minds. Whoever has that kind of change in his life will get his praise from God, even if not from you.

—Romans 2:28–29 (TLB)

Are you a true Jew?

A true Jew, a true son or daughter of Abraham, is someone whose heart and life has been changed by God, someone who seeks the approval of God and obeys God.

Genesis 17:9 reminds us of this responsibility: "Then God said to Abraham, 'Your responsibility is to obey the terms of the covenant. You and all your descendants have this continual responsibility'" (NLT).

The original covenant was written on tablets of stone, whereas the new covenant is written deep within a person's heart and on his or her mind (Jeremiah 31:33; Hebrews 8:10; Hebrews 10:16). A true Jew also has a servant's heart.

Romans 15:8 tells us, "Remember that Christ came as a servant to the Jews to show that God is true to the promises he made to their ancestors" (NLT). A true Jew is someone with a changed life. And we know that changed hearts equal changed lives. It is that simple.

May your life and my life be a reflection of our true Jewish heritage each and every day.

AUGUST 13

Boundless Love

For I am convinced that nothing can ever separate us from his love. Death can't, and life can't. The angels won't, and all the powers of hell itself cannot keep God's love away. Our fears for today, our worries about tomorrow, or where we are—high above the sky, or in the deepest ocean—nothing will ever be able to separate us from the love of God demonstrated by our Lord Jesus Christ when he died for us.

—Romans 8:38–39 (TLB)

God's love for us is something so amazing, so incomprehensible, that our human minds cannot totally grasp it. His love is boundless, limitless. There is no power that has ever been created, or that ever will be created, that can or will come close to destroying God's love. If that doesn't drop you to your knees in humble adoration of Him and gratitude toward Him, I don't know what will.

David often described God's love as a shield and a shelter. In Psalm 5:12, he tells us, "For you bless the godly, O Lord; you surround them with your shield of love" (NLT). And in Psalm 36:7 we read, "How precious is your unfailing love, O God! All humanity finds shelter in the shadow of your wings" (NLT).

It is true. Do you know this love? Have you felt it? When we know His love, it is enough. He is enough.

The greatest demonstration of this love was in the giving of God's Son. As Romans 5:8 tells us, "But God showed his great love for us by sending Christ to die for us while we were still sinners" (NLT).

O that we would crawl across broken glass, swim through shark-infested waters, or simply walk across the street to tell others of His boundless love.

AUGUST 14

A Bitter Pill

Stop being mean, bad-tempered, and angry. Quarreling, harsh words, and dislike of others should have no place in your lives.

—Ephesians 4:31 (TLB)

Have you ever had bitter pills to swallow in life—you know, those things that weren't pleasant and that you didn't really do anything to cause or deserve? Some folks receive more than their fair share of bitter pills in life.

But there is something amazing and beautiful that happens when we give our lives to Jesus Christ. He takes all of those bitter negative events and weaves them into an amazing tapestry of beauty. Then, we have a depth of maturity and understanding we would not otherwise know or have, and there is a level of compassion that is deeper than the deepest ocean.

Romans 8:28 tells us, "And we know that God causes everything to work together for the good of those who love God and are called according to his purpose for them" (NLT).

God takes bitter pills and makes them sweet as honey in your life and mine.

O that we might give Him every pain, every trial, and every bitterness, allowing Him to turn them into sweetness and beauty, both now and forevermore.

AUGUST 15

Temper, Temper

Stop your anger! Turn off your wrath. Don't fret and worry—it only leads to harm.

—Psalm 37:8 (TLB)

When I was taking a chocolate-making class, one of the techniques I and my fellow students had to master was that of tempering chocolate. Through much trial and error, I learned how difficult it was to keep the chocolate perfectly in temper for extended periods of time.

How about you? Do you find it difficult to keep your temper in check for extended periods of time?

The Holy Bible has a great deal to say about controlling our tempers.

Ecclesiastes 7:9 says, "Control your temper, for anger labels you a fool" (NLT).

Proverbs 14:29 explains, "People with understanding control their anger; a hot temper shows great foolishness" (NLT).

Proverbs 19:11 tells us, "Sensible people control their temper; they earn respect by overlooking wrongs" (NLT).

Proverbs 22:24–25 warns us, "Don't befriend angry people or associate with hot-tempered people, or you will learn to be like them and endanger your soul" (NLT).

May the Holy Spirit fill our lives so completely that our tempers are easily held in check.

AUGUST 16

The Law of Kindness

And he has showered down upon us the richness of his grace—for how well he understands us and knows what is best for us at all times.

—Ephesians 1:8 (TLB)

Have you ever experienced some great kindness?

When my mother passed away, I was overwhelmed by the kindness of others. Cards, hugs, and words of love and sympathy flooded my life at every turn. The tender hearts of many loving people were a gentle reminder of the kindness God showers upon us all constantly.

Psalm 145:17 tells us, "The Lord is righteous in everything he does; he is filled with kindness" (NLT).

And we are to have this same kindness toward others.

Proverbs 11:17 says, "Your kindness will reward you, but your cruelty will destroy you" (NLT).

Zechariah 7:9 tells us, "This is what the Lord of Heaven's Armies says: Judge fairly, and show mercy and kindness to one another" (NLT).

God's continued kindness does come with a requirement, namely, that we continue to trust and obey Him. As Romans 11:22 reminds us, "Notice how God is both kind and severe. He is severe toward those who disobeyed, but kind to you if you continue to trust in his kindness. But if you stop trusting, you also will be cut off" (NLT).

May we freely bestow kindness on others as Christ has poured kindness upon us. And may we never test His kindness, trusting and walking always in obedience of Him.

AUGUST 17

Master Service Agreement

You slaves must always obey your earthly masters, not only trying to please them when they are watching you but all the time; obey them willingly because of your love for the Lord and because you want to please him.

—Colossians 3:22 (TLB)

In the field of risk management, in which I have worked for many years, there are many contracts to review. Many of those contracts are master service agreements, which lay out the terms for a long-standing business relationship.

There is a master service agreement we have with the heavenly Father, too. And it's written down. It's called the Holy Bible, and it contains all of the principles necessary for us to have a successful relationship with the Father.

Our master service agreement with God has one primary governing principle. That principle is love. And that principle should govern every relationship we ever have in our lives.

Romans 13:10 tells us, "Love does no wrong to others, so love fulfills the requirements of God's law" (NLT).

Have you read your Master's service agreement lately? Perhaps it's time to do that on a regular basis so that you are daily reminded of His love and all that He requires of you.

AUGUST 18

Looking for the Open Window

I will give him the key to the house of David—the highest position in the royal court. When he opens doors, no one will be able to close them; when he closes doors, no one will be able to open them.

—Isaiah 22:22 (NLT)

There is an old saying that goes, "When God closes a door, He opens a window." But what if you can't seem to find that open window? What then?

God longs to be with us, to commune with us, to teach us. He wants us to ask Him, to seek Him, to find Him, to follow Him.

Matthew 7:7–8 tells us, "Keep on asking, and you will receive what you ask for. Keep on seeking, and you will find. Keep on knocking, and the door will be opened to you. For everyone who asks, receives. Everyone who seeks, finds. And to everyone who knocks, the door will be opened" (NLT).

We are reminded that God is not far from any one of us, as Acts 17:27 tells us, "His purpose was for the nations to seek after God and perhaps feel their way toward him and find him—though he is not far from any one of us" (NLT).

He will show us the way, as He did the Israelites in Isaiah 30:21, which reads, "Your own ears will hear him. Right behind you a voice will say, 'This is the way you should go,' whether to the right or to the left" (NLT).

When you can't seem to find Him, seek after Him with all your heart, and remember that He is closer than you know.

AUGUST 19

Politically Correct

"Watch out!" Jesus warned them. "Beware of the yeast of the Pharisees and Sadducees."

—Matthew 16:6 (TLB)

The concept of saying and doing things in a politically correct fashion is not new. It was around in Jesus's day with the Pharisees and Sadducees. The selfishness and power struggles that breed highways of deceit all around us have, unfortunately, existed since humanity began.

Jesus warned the people to "beware of the yeast of the Pharisees and Sadducees," but He wasn't talking about leavening bread. In referring to the fact that a very small amount of yeast can impact a very large amount of dough, He was saying that the attitudes and practices of certain individuals in positions of church leadership can negatively affect a whole faith community.

It is the same for us today. A few bad apples can spoil the whole bunch. Have you noticed this truth in the world around you?

What can be done about it? Hebrews 3:12–14 (NLT) gives us the key:

Be careful then, dear brothers and sisters. Make sure that your own hearts are not evil and unbelieving, turning you away from the living God. You must warn each other every day, while it is still "today," so that none of you will be deceived by sin and hardened against God. For if we are faithful to the end, trusting God just as firmly as when we first believed, we will share in all that belongs to Christ.

May we heed the warning of Jesus, and warn our fellow believers daily about the subtle deception all around us. In this, may we be faithful to the end.

AUGUST 20

The Reality of Everything

But we know that there is only one God, the Father, who created all things and made us to be his own; and one Lord Jesus Christ, who made everything and gives us life.

—1 Corinthians 8:6 (TLB)

The world is full of theories. There are theories about time, about space, and about psychology. The list could go on and on.

But there is one reality that reigns supreme above all theories.

Psalm 97:9 tells us, "For you, O Lord, are supreme over all the earth; you are exalted far above all gods" (NLT).

God is the reality of all things.

Acts 17:28 tells us, "For in him we live and move and exist. As some of your own poets have said, 'We are his offspring'" (NLT).

He was there before time began.

As John 1:1–2 teaches us, "In the beginning the Word already existed. The Word was with God, and the Word was God. He existed in the beginning with God" (NLT).

Jesus Christ, the eternal Word, is the reality of everything.

AUGUST 21

Beware of the Dog

Watch out for those wicked men—dangerous dogs, I call them— who say you must be circumcised to be saved.

—Philippians 3:2 (TLB)

Have you ever been bitten by a dog?

As a toddler, I tried to force-feed our schipperke named Snoopy, despite my mother's constant effort to stop me. And much to my surprise, Snoopy did exactly what my mother warned me he would do: he bit me.

And it hurt.

When the evil dogs of this world bite, it hurts, too.

Consider what they did to Jesus, as prophesied in Psalm 22:16: "My enemies surround me like a pack of dogs; an evil gang closes in on me. They have pierced my hands and feet" (NLT).

Paul warned us to beware of the dogs, those who tell us things that are not true and whose desire is to harm us. They do nothing but evil.

There is a day coming when we will no longer have to worry about the dogs of this world, as Revelation 22:14–15 tells us: "Blessed are those who wash their robes. They will be permitted to enter through the gates of the city and eat the fruit from the tree of life. Outside the city are the dogs—the sorcerers, the sexually immoral, the murderers, the idol worshipers, and all who love to live a lie" (NLT).

May we wash our robes so that we may be permitted to enter the gates of the city, leaving the dogs behind.

AUGUST 22

Hearing, Doing, and Having Faith

Remember, too, that knowing what is right to do and then not doing it is sin.

—JAMES 4:17 (TLB)

It seems that every day I hear people laughing about and making excuses for not doing what they know they ought to do—what they *know* is right.

My friend, this not doing what we ought to do is sin. There is no sugarcoating it.

James 1:22 tells us, "But don't just listen to God's word. You must do what it says. Otherwise, you are only fooling yourselves" (NLT).

Our failure to do what we are commanded to do is a reflection of our heart's condition. It says, "I don't *really* want to follow God. What I *really* want is to go my own way."

Actions speak louder than words. What are your actions saying?

What is your faith saying? James 2:14–17 (NLT) imparts the following:

What good is it, dear brothers and sisters, if you say you have faith but don't show it by your actions? Can that kind of faith save anyone? Suppose you see a brother or sister who has no food or clothing, and you say, "Goodbye and have a good day; stay warm and eat well"—but then you don't give that person any food or clothing. What good does that do? So you see, faith by itself isn't enough. Unless it produces good deeds, it is dead and useless.

May our lives be a constant reflection of our heart's commitment to Christ.

AUGUST 23

The Triumph of the Holy Spirit

As Samson and his captors arrived at Lehi, the Philistines shouted with glee; but then the strength of the Lord came upon Samson, and the ropes with which he was tied snapped like thread and fell from his wrists!

—JUDGES 15:14 (TLB)

We love to boast about the triumph of the human spirit, but that is nothing compared to the triumph of the Holy Spirit.

First John 4:4 tells us, "But you belong to God, my dear children. You have already won a victory over those people, because the Spirit who lives in you is greater than the spirit who lives in the world" (NLT).

God's Spirit is all-powerful, giving us victory over sin and even over the sting of death, as one day, when Christ comes again, we will be resurrected with new bodies.

First Corinthians 15:56–57 says, "For sin is the sting that results in death, and the law gives sin its power. But thank God! He gives us victory over sin and death through our Lord Jesus Christ" (NLT).

Do you know the triumphant power of the Holy Spirit and the hope that He gives? Every good and perfect gift comes from Him and Him alone (James 1:17).

My prayer for you is that which Paul prayed for the Christians in Rome, as recounted in Romans 15:13: "I pray that God, the source of hope, will fill you completely with joy and peace because you trust in him. Then you will overflow with confident hope through the power of the Holy Spirit" (NLT).

AUGUST 24

Never Wasted

So, my dear brothers, since future victory is sure, be strong and steady, always abounding in the Lord's work, for you know that nothing you do for the Lord is ever wasted as it would be if there were no resurrection.

—1 Corinthians 15:58 (TLB)

This is a powerful, encouraging, and life-changing verse our Lord is ever wasted. Did you get that?

Nothing we do for

In this world where people are constantly looking for meaning and purpose, and where we cringe to consider time that is wasted, this verse gives us a supreme hope and assurance that the things we do for Christ are never wasted.

Doing the will of God is never a waste.

Ephesians 5:16–17 encourages us, "Make the most of every opportunity in these evil days. Don't act thoughtlessly, but understand what the Lord wants you to do" (NLT).

And indeed, beyond that, only what's done for Christ and through Him will last.

Psalm 127:1 reminds us, "Unless the Lord builds a house, the work of the builders is wasted. Unless the Lord protects a city, guarding it with sentries will do no good" (NLT).

May we live every moment of every day in the center of God's will so that we may be good stewards of the days our loving heavenly Father has granted to us.

AUGUST 25

Places in the Heart

Dear children, keep away from anything that might take God's place in your hearts.

—1 John 5:21 (TLB)

There is no question that God desires, needs, and must have first place in our hearts if we want to walk in obedience to Him.

But giving Him first place isn't always easy.

The world is full of distractions that Satan uses to tempt us into moving God out of His rightful place in our hearts and lives.

If we want to keep Satan out, then we must guard our hearts.

Proverbs 4:23 tells us, "Guard your heart above all else, for it determines the course of your life" (NLT).

Are you guarding your heart?

Maybe you haven't done a very good job of guarding your heart in the past. If so, don't give up hope. You can start today.

"Only in returning to me and resting in me will you be saved" (Isaiah 30:15 NLT).

May we give God first place and every place in our hearts, each and every day.

AUGUST 26

The Coal Miner's Daughter

Now set it empty on the coals to scorch away the rust and corruption.

—Ezekiel 24:11 (TLB)

I am proud to be the Coal Miner's daughter.

No, I wasn't born in a cabin on a hill in Butcher Holler. And my earthly father was no coal miner. But my heavenly Father spied this dirty lump of coal and saw instead a diamond in the rough. Then He picked me up. And each day, He burns away more of the filth and corruption in my life, shining and polishing as He goes.

Not everyone sees the diamond I am becoming. Some still see the coal and the ash scattered around. But that's okay, because the Holy Bible tells me what God has done for Israel, and I know He will do the same for me.

As Isaiah 61:3 tells us, "To all who mourn in Israel, he will give a crown of beauty for ashes, a joyous blessing instead of mourning, festive praise instead of despair. In their righteousness, they will be like great oaks that the Lord has planted for his own glory" (NLT).

Colossians 3:4 reminds us of what will happen one day when God is finished transforming us: "And when Christ, who is your life, is revealed to the whole world, you will share in all his glory" (NLT).

How blessed we are to be mined and polished by the Master.

AUGUST 27

Bible-Based Risk Management

Send your grain across the seas, and in time, profits will flow back to you. But divide your investments among many places, for you do not know what risks might lie ahead.

—Ecclesiastes 11:1–2 (NLT)

The Holy Bible is our manual for life, every aspect of it, including investing and managing money.

In this passage of scripture, we see the tried-and-true method of investing and risk management laid out clearly for us. God's Word teaches that we are not to put all our eggs in one basket, but rather divide them up to effectively manage the unknown risks ahead.

Scripture also teaches us not to hoard wealth. Ecclesiastes 5:13–15 (NLT) teaches us as follows:

There is another serious problem I have seen under the sun. Hoarding riches harms the saver. Money is put into risky investments that turn sour, and everything is lost. In the end, there is nothing left to pass on to one's children. We all come to the end of our lives as naked and empty-handed as on the day we were born. We can't take our riches with us.

And we are also taught to give freely throughout God's Word.

Malachi 3:10 promises, "'Bring all the tithes into the storehouse so there will be enough food in my Temple. If you do,' says the Lord of Heaven's Armies, 'I will open the windows of heaven for you. I will pour out a blessing so great you won't have enough room to take it in! Try it! Put me to the test'" (NLT)!

Are you practicing biblical risk management? If not, ask God to help you start today.

AUGUST 28

Waging War

It is true that I am an ordinary, weak human being, but I don't use human plans and methods to win my battles. I use God's mighty weapons, not those made by men, to knock down the devil's strongholds.

—2 Corinthians 10:3–4 (TLB)

You and I are involved in a war. It is a war for our souls. It is a war that requires patience and faithfulness. It is a war that we must endure to the end.

Revelation tells us about another war that is coming, this one near the end of time. Revelation 13:7 tells us, "And the beast was allowed to wage war against God's holy people and to conquer them. And he was given authority to rule over every tribe and people and language and nation" (NLT).

If we stop there and read no further, we might become discouraged. But Revelation 17:14 tells us, "Together they will go to war against the Lamb, but the Lamb will defeat them because he is Lord of all lords and King of all kings. And his called and chosen and faithful ones will be with him" (NLT).

God is always faithful to us. Isaiah 54:10 says, "'For the mountains may move and the hills disappear, but even then my faithful love for you will remain. My covenant of blessing will never be broken,' says the Lord, who has mercy on you" (NLT).

Will you remain faithful to Him?

May we be able to say with Paul, as 2 Timothy 4:7 recounts, "I have fought the good fight, I have finished the race, and I have remained faithful" (NLT).

AUGUST 29

Beyond Imagination

Now glory be to God, who by his mighty power at work within us is able to do far more than we would ever dare to ask or even dream of—infinitely beyond our highest prayers, desires, thoughts, or hopes.

—Ephesians 3:20 (TLB)

Are you aware of God's power? Have you seen it in your life and the lives of others?

Recently, I heard Alex Kendrick share of the power of God at work in his life and the life of his church in light of his accomplishing much more than he could ever ask for or imagine by releasing several Christian low-budget movies. God had placed the vision, the dream, and the desire upon his heart to make them. And when God places those dreams within us, He never fails to accomplish His purposes.

But before God can effectively use us, we must get rid of the strongholds of sin in our lives.

Acts 3:19–20 instructs us, "Now repent of your sins and turn to God, so that your sins may be wiped away. Then times of refreshment will come from the presence of the Lord, and he will again send you Jesus, your appointed Messiah."

When we repent of our sin, it shows that we are delighting in the law of our Lord. When we do this, God grants us the desires of our heart, because they are one and the same as His desires.

Psalm 37:4 promises us, "Take delight in the Lord, and he will give you your heart's desires" (NLT).

Give everything you have and are to Jesus Christ today, and watch Him move beyond your wildest imagination.

AUGUST 30

Crunchy or Smooth?

But for good men the path is not uphill and rough! God does not give them a rough and treacherous path, but smooths the road before them.

—Isaiah 26:7 (TLB)

When it comes to peanut butter, I prefer smooth. I don't care much for the crunchy stuff. It's a bit too much work, requiring more chewing, and it often gets stuck in the cracks and crevices of my teeth.

In life, I am the same way. I prefer the smooth road and don't much care for the rough stuff I often encounter as a result of unconfessed sin in my life.

What about you? Are you in the habit of doing things the hard way? Do you follow a crunchy path of your own making, or are you on the smooth path that God has laid out for you?

When we repent of our sin and turn to Christ, He is right there waiting to lead us back home

The Holy Bible tells us in Jeremiah 31:9 what God did for the children of Israel when they turned their hearts back to Him. The verse reads, "Tears of joy will stream down their faces, and I will lead them home with great care. They will walk beside quiet streams and on smooth paths where they will not stumble. For I am Israel's father, and Ephraim is my oldest child" (NLT).

He can do the same for you and for me.

May we remain close to our Father all the days of our life so that we may walk the smooth road with Him for all of our days.

AUGUST 31

Of Masters and Servants

He will be severely punished, for though he knew his duty he refused to do it.

—Luke 12:47 (TLB)

Do you know what God wants from you, what He expects from you?

This passage of scripture reminds us that if we know what God wants from us but we're not prepared for and don't carry out those instructions, we will be severely punished.

I would have to say that I am not a glutton for punishment. I want to do the will of my Father in heaven. And when I read His Word, He tells me His will for my life. He guides me along the path that I should take. And when the way begins to get too rough, He smooths out the road ahead of me.

Psalm 23:3 tells us, "He renews my strength. He guides me along right paths, bringing honor to his name" (NLT).

And Proverbs 24:12 warns us, "Don't excuse yourself by saying, 'Look, we didn't know.' For God understands all hearts, and he sees you. He who guards your soul knows you knew. He will repay all people as their actions deserve" (NLT).

There is no excuse for our not doing the will of the One who sent us, whose love for us knows no bounds.

May we walk in accordance with His will for our lives, and be doers of His Word, rather than just hearers only (James 1:22).

SEPTEMBER 1

New Every Morning

His compassion never ends. It is only the Lord's mercies that have kept us from complete destruction. Great is his faithfulness; his loving-kindness begins afresh each day.

—LAMENTATIONS 3:22–23 (TLB)

How beautiful and wonderful to receive the mercies of God afresh and new every morning, and to know that His divine love for us never, ever ends.

Human love can often be fleeting—here one day and gone the next. And humans often run out of mercy for us, especially when we've burned them one too many times.

But such is not the case with God.

Isaiah 54:10 promises us, "'For the mountains may move and the hills disappear, but even then my faithful love for you will remain. My covenant of blessing will never be broken,' says the Lord, who has mercy on you."

Are you in need of God's mercy today? What about His love?

Isaiah 63:9 says, "In all their suffering he also suffered, and he personally rescued them. In his love and mercy he redeemed them. He lifted them up and carried them through all the years" (NLT).

God did this for Israel, and He can do it for you, too.

SEPTEMBER 2

Complete Dependence upon God

Oh, come back to God. Live by the principles of love and justice, and always be expecting much from him, your God.

—Hosea 12:6 (TLB)

Have you ever been hurt by someone, *really* hurt?

Have you depended upon someone who let you down in a big way?

Chances are pretty high that if you've lived for a bit of time in this ol' fallen world, you've experienced hurt and disappointment.

Painful wounds we receive from those close to us are often enough to make us determined not to depend on anyone ever again.

But God is not like people—the ones who hurt us and let us down. He never leaves us or forsakes us (Hebrews 13:5).

He wants us to be dependent upon Him. Completely dependent.

Lamentations 3:25 tells us, "The Lord is good to those who depend on him, to those who search for him" (NLT).

Take your wounds to the Master. He can heal them.

And may you find rest by completely depending upon Him in faith today and every day of your life.

SEPTEMBER 3

With All Your Heart

But you will also begin to search again for Jehovah your God, and you will find him when you search for him with all your heart and soul.

—Deuteronomy 4:29 (TLB)

Do you seek God with all your heart?

The Holy Bible tells us that if we seek God with all our heart and all our soul, we will find Him (Deuteronomy 4:29).

Do you love God with all your heart?

Matthew 22:37–38 tells us, "Jesus replied, 'You must love the Lord your God with all your heart, all your soul, and all your mind.' This is the first and greatest commandment" (NLT).

Do you trust God with all your heart?

Proverbs 3:5 tells us we should do so, and not lean on our own understanding. Do you keep God's commands?

The Holy Bible tells us that if we keep His commandments, we will live (Proverbs 4:4) and we will be blessed (Psalm 119:2).

Do you praise God with your whole heart?

Psalm 103:1 says, "Let all that I am praise the Lord; with my whole heart, I will praise his holy name" (NLT).

O that we would not hold back any part of our heart from Him.

SEPTEMBER 4

Sickened by Sin

Because of your anger, my body is sick, my health is broken beneath my sins. They are like a flood, higher than my head; they are a burden too heavy to bear.

—Psalm 38:3–4 (TLB)

Have you ever felt physically sick by the very thought of your own sin? I have.

In this passage of scripture, King David does, too. He lusted after another man's wife, which led to adultery, and eventually murder of the woman's husband. It was an unthinkable series of sins for the "man after God's own heart" (Acts 13:22 NLT).

The Holy Bible tells us in James 1:14–15, "Temptation comes from our own desires, which entice us and drag us away. These desires give birth to sinful actions. And when sin is allowed to grow, it gives birth to death" (NLT).

The consequences for our sins are often lasting and irreversible. But there is hope.

First John 1:9 tells us, "But if we confess our sins to him, he is faithful and just to forgive us our sins and to cleanse us from all wickedness" (NLT).

Now, that is reason to shout.

May we confess our sins to Him, and may our hearts be filled with thankfulness for the faithfulness, forgiveness, and cleansing we receive freely from our loving and merciful heavenly Father.

SEPTEMBER 5

Pure Reverence

God's laws are pure, eternal, just.

—Psalm 19:9 (TLB)

Reverence is having a very deep respect and awe for someone.

Do you have that for God? Are you in awe of Him? Do you respect Him purely, with no apprehension in your thought of Him, your trust in Him?

The Holy Bible tells us in Philippians 2:12, "Dear friends, you always followed my instructions when I was with you. And now that I am away, it is even more important. Work hard to show the results of your salvation, obeying God with deep reverence and fear" (NLT).

Jesus is the perfect example of deep reverence and fear. He showed this for the Father every moment of His life on earth.

Hebrews 5:7 reminds us of Jesus's reverence for the Father: "While Jesus was here on earth, he offered prayers and pleadings, with a loud cry and tears, to the one who could rescue him from death. And God heard his prayers because of his deep reverence for God" (NLT).

If we have reverence for the Lord in its purest form, it will be evident in every area of our lives. We will approach relationships with others differently, soberly.

May we worship the Lord in wisdom, showing reverence to Him always.

SEPTEMBER 6

The Big Bang

By faith—by believing God—we know that the world and the stars—in fact, all things—were made at God's command; and that they were all made from things that can't be seen.

—Hebrews 11:3 (TLB)

"In the beginning God created the heavens and the earth" (Genesis 1:1 NLT).

There are many theories regarding the creation of the universe. None of us happened to be there at the time, but by faith we believe what the Holy Bible tells us. Plus, science has proven God's Word to be true.

Psalm 33:6 tells us, "The Lord merely spoke, and the heavens were created. He breathed the word, and all the stars were born" (NLT).

But God does not want us to waste time arguing with others about such things.

First Timothy 6:20 reminds us all, "Timothy, guard what God has entrusted to you. Avoid godless, foolish discussions with those who oppose you with their so-called knowledge" (NLT).

I do not know if there was a bang or an explosion when God spoke creation into existence, when His light flooded all of existence. But I do know who made all of creation.

"Let every created thing give praise to the Lord, for he issued his command, and they came into being" (Psalm 148:5 NLT).

SEPTEMBER 7

The Unseen World

For we are not fighting against people made of flesh and blood, but against persons without bodies—the evil rulers of the unseen world, those mighty satanic beings and great evil princes of darkness who rule this world; and against huge numbers of wicked spirits in the spirit world.

—Ephesians 6:12 (TLB)

The world in which we live is composed of forces that are seen and also of forces that are unseen. To deny this is to deny reality, the reality of all that God created.

Colossians 1:15–16 (NLT) tells us the following:

Christ is the visible image of the invisible God. He existed before anything was created and is supreme over all creation, for through him God created everything in the heavenly realms and on earth. He made the things we can see and the things we can't see—such as thrones, kingdoms, rulers, and authorities in the unseen world. Everything was created through him and for him.

Before we knew Christ and when we walked in sin and disobedience, our spirit was controlled by Satan, as Ephesians 2:2 reminds us: "You used to live in sin, just like the rest of the world, obeying the Devil—the commander of the powers in the unseen world. He is the spirit at work in the hearts of those who refuse to obey God" (NLT).

But praise be to God, who has given us victory over the spiritual forces of evil in the heavenly places through His Son, Jesus Christ! Ephesians 3:10 explains to us the mystery of His purpose: "God's purpose in all this was to use the church to display his wisdom in its rich variety to all the unseen rulers and authorities in the heavenly places" (NLT).

May our lives display His wisdom, His light, and His majesty to all the world—both seen and unseen—so that all may know the eternal King who reigns forever.

SEPTEMBER 8

Spirit, Soul, and Body

May the God of peace himself make you entirely pure and devoted to God; and may your spirit and soul and body be kept strong and blameless until that day when our Lord Jesus Christ comes back again.

—1 Thessalonians 5:23 (TLB)

You and I are each made up of three parts. Our body is that fleshly part of us that will one day die and decay, becoming dust once again. Our soul is that part of us that contains our mind, will, emotions, and personality, and all of those aspects of ourselves that make us unique. And our spirit is the part of us that lives forever.

God is made up of three parts too. First, there is Jesus, the visible essence of the unseen God. Then, there is the Holy Spirit, our Comforter, who will never leave us or forsake us. Finally, there is God the Father, the Creator of all. When we accept Jesus Christ as our Savior, He promises us a new, resurrected body when Christ returns.

First Corinthians 15:45–49 reads as follows:

The Scriptures tell us, "The first man, Adam, became a living person." But the last Adam—that is, Christ—is a life-giving Spirit. What comes first is the natural body, then the spiritual body comes later. Adam, the first man, was made from the dust of the earth, while Christ, the second man, came from heaven. Earthly people are like the earthly man, and heavenly people are like the heavenly man. Just as we are now like the earthly man, we will someday be like the heavenly man.

And as our spirits become more like Christ's, His righteousness is infused into our souls, making us more like Him in personality, and our natural bodies radiate this righteousness, this light, to the world around us.

O that our whole being, spirit and soul and body, may be kept blameless until that day when Christ returns.

SEPTEMBER 9

Rich Man, Poor Man

Some he causes to be poor and others to be rich. He cuts one down and lifts another up.

—1 Samuel 2:7 (TLB)

Are you someone who treats poor people different from the rich? You may not really think about it, but perhaps you are a respecter of persons based on economics.

The Holy Bible warns us very strongly against showing partiality to people based on wealth.

James 2:1 tells us, "My dear brothers and sisters, how can you claim to have faith in our glorious Lord Jesus Christ if you favor some people over others" (NLT)?

Scripture goes on to tell us the advantages that each, rich and poor, has over the other so that we may keep such judgments in check.

James 2:5 says, "Listen to me, dear brothers and sisters. Hasn't God chosen the poor in this world to be rich in faith? Aren't they the ones who will inherit the Kingdom he promised to those who love him" (NLT)?

And Proverbs 10:15 instructs, "The wealth of the rich is their fortress; the poverty of the poor is their destruction" (NLT).

We must remember it is the Lord who made us all.

May we say, as does Solomon in Proverbs 30:8, "First, help me never to tell a lie. Second, give me neither poverty nor riches! Give me just enough to satisfy my needs" (NLT).

SEPTEMBER 10

The Cream of the Crop

You belong exclusively to the Lord your God, and he has chosen you to be his own possession, more so than any other nation on the face of the earth.

—Deuteronomy 14:2 (TLB)

What does it mean to be the cream of the crop?

It comes from the French expression *crème de la crème*, meaning "the best of the best."

My mother said often, "The cream always rises to the top."

During the Babylonian exile, Daniel (Belteshazzar) and his friends Shadrach, Meshach, and Abednego were selected for service to the king in the royal palace because they were considered to be the cream of the crop. They received special training for three years before entering the king's service.

When we accept Jesus Christ as our personal Savior, we are set apart as holy to the Lord. We are His special treasure, being sanctified for His divine purposes. He personally trains us for His special service.

Psalm 18:34 tells us, "He trains my hands for battle; he strengthens my arm to draw a bronze bow" (NLT).

Ephesians 2:10 blesses us with the following promise: "For we are God's masterpiece. He has created us anew in Christ Jesus, so we can do the good things he planned for us long ago" (NLT).

May we live in the knowledge of our true identity in Jesus Christ today and every day.

SEPTEMBER 11

Calling All Workers

These were his instructions to them: "Plead with the Lord of the harvest to send out more laborers to help you, for the harvest is so plentiful and the workers so few."

—Luke 10:2 (TLB)

Are you a worker bee, or are you more interested in being the queen or king?

God needs us to be workers in His kingdom. There is a task, a purpose, for each of us to carry out in His beautiful master plan. There are no couch potatoes in God's kingdom, and no chair warmers. Instead, each and every task is uniquely and specifically designed with both you and me in mind.

John 9:4 says, "We must quickly carry out the tasks assigned us by the one who sent us. The night is coming, and then no one can work" (NLT).

And God's work is not overwhelming or burdensome. His yoke is easy and His burden is light (Matthew 11:30).

God's Word also teaches us that those who wish to be the greatest in His kingdom must be servant to all.

Matthew 23:11–12 tells us, "The greatest among you must be a servant. But those who exalt themselves will be humbled, and those who humble themselves will be exalted" (NLT).

May we say along with the author of Acts 20:24, "But my life is worth nothing to me unless I use it for finishing the work assigned me by the Lord Jesus—the work of telling others the good news about the wonderful grace of God" (NLT).

SEPTEMBER 12

Mirror, Mirror

And remember, it is a message to obey, not just to listen to. So don't fool yourselves. For if a person just listens and doesn't obey, he is like a man looking at his face in a mirror; as soon as he walks away, he can't see himself anymore or remember what he looks like.

—James 1:22–24 (TLB)

"Mirror, mirror, on the wall, who's most obedient of them all?"

That should be our goal, to be obedient to Christ. We see this theme repeated throughout scripture. Yet if you do so, the people of the world in which we live will call you a fool, a doormat, a moron, a radical, or a myriad of other labels, claiming that in obeying Christ, you have no mind of your own.

The mind that scripture tells us we are to have is the mind of Christ.

First Corinthians 2:15–16 instructs us, "Those who are spiritual can evaluate all things, but they themselves cannot be evaluated by others. For, 'Who can know the Lord's thoughts? Who knows enough to teach him?' But we understand these things, for we have the mind of Christ" (NLT).

Do you see yourself in the mirror the way that God sees you? No, but one day you shall. As 1 Corinthians 13:12 reminds us, "Now we see things imperfectly, like puzzling reflections in a mirror, but then we will see everything with perfect clarity. All that I know now is partial and incomplete, but then I will know everything completely, just as God now knows me completely" (NLT).

May we walk in obedience so that we might gain a heart of wisdom and the mind of Christ, lighting a path directly to the Father in heaven.

SEPTEMBER 13

Having My Way

You want what you don't have, so you kill to get it. You long for what others have, and can't afford it, so you start a fight to take it away from them. And yet the reason you don't have what you want is that you don't ask God for it.

—James 4:2 (TLB)

Are you a selfish person?

I would venture to say that all relationship problems are caused by selfishness on the part of one person or the other.

Philippians 2:3 says, "Don't be selfish; don't try to impress others. Be humble, thinking of others as better than yourselves" (NLT).

The world says, "Look out for number one." It says, "If you don't put yourself first, you'll get steamrolled."

But that's not God's way. God's way is different. God's way is better.

God's way says, "For jealousy and selfishness are not God's kind of wisdom. Such things are earthly, unspiritual, and demonic" (James 3:15 NLT).

God's way says, "But the wisdom from above is first of all pure. It is also peace loving, gentle at all times, and willing to yield to others. It is full of mercy and the fruit of good deeds. It shows no favoritism and is always sincere" (James 3:17 NLT).

Are you willing to yield to others? Beyond the willingness, do you, in fact, yield to others?

May the fruit of His Spirit be evident to all as you yield your way to His way, today and every day.

SEPTEMBER 14

A Generous Spirit

He generously poured out the Spirit upon us through Jesus Christ our Savior.

—Titus 3:6 (NLT)

Do you have a generous spirit, or are you a hoarder of both spiritual and material blessings?

God is the absolute and complete picture of generosity in all of His dealings. Think about the Israelites. Through scripture, in both the Old Testament and the New Testament, God shows His generosity to the children of Israel though they forsake Him time and time again.

Isaiah 32:8 tells us, "But generous people plan to do what is generous, and they stand firm in their generosity" (NLT).

Do you stand firm in your generosity?

The ultimate act of generosity toward all of us was the sacrifice of Jesus Christ on the cross for your sins and mine. There could be no greater act of generosity.

Do you long to be generous?

Ask God to produce a great harvest of generosity in you. Second Corinthians 9:10–11 (NLT) promises us as follows:

For God is the one who provides seed for the farmer and then bread to eat. In the same way, he will provide and increase your resources and then produce a great harvest of generosity in you. Yes, you will be enriched in every way so that you can always be generous. And when we take your gifts to those who need them, they will thank God.

SEPTEMBER 15

Hold Your Tongue

O lying tongue, what shall be your fate?

—Psalm 120:3 (TLB)

Do you have difficulty controlling your tongue?

The Holy Bible tells us in James 3:8, "But no one can tame the tongue. It is restless and evil, full of deadly poison" (NLT).

And James 3:2 says, "Indeed, we all make many mistakes. For if we could control our tongues, we would be perfect and could also control ourselves in every other way" (NLT).

Though the tongue may not be tamed, through the Holy Spirit's power, it can be controlled, as it must be.

James 1:26 tells us, "If you claim to be religious but don't control your tongue, you are fooling yourself, and your religion is worthless" (NLT).

The Holy Spirit dwelling within produces the fruit of love, joy, peace, patience, kindness, goodness, faithfulness, gentleness, and self-control (Galatians 5:22–23). Self-control manifests itself in control of the things we say and the manner in which we say them.

God rewards us when we control our tongues, as Proverbs 13:3 teaches us: "Those who control their tongue will have a long life; opening your mouth can ruin everything" (NLT).

May we seek the Holy Spirit to set a guard about our mouth, so that we might stay out of trouble and have a long life (Psalm 21:23; Proverbs 13:3).

SEPTEMBER 16

The Real You

In their blind conceit, they cannot see how wicked they really are.

—Psalm 36:2 (NLT)

Who are you, *really?*

In the quiet moments when you are all alone with no one watching except God, are you focused on Him?

Does your heart and life exhibit His love?

Romans 12:3 offers a warning with regard to how we should measure ourselves. It says, "Because of the privilege and authority God has given me, I give each of you this warning: Don't think you are better than you really are. Be honest in your evaluation of yourselves, measuring yourselves by the faith God has given us" (NLT).

It is important for us to take a close look at ourselves, examine what we are really made of, and discern who we really are in Christ.

Second Corinthians 13:5 tells us, "Examine yourselves to see if your faith is genuine. Test yourselves. Surely you know that Jesus Christ is among you; if not, you have failed the test of genuine faith" (NLT).

In spite of his sin, there is little wonder why David was a man after God's own heart (1 Samuel 13:14), because he said, "Then I pray to you, O Lord. I say, 'You are my place of refuge. You are all I really want in life'" (Psalm 142:5 NLT).

May God be all any of us really ever want in life.

SEPTEMBER 17

The Power of Prayer

Admit your faults to one another and pray for each other so that you may be healed. The earnest prayer of a righteous man has great power and wonderful results

—JAMES 5:16 (TLB)

Prayer is very underestimated and underutilized. If we truly knew and understood the power of prayer, then our lives would improve and our world would be a totally different place.

Our heavenly Father *longs* for us to know and understand this most powerful form of communication with Him.

He gave us a model for prayer in Matthew 6:9–13. Jesus even tells us how *not* to pray in Matthew 6:7.

And he tells us how much and how often to pray in Matthew 7:7 and 1 Thessalonians 5:17.

Time after time throughout the Holy Bible, and in our lives today, *God answers prayer.*

Psalm 65:5 tells us, "You faithfully answer our prayers with awesome deeds, O God our savior. You are the hope of everyone on earth, even those who sail on distant seas" (NLT).

And when we pray in the Holy Spirit, we keep each other safe in God's love, as Jude 1:20–21 tells us: "But you, dear friends, must build each other up in your most holy faith, pray in the power of the Holy Spirit, and await the mercy of our Lord Jesus Christ, who will bring you eternal life. In this way, you will keep yourselves safe in God's love" (NLT).

O that we might *really* know the power of prayer in our lives today.

SEPTEMBER 18

Haters Gonna Hate

Listen, all of you. Love your enemies. Do good to those who hate you. Pray for the happiness of those who curse you; implore God's blessing on those who hurt you.

—Luke 6:27–28 (TLB)

Some people are just full of hate. They spew bitterness, venom, and negativity on everyone around them, unable to find a positive thing to say about anyone or anything.

It can be hard to love these people.

Notice what 1 John 3:15 tells us about them. It says, "Anyone who hates another brother or sister is really a murderer at heart. And you know that murderers don't have eternal life within them" (NLT).

You can't say it any plainer than that.

First John 2:9 tells us, "If anyone claims, 'I am living in the light,' but hates a fellow believer, that person is still living in darkness" (NLT).

There is no place for hate in the heart of a Christian, unless it is the hatred of sin. Instead, we are to bless those who curse us, and pray for those who hurt us. This kind of love is an overflow of the generous heart God places within each of His children. It is a part of our new nature.

Those whose lives are filled with hate for others do not have the love of God in them. For God's love is light, and in Him there is no darkness, no sin.

May Christ within us be love and light to the world around us—including the haters.

SEPTEMBER 19

Rooted and Grounded in Love

I pray that from his glorious, unlimited resources he will empower you with inner strength through his Spirit. Then Christ will make his home in your hearts as you trust in him. Your roots will grow down into God's love and keep you strong.

—Ephesians 3:16–17 (NLT)

There is an oak tree in the front yard of the school my children attend that is enormous. The trunk of the tree is probably three feet in diameter. This tree is planted so firmly in the ground that it is unshakable even amid the strongest storm. Its roots grow down deep, China deep, making it immovable.

When we allow God to take up residence in our hearts, He fills us with His strength and power as we trust Him more.

The more we trust Him, the deeper our roots grow down into God's love. We become like that oak tree—immovable, unshakable, and strong.

Colossians 2:7 tells us, "Let your roots grow down into him, and let your lives be built on him. Then your faith will grow strong in the truth you were taught, and you will overflow with thankfulness" (NLT).

May we trust in our Savior so that our roots may grow down deep into His love, keeping us strong throughout all our days.

SEPTEMBER 20

The Tune of the Hickory Stick

If you refuse to discipline your son, it proves you don't love him; for if you love him, you will be prompt to punish him.

—Proverbs 13:24 (NLT)

There is an old song that I and my fellow students sang in school many years back called "School Days." The lyrics to the song, written in 1907 by Will Cobb and Gus Edwards, are as follows:

School days, school days, Dear old golden rule days.

Reading and 'riting and 'rithmetic Taught to the tune of the hick'ry stick. You were my queen in calico;

I was your bashful, barefoot beau.

And you wrote on my slate, "I Love You, Joe," When we were a couple o' kids.

The hickory stick referred to in this song was used by teachers for instruction, and also for discipline. In my day, the yardstick was used by teachers for instruction, and a wooden paddle was used for discipline. One of my teachers had "The Board of Education" painted across the paddle that hung behind her desk. We knew she loved us enough to use it, if necessary.

O how we need a return to that kind of love—the kind that is not afraid to use the hickory stick.

Proverbs 26:3 tells us, "Guide a horse with a whip, a donkey with a bridle, and a fool with a rod to his back" (NLT)!

May we love our children enough to discipline them when they need it.

SEPTEMBER 21

Livin' Large

But the people living there are powerful, and their cities are fortified and very large; and what's more, we saw Anakim giants there!

—Numbers 13:28 (TLB)

After Moses sent twelve scouts to explore the Promised Land of Canaan for forty days before the Israelites went in to take possession, they brought back a very interesting report.

They noted that the land was indeed bountiful, showing the people a cluster of grapes so large that it took two men to carry it on a pole between them. The scouts from the twelve tribes told the people that Canaan was a land flowing with milk and honey, just as they had been promised.

There was just one problem Not only was the fruit and bounty of the land large, but also the people were large. They were giants, descendants of Anak. Eleven of the twelve scouts were terrified, and spread a bad report throughout the camp. There was one scout from the tribe of Judah named Caleb who knew that God was larger than any ol' giant.

Numbers 13:30 tells us, "But Caleb tried to quiet the people as they stood before Moses. 'Let's go at once to take the land,' he said. 'We can certainly conquer it'" (NLT)!

The Israelites eventually did take the land, but their lack of faith made the process much longer and harder than it should have been.

Are there giants in your land today?

Have faith, like Caleb, to believe God is larger, and then go at once to claim the victory.

SEPTEMBER 22

The Supreme Court

When Christ has finally won the battle against all his enemies, then he, the Son of God, will put himself also under his Father's orders, so that God who has given him the victory over everything else will be utterly supreme.

—1 Corinthians 15:28 (TLB)

In the case of *United States v. Windsor* (2013), the United States Supreme Court essentially decided to change the definition of marriage. No longer does the United States Supreme Court define marriage as being the union of one man and one woman in accordance with God's holy Word (Genesis 2:24).

But the US Supreme Court is not *the* supreme court.

The supreme court isn't in Washington, DC. It is in God's holy place, and the chief justice of this supreme court does not bow to peer pressure, social norms, or the latest acceptable pet sins.

Sadly, those who do wrong and temporarily get away with it tend to boast about their crimes. But take heart. Such boasting will be short-lived.

Psalm 52:1 tells us, "Why do you boast about your crimes, great warrior? Don't you realize God's justice continues forever" (NLT)?

Are you in need of justice from the chief justice of the real supreme court?

Psalm 135:14 says, "For the Lord will give justice to his people and have compassion on his servants" (NLT).

May you find comfort in the promises of God's holy Word.

SEPTEMBER 23

Don't Give Up

And let us not get tired of doing what is right, for after a while we will reap a harvest of blessing if we don't get discouraged and give up.

—GALATIANS 6:9 (TLB)

Do you ever get discouraged in taking the high road, observing that no one else seems to care?

God cares. And He's the one that matters.

Are you surrounded by people who constantly do what is wrong and never seem to get caught? In fact, they seem to prosper more than the folks who are doing what is right.

Take heart, my friend. God sees them too.

Psalm 37:7 tells us, "Be still in the presence of the Lord, and wait patiently for him to act. Don't worry about evil people who prosper or fret about their wicked schemes" (NLT).

Waiting can be hard. Don't give up.

Have faith in the One who answers our prayers with awesome deeds. He is the hope of everyone on earth, even those who sail on distant seas (Psalm 65:5).

SEPTEMBER 24

While You're Waiting

Wait until the bridal week is over and you can have Rachel too—if you promise to work for me another seven years!

—Genesis 29:27 (TLB)

Jacob loved Rachel. He worked seven years for her father, Laban, so that he could have her as his wife. At the end of the seven years, Laban did a switcheroo on Jacob, and gave him Rachel's older sister, Leah, to wed. Jacob ended up having to wait until the end of the bridal week for Rachel, and he also had to work for Laban seven more years.

Sarah waited ninety years to have her one and only child.

The Israelites waited forty years to see the Promised Land of Canaan. But what did all of these people do while they were waiting?

Does it matter? It matters.

Second Peter 3:14 tells us, "And so, dear friends, while you are waiting for these things to happen, make every effort to be found living peaceful lives that are pure and blameless in his sight" (NLT).

Often our times of waiting are times when God is growing us, pruning us, and making us into all that He wants us to be.

May God help us not to grumble, not to mumble, and to have faith in the One who never fails us, even while we are waiting.

SEPTEMBER 25

Living in the Land of the Lost

We—every one of us—have strayed away like sheep! We, who left God's paths to follow our own. Yet God laid on him the guilt and sins of every one of us!

—Isaiah 53:6 (TLB)

The world in which we live is filled with lost people. We are surrounded by them each and every day.

So how do we approach the lost world in which we live? How are we to act each and every day?

The Holy Bible provides us with the answers to these questions, as well as the perfect example to follow, Jesus. When Jesus interacted with others, He always met them at their point of need. He met their physical needs, spoke in a way that was relatable, and never shied away from or failed to address their spiritual needs.

In John 4:1–42, we see Jesus doing exactly this with a Samaritan woman. The woman did not even realize she had a need. But Jesus did.

Both Jesus and the woman were both in need of water, so Jesus used the water to relate to the woman, and to address the spiritual needs she was not even aware that she had.

There are people whom you and I come into contact with each and every day who have no awareness of their need for Jesus Christ. But we can relate to them, love them, and meet them at their point of need as we share the gospel with them.

May we not pass them by.

SEPTEMBER 26

Spiritual Circumcision

When you came to Christ, he set you free from your evil desires, not by a bodily operation of circumcision but by a spiritual operation, the baptism of your souls.

—Colossians 2:11 (TLB)

The act of circumcision has been a tradition for Jewish males since the days of Abraham. The term comes from the Latin word *circumcidere*, which means "to cut around."[3]

Abraham's circumcision and the circumcision of all the Jewish males was a sign of God's covenant with the people, and their promise to obey Him.

When Jesus Christ came as the one everlasting atoning sacrifice for our sins, the need for an outward mark—a physical circumcision—changed too.

When we accept Jesus Christ as our Lord, our Savior, and our Master, He performs a circumcision of the heart. He writes His law upon our hearts, and cuts away the old nature of sin, replacing it with a new nature. The new nature wants only to love and obey Christ.

And though this new nature is not evidenced by a physical mark upon our flesh, it is seen in every aspect of our lives and through every pore in our being, every word that we say, every thought in our mind, and every action that we take—day after day after day.

May your life and mine be a reflection of our spiritual circumcision of the heart.

---

[3] World Health Organization, *Male circumcision: Global trends and determinants of prevalence, safety, and acceptability* (Geneva: WHO Press, 2007), accessed December 9, 2016, whqlibdoc.who.int/publications/2007/9789241596169_eng.pdf.

SEPTEMBER 27

My Hiding Place

You are my hiding place from every storm of life; you even keep me from getting into trouble! You surround me with songs of victory.

—Psalm 32:7 (TLB)

Do you ever wish that you could just run away and hide from the cold, cruel world?

I have felt that way on many occasions. In each and every instance, God has been my hiding place, my protection, my shelter from the storm.

In the Holy Bible, David understood trouble. He understood what it meant to be surrounded by and chased by enemies.

In Psalm 27:4–5, David tells us, "The one thing I ask of the Lord—the thing I seek most—is to live in the house of the Lord all the days of my life, delighting in the Lord's perfections and meditating in his Temple.

For he will conceal me there when troubles come; he will hide me in his sanctuary. He will place me out of reach on a high rock" (NLT).

Psalm 64:2 says, "Hide me from the plots of this evil mob, from this gang of wrongdoers" (NLT).

And Psalm 143:9 tells us, "Rescue me from my enemies, Lord; I run to you to hide me" (NLT).

Are you in need of God's hiding place today?

May you run to the One who is our hiding place so that He may protect you when trouble comes.

SEPTEMBER 28

Bonded Together

Try always to be led along together by the Holy Spirit and so be at peace with one another.

—Ephesians 4:3 (TLB)

There many different kinds of bonds. There are surety bonds, financial bonds, bail bonds, bonds between friends, bonds between siblings, bonds between Christians, and bonds between parents and children. The list goes on.

One bond that is deeper and stronger than any other is the bond of love. And since we know that God is love (1 John 4:8), we know that the bond of love is from Him.

Colossians 3:14 tells us, "Above all, clothe yourselves with love, which binds us all together in perfect harmony."

The Holy Bible tells us that the bond of love is the one principle that sums up all the law and the prophets (Galatians 5:14).

Romans 13:8 puts it this way: "Owe nothing to anyone—except for your obligation to love one another. If you love your neighbor, you will fulfill the requirements of God's law" (NLT).

When we have God in our hearts, we have love. And where there is love, there is also peace.

May our bond for one another grow as our love for God grows. "May God give you more and more mercy, peace, and love" (Jude 1:2 NLT).

SEPTEMBER 29

Being Different

Do you think you deserve credit for merely loving those who love you? Even the godless do that! And if you do good only to those who do you good—is that so wonderful? Even sinners do that much!

—Luke 6:32–33 (TLB)

Are you different?

Sometimes it's hard to be different.

Different isn't popular, and it is sometimes hard for people to understand.

God's way is different. God's way isn't popular. It goes against socially and culturally accepted norms. It goes against the way of the world, the way of the crowd. It doesn't scream and demand its way. It whispers to us, calling us out to march to the beat of a different drum, a different drummer.

God's way calls us to love the unlovable. His way calls us to do good to the person who stabbed us in the back yesterday and today.

No one said it was easy. But being different is refreshing, magnetic, when it's God's way.

It's different.

In Matthew 5:47, Jesus says, "If you are kind only to your friends, how are you different from anyone else? Even pagans do that" (NLT).

May God enable you in all ways to be different today.

SEPTEMBER 30

Paybacks Are Heaven

Love your enemies! Do good to them! Lend to them! And don't be concerned about the fact that they won't repay. Then your reward from heaven will be very great, and you will truly be acting as sons of God: for he is kind to the unthankful and to those who are very wicked.

—Luke 6:35 (TLB)

Have you ever been done wrong—I mean, really, really wrong?

The world would say that we should pay the person back who wronged us, take matters into our own hands, get revenge.

But that's not what God says.

God commands us to love our enemies—not just our neighbors, but also our enemies.

This world is full of evil, ungrateful, wicked people who will rob you blind at the drop of a hat, and God is kind to them. He wants us to be kind to them too, and never to take revenge (Romans 12:19). This mind-set and practice goes against everything the world would have us believe and do.

God even tells us to lend to our enemies without expecting to be repaid. And believe you me, some people have no intention of repaying you with anything good—ever.

But guess what? You'll get paid back (and so will they). Your payback will be heaven.

OCTOBER 1

Demonstrating Peace

Never pay back evil for evil. Do things in such a way that everyone can see you are honest clear through. Don't quarrel with anyone. Be at peace with everyone, just as much as possible.

—Romans 12:17–18 (TLB)

Have you ever noticed that some people are next to impossible to be at peace with?

This verse doesn't tell us that we have to live in peace with everyone, but it does tell us to do everything within our power to live in peace with others. There's a difference. But what does it look like to do all that we can to live in peace?

It looks like Pam, who quietly gets dinner ready for her husband when he comes in the door, though he is negative and critical of her every move. And she prays.

It looks like Chris, who smiles at the bully scowling back at him every day. Chris kindly says, "Good morning," receiving nothing but the continued scowl in reply.

It looks like Linda, who doesn't drink alcohol but takes no issue with those who do so in moderation. She doesn't act self-righteous about it, either.

Does your life demonstrate peace, *real* peace?

Ephesians 4:3 tells us, "Make every effort to keep yourselves united in the Spirit, binding yourselves together with peace" (NLT).

May the Holy Spirit fill our lives, uniting us together in peace.

OCTOBER 2

Rock Beats Scissors

Don't let evil get the upper hand, but conquer evil by doing good.

—Romans 12:21 (TLB)

Do you remember the game rock, paper, scissors? I've always loved playing that game. And it has a real-life application.

The world can be a cold, cruel place. Evil can cut us to the quick, leaving us feeling down and defeated—especially when evil appears to win for the moment.

When we try to do things our own way or the world's way, we end up losing. We become nothing but paper going up against scissors.

But when we put our hope in the Solid Rock, doing things *His* way, we have the assurance that good conquers evil, even when we don't see it right away.

The Holy Bible tells us in 1 John 5:4, "For every child of God defeats this evil world, and we achieve this victory through our faith" (NLT).

Proverbs 29:25 tells us, "Fearing people is a dangerous trap, but trusting the Lord means safety" (NLT).

May we always remember that Rock beats scissors—every time.

OCTOBER 3

Shoring Up the Foundation

All who listen to my instructions and follow them are wise, like a man who builds his house on solid rock.

—Matthew 7:24 (TLB)

Are there cracks in your foundation?

The house was about forty years old. It had seen many storms, including Hurricanes Alicia and Rita. It had been through Tropical Storm Allison, too, and years of intensely hot summers and cold winters, and summer droughts and springtime floods. All these events had revealed some weakness in the foundation that was originally laid.

There were a few barbs missing when the foundation was poured, and although it was not apparent early on, there was no denying it now. If the house was going to stand, that foundation was going to have to be repaired.

How is your foundation? Has your life seen some fierce storms, hurricanes, and times of drought, flood, heat, and cold?

Proverbs 10:25 tells us, "When the storms of life come, the wicked are whirled away, but the godly have a lasting foundation" (NLT).

Are there barbs missing from your foundation?

First Corinthians 3:10 cautions us, "Because of God's grace to me, I have laid the foundation like an expert builder. Now others are building on it. But whoever is building on this foundation must be very careful" (NLT).

May we be careful to build our foundation upon the rock of God's truth so that our lives may withstand any storm that comes our way.

OCTOBER 4

Renewed

That is why we never give up. Though our bodies are dying, our inner strength in the Lord is growing every day.

—2 Corinthians 4:16 (TLB)

Each of us is closer to eternity than we realize.

Psalm 102:11 tells us, "My life passes as swiftly as the evening shadows. I am withering away like grass" (NLT).

This verse reminds us that though our physical bodies are dying, our spirits are being renewed day by day. What a glorious promise!

But what does that really mean?

Colossians 5:4–5 (NLT) answers this question for us. It reads as follows: While we live in these earthly bodies, we groan and sigh,

but it's not that we want to die and get rid of these bodies that clothe us. Rather, we want to put on our new bodies so that these dying bodies will be swallowed up by life. God himself has prepared us for this, and as a guarantee he has given us his Holy Spirit.

We must always remember that God's Spirit within us gives us life. When we do remember, we are able to properly shift our focus to the things of heaven, living in all the fullness of joy that God intended for us to experience here on earth—regardless of our circumstance.

Colossians 3:2 tells us, "Think about the things of heaven, not the things of earth" (NLT).

May we live by believing, not by seeing (2 Corinthians 5:7), and may we always live this life in such a way as to please Him.

OCTOBER 5

When Life Is Uncertain

God's ways are as mysterious as the pathway of the wind and as the manner in which a human spirit is infused into the little body of a baby while it is yet in its mother's womb.

—ECCLESIASTES 11:5 (TLB)

Sometimes life doesn't make sense.

We reason, theorize, theologize, and suppose. We guess, suspect, conjecture, and speculate. But it still doesn't make sense.

It is at these times that we must simply trust. We must trust God.

Proverbs 3:5 tells us, "Trust in the Lord with all your heart; do not depend on your own understanding" (NLT).

Is doing this easy? No.

It is an act of the will, enabled by the Spirit. And as we exercise this trust, it will become stronger and grow deeper, enabling us to see past the storm to our eternity with Him.

Romans 15:13 says, "I pray that God, the source of hope, will fill you completely with joy and peace because you trust in him. Then you will overflow with confident hope through the power of the Holy Spirit" (NLT).

May we not allow the uncertainties of life to tarnish our trust in Him. As Hebrews 3:14 tells us, "For if we are faithful to the end, trusting God just as firmly as when we first believed, we will share in all that belongs to Christ" (NLT).

OCTOBER 6

Bloom Where You're Planted

Yes, there will be an abundance of flowers and singing and joy! The deserts will become as green as the Lebanon mountains, as lovely as Mount Carmel's pastures and Sharon's meadows; for the Lord will display his glory there, the excellency of our God.

—Isaiah 35:2 (TLB)

Growing up, I often complained to my mother about various things I had to do and places I had to go.

"Bloom where you're planted," she would say.

"But I don't want to be a flower in the junkyard," I protested in return.

My mother, in her wisdom, would remind me that junkyards need flowers,

too. And she would go on to tell me how much more noticeable and appreciated was the single flower in the junkyard, versus the flower in the garden flower bed.

Do you find yourself in a place that is not of your choosing?

Remember that God's ways are not our ways and that His plans are not our plans. His are so much better (Isaiah 55:9).

Ephesians 3:20 tells us, "Now all glory to God, who is able, through his mighty power at work within us, to accomplish infinitely more than we might ask or think" (NLT).

Jeremiah 29:11 reads as follows: "'For I know the plans I have for you,' says the Lord. 'They are plans for good and not for disaster, to give you a future and a hope'" (NLT).

May we choose to bloom wherever God may plant us.

OCTOBER 7

One Day at a Time

So don't be anxious about tomorrow. God will take care of your tomorrow too. Live one day at a time.

—Matthew 6:34 (TLB)

Do you have a tendency to borrow tomorrow's troubles?

For many years I had this habit, thinking of what-if scenarios, working diligently to prevent and protect that which was clearly out of my control.

My own efforts never left me feeling as though I had peace and comfort. On the contrary, I felt conviction for attempting to control things I both couldn't and shouldn't control.

Philippians 4:6 tells us, "Don't worry about anything; instead, pray about everything. Tell God what you need, and thank him for all he has done" (NLT).

God will never disappoint us. He will never let us down. He has a proven track record.

He always meets us at our point of need, and He will take every opportunity to lovingly teach us how to trust Him more—one day at a time.

"But each day the Lord pours his unfailing love upon me, and through each night I sing his songs, praying to God who gives me life" (Psalm 42:8 NLT).

OCTOBER 8

Free-Flying

And this has a real advantage: I am not bound to obey anyone just because he pays my salary; yet I have freely and happily become a servant of any and all so that I can win them to Christ.

—1 Corinthians 9:19 (TLB)

There is an amazing freedom that comes from knowing Christ as our Savior.

No longer does sin have a death grip on our lives. His love is the wind beneath our wings, enabling us to soar to amazing new heights, to live victorious lives of freedom.

John 8:36 tells us, "So if the Son sets you free, you are truly free" (NLT). But that freedom is not a license to sin. It is a license to love.

Galatians 5:13 says, "For you have been called to live in freedom, my brothers and sisters. But don't use your freedom to satisfy your sinful nature. Instead, use your freedom to serve one another in love" (NLT).

Praise Him, our glorious Master, who has freed us from sin and death and made us alive to His love!

May we take up our cross daily and follow Him (Luke 9:23). And may others see Jesus in you today.

OCTOBER 9

The Fine Art of Shutting Up

A rebel shouts in anger; a wise man holds his temper in and cools it.

—Proverbs 29:11 (TLB)

I often speak when I shouldn't, and then I say the wrong things. Do you ever do that?

Regardless, silence is not always golden. Sometimes we need to speak up rather than shut up.

Do you know the difference? It is a fine art.

Proverbs 18:20 says, "Wise words satisfy like a good meal; the right words bring satisfaction" (NLT).

Cooking a good meal, like any art, must be practiced. It is the same with shutting up. And what flows out of a man or woman is that which is inside.

Luke 6:45 tells us, "A good person produces good things from the treasury of a good heart, and an evil person produces evil things from the treasury of an evil heart. What you say flows from what is in your heart" (NLT).

May God fill our hearts and guide us all as we choose our words carefully before speaking.

OCTOBER 10

The Cattle Prod of God

The wise man's words are like goads that spur to action. They nail down important truths. Students are wise who master what their teachers tell them.

—ECCLESIASTES 12:11 (TLB)

Have you ever felt the painful but helpful cattle prod of God?

Sometimes He places wise people in our path. He does this so these people can prod us in the right direction.

Often the words of the wise are painful to hear.

Hebrews 12:11 tells us, "No discipline is enjoyable while it is happening—it's painful! But afterward there will be a peaceful harvest of right living for those who are trained in this way" (NLT).

Sometimes we need help to get moving in the right direction. Like sheep without a shepherd, we often wander away from the right path, unable to find our way back.

Yet God lovingly calls us back to Him by name.

John 10:3 says, "The gatekeeper opens the gate for him, and the sheep recognize his voice and come to him. He calls his own sheep by name and leads them out" (NLT).

May we recognize the cattle prod of God for the blessing that it is, and may we stay close beside the Good Shepherd.

OCTOBER 11

Constrained by Humanness

Under the old system, even the high priests were weak and sinful men who could not keep from doing wrong, but later God appointed by his oath his Son who is perfect forever.

—Hebrews 7:28 (TLB)

As humans, we face the limitations of our humanness each and every day.

We are imperfect, and confined by the natural laws that govern our world, like time and gravity, as well as by physics, the finite nature of the world, and sin.

We often forget that God is not limited or constrained by the same limitations and weakness.

When God sent His Son, Jesus, to the world, the latter was constrained by humanness in many ways. He was in a human body, limited by the same natural laws that impact us all today. Yet look at all of the miracles He performed!

James 5:17 tells us, "Elijah was as human as we are, and yet when he prayed earnestly that no rain would fall, none fell for three and a half years" (NLT)!

We must remember that our Master, our Savior, is not confined by human limitations like we are.

John 14:12 promises us, "I tell you the truth, anyone who believes in me will do the same works I have done, and even greater works, because I am going to be with the Father" (NLT).

May we remember the power available to us through Jesus, who has gone to be with the Father, if only we will believe.

OCTOBER 12

The End of the Story

Here is my final conclusion: fear God and obey his commandments, for this is the entire duty of man. For God will judge us for everything we do, including every hidden thing, good or bad.

—Ecclesiastes 12:13–14 (TLB)

The story of life reads better than any novel. There is the perfect protagonist. The plot is full of nearly unbelievable twists and turns, climaxes, and stomach-snatching drops. And—spoiler alert—we know who wins in the end.

But there is much more to the story.

It's not fiction, and our existence is not just a novel that ends once this lifetime is over.

We are here to learn how to love and obey Christ. And God will judge us for everything we do, good or bad, seen or unseen.

Are you ready to face the story's conclusion?

"Look, I will come as unexpectedly as a thief! Blessed are all who are watching for me, who keep their clothing ready so they will not have to walk around naked and ashamed" (Revelation 16:15 NLT).

And that's just the beginning of the story.

OCTOBER 13

Don't Hold Back

And I can't quit! For if I say I'll never again mention the Lord— never more speak in his name—then his word in my heart is like fire that burns in my bones, and I can't hold it in any longer!

—Jeremiah 20:9 (TLB)

Have you ever felt like Jeremiah in this passage of scripture? I have.

There are times in my life when God's Word burns in my heart like a fire and I have to let the words loose. Sometimes the words are difficult for the listener, and both our hearts ache while I am talking. In speaking words like these, our chief concern should always be acting in love and obedience to Christ.

The Holy Bible tells us in Isaiah 55:11, when talking about God's use of all things for His purposes, "It is the same with my word. I send it out, and it always produces fruit. It will accomplish all I want it to, and it will prosper everywhere I send it" (NLT).

When God lays His Word upon our heart, it is for a specific purpose, although we may not know what that purpose is.

Proverbs 25:11 tells us, "Timely advice is lovely, like golden apples in a silver basket" (NLT).

In John 6:63, Jesus tells us, "The Spirit alone gives eternal life. Human effort accomplishes nothing. And the very words I have spoken to you are spirit and life" (NLT).

It is never about us. It is always about God. May God bless the speaking of His Word.

OCTOBER 14

Batting Order

I replied, "But my work for them seems all in vain; I have spent my strength for them without response. Yet I leave it all with God for my reward."

—Isaiah 49:4 (TLB)

I like to play softball with the boys, but I'm really no good, not even for a girl.

When I was a fresh college graduate, the company I worked for had a women's softball team. For some reason, they allowed me on the team. Each week, I would eagerly run, glove in hand, to check the batting order, but my name wouldn't be on the sheet.

Week after week I practiced. And week after week, I warmed the bench, keeping score and sometimes fetching water for the other women on the team.

Sometimes our spiritual life can seem a bit like that.

Each week we study God's Word, looking for an opportunity to be used by Him. And each week, that opportunity we have in our mind fades away. It never materializes.

But what we fail to realize is that God *is* using us. He is using us in ways we overlook.

There is always someone watching.

Will you trust Him with your life's work even when that work seems useless? Will you trust Him even when you're not in the batting order?

May we learn to leave everything in God's hands, trusting Him for our reward.

OCTOBER 15

Keeping Our Eyes on Jesus

Keep your eyes on Jesus, our leader and instructor. He was willing to die a shameful death on the cross because of the joy he knew would be his afterwards; and now he sits in the place of honor by the throne of God.

—Hebrews 12:2 (TLB)

Whom are you watching? Are you watching the world? Who is your example?

When life gets hard, it is important for us to keep our eyes on Jesus, the author and finisher of our faith, the champion who initiates and perfects our faith. Otherwise, we will easily be led astray and corrupted by the world. We will find ourselves on a path that is not what we hoped for but that is of our choosing—whether we recognize it or not.

Proverbs 21:16 says, "The person who strays from common sense will end up in the company of the dead" (NLT).

Sometimes the world's way seems like common sense, but it's not.

Proverbs 17:24 says, "Sensible people keep their eyes glued on wisdom, but a fool's eyes wander to the ends of the earth" (NLT).

May we follow the words of Psalm 123:2, which tells us, "We keep looking to the Lord our God for his mercy, just as servants keep their eyes on their master, as a slave girl watches her mistress for the slightest signal" (NLT).

OCTOBER 16

When the Answer Never Comes

Shall we not expect far greater glory in these days when the Holy Spirit is giving life? If the plan that leads to doom was glorious, much more glorious is the plan that makes men right with God.

—2 Corinthians 3:8–9 (TLB)

Have you ever prayed very hard for something for a long, long time without getting the answer you wanted?

Sometimes when we pray, asking God for something, we are sure that He will answer the way we want because we believe that what we request is the best possible outcome. We believe our prayer to be in keeping with God's will for the situation. We can't imagine anything else.

In the passage of scripture above, Paul couldn't imagine a better outcome, either. But there *was* a better outcome, and God revealed it to Paul. Sometimes our prayers are hindered because of our disobedience (1 Peter 3:7).

Sometimes our prayers go unanswered because we waver in our belief and our loyalty is divided (James 1:6–7). But Jesus taught us in the parable of the persistent widow (Luke 18:1–8) that we should always pray and never give up.

Second Peter 3:9 tells us, "The Lord isn't really being slow about his promise, as some people think. No, he is being patient for your sake. He does not want anyone to be destroyed, but wants everyone to repent."

May we continue to pray, leaving the outcome in the hands of our loving and merciful God.

OCTOBER 17

Which Seed Are You?

The good ground represents the heart of a man who listens to the message and understands it and goes out and brings thirty, sixty, or even a hundred others into the Kingdom.

—Matthew 13:23 (TLB)

In the parable of the sower, Jesus tells of the farmer scattering seed. In Matthew 13:1–23, He gives the account of what happens to four different groups of seeds.

The first seeds in the story fall along the sidewalk, where the birds come and eat them. These seeds represent those who hear the gospel but don't understand it. The Devil comes and snatches the good news planted in these people's hearts.

The second seeds that land on rocky soil re resent those who immediately receive the gospel into their hearts with joy but who don't have deep roots. The minute they hit tough times or persecution, they fall away from God.

The third group of seeds in this parable fall among the thorns. These seeds represent those who hear God's Word but who allow the things of the world to quickly crowd out the message, so there is no fruit produced in their lives.

Finally, the fourth group of seeds, which fall on the good soil, represent those who hear God's Word and believe it. Their lives produce a bountiful harvest of good fruit many times greater than that which was planted.

Have you gotten off course or allowed the things of this world to crowd out God's plan and purpose for your life? May we remain grafted onto the vine of Jesus every day, so that our lives produce much good fruit for the kingdom of God.

OCTOBER 18

The Best Insulation

The Lord is my fort where I can enter and be safe; no one can follow me in and slay me. He is a rugged mountain where I hide; he is my Savior, a rock where none can reach me, and a tower of safety. He is my shield. He is like the strong horn of a mighty fighting bull.

—Psalm 18:2 (TLB)

A recent risk management conference in Houston I attended detailed a new spray-on foam insulation being used in the construction of both commercial and residential buildings. It was touted as the best insulation on the market, protecting internal structures from dramatic temperature changes resulting from the storms of life, regardless of season.

In our personal spiritual lives, we need the best insulation on the market. The storms in our lives can occur in any and every season, and our internal structures need protection from them.

There is no better insulation available to humankind than God, our Savior. And there will never be a better insulator than He.

He is our Rock.

He is our Protector.

He is our shield, the power that saves us. He is our place of safety.

Isaiah 25:4b tells us, "You are a refuge from the storm and a shelter from the heat" (NLT). Praise the God who insulates us.

OCTOBER 19

Laundry Day

Create in me a new, clean heart, O God, filled with clean thoughts and right desires.

—Psalm 51:10 (TLB)

When King David penned these words, it was laundry day.

It was his heart that was dirty. There were some stubborn stains, ground-in dirt. David's adultery with Bathsheba and his murder of her husband had been exposed. He was in need of cleansing.

Are you in need of cleansing?

Perhaps sin has gained a foothold in your life. Others may not know it, but God knows it.

Psalm 90:8 says, "You spread out our sins before you—our secret sins—and you see them all" (NLT).

But God's redemption, love, and cleansing removes even stubborn stains and ground-in dirt.

Psalm 51:2 encourages us: "Wash me clean from my guilt. Purify me from my sin" (NLT).

Psalm 51:7 tells us, "Purify me from my sins, and I will be clean; wash me, and I will be whiter than snow" (NLT).

Is it laundry day at your house?

Our God, our Jesus, is the best cleanser you'll ever find.

OCTOBER 20

In a Little While

After you have suffered a little while, our God, who is full of kindness through Christ, will give you his eternal glory. He personally will come and pick you up, and set you firmly in place, and make you stronger than ever.

—1 Peter 5:10 (TLB)

How much longer?

I have asked God this question repeatedly when suffering with my own personal thorn in the flesh.

There doesn't seem to be an audible answer when I ask God this question, but this verse provides the promise, the hope, the answer that I seek: "After you have suffered a little while."

I'm not really sure how long a little while is to God, but the promise is that he will restore, support, and strengthen me, and that He will place me on a firm foundation.

Have you been suffering for a little while?

Perhaps your little while has lasted ten, twenty, or thirty years—or more.

There is hope in knowing that God is mindful of us. He has called us to share in His eternal glory.

And one day, He will restore, support, and strengthen you, and place you on a firm foundation.

May we be encouraged not to give up.

In a little while is just around the corner.

OCTOBER 21

Written on My Heart

And I delight to do your will, my God, for your law is written upon my heart!

—Psalm 40:8 (TLB)

Long before Jesus came to die for our sins on the cross, ushering in a new covenant, God's laws, His instructions, were being written on humanity's heart.

Yet many a man and woman had hearts too hard, too callous, to feel the pen of God upon them.

Many a man and woman today have hearts too hard and too callous to sense the delicate pen of Christ upon them, too.

What about you? Are you sensitive to the loving gentle touch of the Father upon your heart? Do you take joy in doing His will?

Psalm 19:8 tells us, "The commandments of the Lord are right, bringing joy to the heart. The commands of the Lord are clear, giving insight for living" (NLT).

May He soften your heart to sense His pen upon it. And may you find joy in following His commands.

OCTOBER 22

Running on Empty

Oh, how kind our Lord was, for he showed me how to trust him and become full of the love of Christ Jesus.

—1 Timothy 1:14 (TLB)

Are you running on empty?

Sometimes the pace of life and its circumstances can drain our physical, spiritual, and emotional batteries. When that happens, God calls us to Him. He calls us out to a place of rest and refuge. He calls us away from the frantic pace of life and its exhausting circumstances.

In Jesus's earthly ministry, He and the disciples often experienced this same frantic pace of life and its circumstances. When this happened, Jesus called the disciples away to rest.

Mark 6:31 tells us, "Then Jesus said, 'Let's go off by ourselves to a quiet place and rest awhile.' He said this because there were so many people coming and going that Jesus and his apostles didn't even have time to eat" (NLT).

Can you relate to Jesus and the disciples?

Do you need to find a quiet place to rest a while? Jesus is that place.

Psalm 91:1 says, "Those who live in the shelter of the Most High will find rest in the shadow of the Almighty" (NLT).

Matthew 11:29 encourages us: "Take my yoke upon you. Let me teach you, because I am humble and gentle at heart, and you will find rest for your souls" (NLT).

May we allow Jesus to teach us how to rest and recharge today.

OCTOBER 23

Singing in the Rain

He sends rain upon the mountains and fills the earth with fruit.

—Psalm 104:13 (TLB)

Have you ever felt like singing in the rain?

When God sends down this glorious substance upon the dry, parched ground after weeks of blistering heat, it makes me want to sing.

When He rains down blessings of every kind from heaven, it makes me want to sing.

Psalm 66:8 says, "Let the whole world bless our God and loudly sing his praises" (NLT).

After a rainy Sunday church service one week, I noticed a little rascal about four or five years old who exuberantly yanked off his socks and shoes to go stomping through puddles with a huge smile on his face. He did this all the way to the family car. His dad scooped him up, beaming at his son's enjoyment as he positioned the lad in his car seat.

Deuteronomy 28:12 tells us, "The Lord will send rain at the proper time from his rich treasury in the heavens and will bless all the work you do. You will lend to many nations, but you will never need to borrow from them" (NLT).

How long has it been since you stomped through rain puddles? Perhaps it's been too long.

OCTOBER 24

Purging the Evil

It isn't our job to judge outsiders. But it certainly is our job to judge and deal strongly with those who are members of the church and who are sinning in these ways. God alone is the Judge of those on the outside. But you yourselves must deal with this man and put him out of your church.

—1 Corinthians 5:12–13 (TLB)

Our churches are full of evil people these days who should be purged from our midst, according to this verse. So why don't we have the courage to remove them?

Could it be, perhaps, that we fear our pews will be empty if we remove all who continue to be unrepentant of their sinful acts? Or is it that we are treading on the border of such behavior ourselves, unwilling to repent of our own sin and afraid of being exposed?

Yet scripture is clear on this matter.

First Corinthians 5:11 tells us, "I meant that you are not to associate with anyone who claims to be a believer yet indulges in sexual sin, or is greedy, or worships idols, or is abusive, or is a drunkard, or cheats people. Don't even eat with such people" (NLT).

Are such people members of your church congregation?

First Corinthians 5:7 says, "Get rid of the old 'yeast' by removing this wicked person from among you. Then you will be like a fresh batch of dough made without yeast, which is what you really are" (NLT).

May we have the courage to purge the evil from our midst so that we might not be guilty of spiritual pride.

OCTOBER 25

Demons Are Real

And they cast out many demons and healed many sick people, anointing them with olive oil.

—Mark 6:13 (TLB)

Demons are real.

They are evil spirits doing Satan's bidding, and they are all around us. They have the ability to take possession or control of those who do not know Christ.

The gospels are full of accounts in which Jesus cast out demons that had taken possession of people young and old. Yet in Matthew 17:14–22, when the disciples tried to cast the demon out of a boy whose father had asked for help, they were unable to do it. When they asked Jesus why, He explained that it was because they did not have enough faith.

In another example, as read in Mark 9:14–29, the disciples are unable to cast out a demon from a boy who can't talk, foams at the mouth, grinds his teeth, and becomes rigid as a result of the evil spirit within him. Jesus casts out the demon, and the boy is healed. When the disciples ask why they were unable to do it, Jesus advises them that prayer is the only way to cast out this particular kind of demon.

Ephesians 6:12 tells us, "For we are not fighting against flesh-and-blood enemies, but against evil rulers and authorities of the unseen world, against mighty powers in this dark world, and against evil spirits in the heavenly places" (NLT). Why is it that we would rather explain evil away by attributing it to a syndrome or a new mental illness than calling it what it truly is, an evil spirit?

May we wake up to God's truth, shun evil, and cast out demons in His name.

OCTOBER 26

One of Us

One of his disciples, John, told him one day, "Teacher, we saw a man using your name to cast out demons; but we told him not to, for he isn't one of our group."

—Mark 9:38 (TLB)

Are you in a clique?

The disciples thought they had one. They were quite proud of their exclusive little Jesus club, so much so that when they saw someone casting out demons in His name, they told him to stop, saying that only they were allowed to do that.

Notice Jesus's response in Mark 9:39–41 (NLT):

"Don't stop him!" Jesus said. "No one who performs a miracle in my name will soon be able to speak evil of me. Anyone who is not against us is for us. If anyone gives you even a cup of water because you belong to the Messiah, I tell you the truth, that person will surely be rewarded."

In another instance, the disciples chased off children whose mothers had brought them to Jesus to receive a blessing. Jesus's response was the same: "But Jesus said, 'Let the children come to me. Don't stop them! For the Kingdom of Heaven belongs to those who are like these children'" (Matthew 19:14 NLT).

Jesus doesn't like cliques. He is all about the unity of believers. What about your church? Does it tend to be exclusive and cliquish? And what about you? Do you tend to be exclusive?

May we welcome all believers in the name of Jesus Christ, and may we love them as He has commanded us in 1 John 4:21: "And he has given us this command: Those who love God must also love their fellow believers" (NLT).

OCTOBER 27

Whom Are You Listening To?

So be careful how you listen; for whoever has, to him shall be given more; and whoever does not have, even what he thinks he has shall be taken away from him.

—Luke 8:18 (TLB)

Whom are you listening to? Are you listening to God? Whom you listen to makes a very big difference in your life.

Hebrews 12:25 tells us, "Be careful that you do not refuse to listen to the One who is speaking. For if the people of Israel did not escape when they refused to listen to Moses, the earthly messenger, we will certainly not escape if we reject the One who speaks to us from heaven" (NLT)!

We should also be careful to avoid listening to those who are bad influences.

First Corinthians 15:33 reminds us, "Don't be fooled by those who say such things, for 'bad company corrupts good character'" (NLT).

Remember that God's voice is on the FM (for Me) frequency, and that evil's voice is on the AM (against Me) frequency.

May we listen to the voice of all that is good, all that is God, today and every day.

OCTOBER 28

Lean on Me

Share each other's troubles and problems, and so obey our Lord's command.

—GALATIANS 6:2 (TLB)

We need each other.

In the words of a famous poem by John Donne, "No man is an island."[4]

The referenced passage of scripture reminds us of the importance of looking beyond ourselves to help each other in times of need, specifically when it comes to times of temptation. When we get off track, we often need someone to lovingly come alongside us and direct us back to the light. Satan is crafty, so we need to look out for one another.

Do you know someone in need of help? May that person lean on you? Perhaps you're the one struggling with sin. Is there someone you can lean on?

Romans 12:13 tells us, "When God's people are in need, be ready to help them. Always be eager to practice hospitality" (NLT).

Ecclesiastes 4:9–10 says, "Two people are better off than one, for they can help each other succeed. If one person falls, the other can reach out and help. But someone who falls alone is in real trouble" (NLT).

May we pay attention to those in need around us, providing them with a shoulder, and may we reach for the shoulder of a Christian brother or sister when we find ourselves in need.

---

[4] From the poem "Meditation XVII."

OCTOBER 29

The Witches' Eternal Cauldron

But cowards who turn back from following me, and those who are unfaithful to me, and the corrupt, and murderers, and the immoral, and those conversing with demons, and idol worshipers and all liars—their doom is in the Lake that burns with fire and sulphur. This is the Second Death.

—Revelation 21:8 (TLB)

On a family vacation a few years back, my family was shocked to encounter a coven of witches on a train at the amusement park we were visiting.

It is a sad fact that witches, those who practice witchcraft, do exist.

Many poke fun at the idea of witches, while television and other media paint them as cute, funny, and desirable. But they're not these things. What they practice is evil. First Samuel 15:23 also advises us that rebellion is as sinful as witchcraft.

The Holy Bible tells us exactly where the cowards, the unbelievers, the corrupt people, the murderers, the immoral people, the idol worshipers, the liars, and those who practice witchcraft will end up. They will end up in the fiery lake of burning sulfur. Pretty ironic, considering that these people seem to be stereotypically stirring their own pot of eternal doom.

But there is no need for us to be afraid of any of these workers of iniquity.

Psalm 97:10 tells us, "You who love the Lord, hate evil! He protects the lives of his godly people and rescues them from the power of the wicked" (NLT).

May we hate evil, and find comfort in God's loving protection of His children.

OCTOBER 30

The Exorcist

For people from all over Judea and from Jerusalem and from as far north as the seacoasts of Tyre and Sidon had come to hear him or to be healed. And he cast out many demons.

—Luke 6:18 (TLB)

As I write this, I must confess that the forces of evil would not have you know of the victory, the power, that is found in the name of Jesus Christ.

But it is there.

Satan is real, but so is God. And God is more powerful, most powerful.

The Holy Bible is filled with many wonderful miraculous accounts of Jesus exorcising evil spirits from people so that they might be healed, restored, and able to choose to follow after Christ.

Although we encounter evil spirits around us each and every day, we rarely see anyone willing to cast them out of those in bondage to them.

Do you believe in God's ability to cast out demons?

When Jesus sent out the twelve disciples to share the good news, He said, "Heal the sick, raise the dead, cure those with leprosy, and cast out demons. Give as freely as you have received" (Matthew 10:8)!

In Mark 16:17, Jesus tells us, "These miraculous signs will accompany those who believe: They will cast out demons in my name, and they will speak in new languages" (NLT).

May God grant us the power to believe, so that we may become all that God would have us to be.

OCTOBER 31

That Haunting Feeling

For I admit my shameful deed—it haunts me day and night.

—Psalm 51:3 (TLB)

Are you the rebellious type?

Even if you're not the rebellious type, you have the ability to rebel.

That's what happened to David. Have you ever been in his position? Perhaps you're there now.

If so, you should know that God doesn't mess around when it comes to rebellion. The Holy Bible equates the sin of rebellion with that of witchcraft (1 Samuel 15:23).

Proverbs 17:11 tells us, "Evil people are eager for rebellion, but they will be severely punished" (NLT).

After David's rebellion, he suffered serious consequences. The son who was the product of his rebellious act died, and there was unrest, dysfunction, and violence within his own family until his death.

Second Samuel 12:11–12 (NLT) tells us the result of David's rebellion: This is what the Lord says: Because of what you have done,

I will cause your own household to rebel against you. I will give your wives to another man before your very eyes, and he will go to bed with them in public view. You did it secretly, but I will make this happen to you openly in the sight of all Israel.

May we take up our cross daily, choosing to walk in obedience, rather than rebellion, and may we honor our loving heavenly Father with every word and deed of our life.

NOVEMBER 1

Thanks Much

Then Jesus took the loaves and gave thanks to God and passed them out to the people. Afterwards he did the same with the fish. And everyone ate until full!

—John 6:11 (TLB)

It struck me recently upon reading this verse how truly blessed many of us are in that we can eat as much or as little as we want.

That is not true for everyone.

If it is true for you, have you taken the time to thank God for it? Do you thank Him in your heart each and every time you bring food to your lips?

A grateful attitude is what Jesus exemplifies in this passage of scripture, and we know that the attitude of gratitude is a reflection of the heart. A thankful heart permeates all parts of our being, and it is evident to everyone around us.

Is your thankfulness evident to all?

Colossians 3:16 says, "Let the message about Christ, in all its richness, fill your lives. Teach and counsel each other with all the wisdom he gives. Sing psalms and hymns and spiritual songs to God with thankful hearts" (NLT).

O that our hearts might be filled with much thanks for all that our heavenly Father has given us.

NOVEMBER 2

May I Help You?

May the God of your fathers, the Almighty, bless you with blessings of heaven above and of the earth beneath—blessings of the breasts and of the womb.

—Genesis 49:25 (TLB)

Do you ever need help?

Perhaps you know that you are in need of help but are reluctant to accept it. Maybe you would gladly accept help if you knew where to find it. Or you may be thinking of someone you know who is in desperate need of help.

In any case, there is someone who desires to help us. That someone is God.

Isaiah 59:1 tells us, "Listen! The Lord's arm is not too weak to save you, nor is his ear too deaf to hear you call" (NLT).

And if someone is too weak to call upon the name of the Lord, won't you intercede on that person's behalf?

First Timothy 2:1 commands us, "I urge you, first of all, to pray for all people. Ask God to help them; intercede on their behalf, and give thanks for them" (NLT).

May we recognize our own need for help and then receive that help. And may we intercede on behalf of others we know are in need.

NOVEMBER 3

Worth Repeating

Give thanks to the Lord, for he is good! His faithful love endures forever.

—1 Chronicles 16:34 (NLT)

The words found in this passage of scripture are found twenty-two times in the New Living Translation of the Holy Bible.

Considering it is found so many times, one would reason that the message is important.

Do you give thanks to the Lord? Whether we say the words audibly or not, our hearts should be in a constant state of gratitude toward our Savior.

Do you recognize His goodness? It is all around us! O that we would open our eyes to see more of His goodness.

And God's love, it is shillyshallies.

faithful. It never wavers, never vacillates, never

There is something else, too.

That faithful love? It lasts forever. It doesn't ever end. It is always there. Even if everyone else in all the world despises you, leaves you, and turns their back on you, God still loves you.

And He won't ever stop.

O that we would give constant perpetual thanks to God, for He is good! His faithful love endures forever.

NOVEMBER 4

The Pleasure of Knowing Him

You have let me experience the joys of life and the exquisite pleasures of your own eternal presence.

—Psalm 16:11 (TLB)

It is such a joy to have the pleasure of knowing God!

Each and every day, He reveals more of Himself to us, sharing more of His amazing divine nature and unconditional love.

As we grow deeper in our relationship with Him, we are able to become more like Him. We are a reflection of Him, and others are able to see that.

Do others see Jesus in you?

Psalm 104:31 tells us, "May the glory of the Lord continue forever! The Lord takes pleasure in all he has made" (NLT)!

We are God's creation, and He takes pleasure in us.

When we take the time to have a deep personal relationship with Him, we take pleasure in Him, too.

He is awesome. He is wonderful!

Living in His presence fills our lives with unspeakable joy.

Isaiah 35:5–6 says, "And when he comes, he will open the eyes of the blind and unplug the ears of the deaf. The lame will leap like a deer, and those who cannot speak will sing for joy" (NLT)!

O that we would find all of life's pleasure fulfilled in knowing Him.

NOVEMBER 5

I Was Wrong

Blessed is the man who reveres God, but the man who doesn't care is headed for serious trouble.

—Proverbs 28:14 (TLB)

Are you afraid of doing wrong? I am.

I remember it well. It was a new job, and my supervisor was anything but kind. She was downright rude, inconsiderate, and condescending, and I didn't like it one bit. So I acted snotty and responded sarcastically to her rudeness. She noticed, and called me on it.

But I was unrepentant. I felt justified in my retaliation.

I ended up taking another job, but I was just as snotty on the way out as I had been on the way in. My behavior was wrong in every way. God convicted me of my sin, and I confessed it to Him.

First John 1:9 promises, "But if we confess our sins to him, he is faithful and just to forgive us our sins and to cleanse us from all wickedness" (NLT).

But that wasn't all. God spoke to my heart, telling me that I needed to apologize to the supervisor I had wronged. God had instilled in me a healthy fear of not responding to His loving nudge.

Proverbs 28:13 tells us, "People who conceal their sins will not prosper, but if they confess and turn from them, they will receive mercy."

When I called my former supervisor and apologized, she was very merciful and kind—even complimentary.

May God fill our hearts with a healthy fear of doing wrong, so that we may be blessed in all things.

NOVEMBER 6

A Chill in the Air

Sin will be rampant everywhere and will cool the love of many.

—Matthew 24:12 (TLB)

Have you noticed the chill in the air? I'm not talking about the change in the temperature of the atmosphere. I'm talking about the change in the temperature of the human spirit, which is a reflection of the soul within.

It seems as though the vast majority of people have forgotten what it means to love, how to do it, and the Author of it.

Have you?

First Thessalonians 4:9 says, "But we don't need to write to you about the importance of loving each other, for God himself has taught you to love one another" (NLT).

Do you need a refresher course? Perhaps a little encouragement will do the trick.

Hebrews 10:24 tells us, "Let us think of ways to motivate one another to acts of love and good works" (NLT).

May the chill in our hearts be replaced with the warmth of God's love, and may we discover the joy and the immense pleasure of God Himself, the very definition of love.

NOVEMBER 7

Our Father's Patience

Don't you realize how patient he is being with you? Or don't you care? Can't you see that he has been waiting all this time without punishing you, to give you time to turn from your sin? His kindness is meant to lead you to repentance.

—ROMANS 2:4 (TLB)

Our loving heavenly Father has patience with us beyond any amount of human patience. His is a patience borne of love for us, compassion for us, and kindness toward us. And this patience should never be taken for granted.

There are times when I have wondered why God allows certain people, evil people, to stay in the world without their seeming to experience the full consequences of their continued rebellion. It is at those times that God lovingly reminds me of His nature, His love, His patience.

Second Peter 3:9 tells us, "The Lord isn't really being slow about his promise, as some people think. No, he is being patient for your sake. He does not want anyone to be destroyed, but wants everyone to repent" (NLT).

God's loving desire is that all of us be a part of His family. Because of this, He gives us every opportunity possible to turn to Him.

Hebrews 10:38 says, "And my righteous ones will live by faith. But I will take no pleasure in anyone who turns away" (NLT).

May we not try our Father's patience, and may we seek to understand His loving-kindness, His patience in dealing with our sin and the sin of others, so that we might all come to repentance.

NOVEMBER 8

Advancing the Kingdom

Well then, if you teach others, why don't you teach yourself? You tell others not to steal, but do you steal?

—ROMANS 2:21 (NLT)

Are you involved in teaching others about God's Word and what it means to be a believer?

In our Christian walk, there comes a point when we must move beyond the basics of learning what is right and wrong and advance to maturity. Like a baby advancing from milk to solid food, a mature Christian is able to grow and develop into a fruitful adult, a tree bearing much fruit for the kingdom of God.

Are you there, or are you in a perpetual state of infancy? First Corinthians 3:2–3 (NLT) tells us the following:

I had to feed you with milk, not with solid food, because you weren't ready for anything stronger. And you still aren't ready, for you are still controlled by your sinful nature. You are jealous of one another and quarrel with each other. Doesn't that prove you are controlled by your sinful nature? Aren't you living like people of the world?

We must advance beyond infancy to effect change and make a positive difference in the lives of others, and for the kingdom of God.

Perhaps you are not on milk but someone close to you is. May you have the love and grace to come alongside that person, helping him or her into maturity so that God's kingdom will flourish.

NOVEMBER 9

Easy Does It

For my yoke is easy to bear, and the burden I give you is light.

—MATTHEW 11:30 (NLT)

Is your life hard right now? It doesn't have to be.

Our loving heavenly Father wants to lighten your load, making it less difficult for you to bear. In fact, He wants to carry your burdens for you.

Psalm 55:22 tells us, "Give your burdens to the Lord, and he will take care of you. He will not permit the godly to slip and fall" (NLT).

Often we misunderstand who God is and how He longs for us to be dependent upon Him. We try to do things and carry things that we are not able or designed to carry. And in doing so, we often inhibit the Holy Spirit's power from working in and through our lives.

Matthew 11:28 says, "Then Jesus said, 'Come to me, all of you who are weary and carry heavy burdens, and I will give you rest'" (NLT).

Do you feel overwhelmed by the weight of all that you are carrying today?

Give all of your burdens, dreams, and broken pieces—and your wounded heart—to Jesus. He will turn your sorrow, pain, and burdens into joy.

NOVEMBER 10

Breath of Life

For the Spirit of God has made me, and the breath of the Almighty gives me life.

—Job 33:4 (TLB)

When my mother was in her early eighties, she suffered a debilitating stroke. As a result of the stroke, she could no longer walk, had difficulty speaking, and had lost the majority of her eyesight.

Doctors decided it best to place my mother on oxygen during the night as the main focus of her care. After one month on oxygen, my mother's eyesight returned, her speech improved, and she was able to walk again—without the use of a walker.

Almighty God is oxygen in your veins and mine.

Without Him, I cannot walk the path that He has laid out for me, I cannot speak the words He would have me to say, and my eyes are blind, unable to see His truth.

Psalm 104:30 tells us, "When you give them your breath, life is created, and you renew the face of the earth" (NLT).

Are you connected to the breath of life?

May we get connected and remain connected to the Source of all life, the breath of life Himself.

NOVEMBER 11

The First Time We Met

Yes, he wrestled with the Angel and prevailed. He wept and pleaded for a blessing from him. He met God there at Bethel face-to-face. God spoke to him.

—Hosea 12:4 (TLB)

I remember the first time we met.

My heart was racing. It nearly leaped from my chest.

I knew He was *the One*. There was not a doubt in my mind. I couldn't believe we were really going to be together—forever.

He was perfect—everything I needed and wanted, and so much more.

I believed every word He said, would do anything for Him, and would follow Him anywhere without hesitation.

Do you remember the first time you met Him, met Jesus?

Are you still just as passionate about Him, for Him, as when you first met, or has your love for Him waxed cold?

Hosea 10:12 reads, "I said, 'Plant the good seeds of righteousness, and you will harvest a crop of love. Plow up the hard ground of your hearts, for now is the time to seek the Lord, that he may come and shower righteousness upon you'" (NLT).

Unlike humans, God never fails us. He never disappoints us. And He will never give us cause to doubt Him.

O that we would remember the first time we met, and may we also grow far beyond that, into a deep, personal, proven relationship with Him.

NOVEMBER 12

Making Every Moment Count

Must you be his inquisitor every morning and test him every moment of the day?

—Job 7:18 (TLB)

Do you make the most of each and every moment you are given?

Psalm 39:4 tells us, "Lord, remind me how brief my time on earth will be. Remind me that my days are numbered—how fleeting my life is" (NLT).

We are all given the same amount of time in each day while we are here. It is what we do with that time that makes the difference. And it is only what we do for Christ that will stand the test of time and last forever.

Psalm 39:5 says, "You have made my life no longer than the width of my hand. My entire lifetime is just a moment to you; at best, each of us is but a breath" (NLT).

Is there someone sitting next to you who does not know Christ? What about a neighbor? A family member?

Are you praying for them? What about your daily witness, your example?

Ephesians 5:16 tells us, "Make the most of every opportunity in these evil days" (NLT).

May we honor God's call upon our lives each and every moment of the day, and may we listen to and obey His voice as it whispers to our heart.

NOVEMBER 13

Living an Honorable Life

It is God's will that your good lives should silence those who foolishly condemn the Gospel without knowing what it can do for them, having never experienced its power.

—1 Peter 2:15 (TLB)

Do you live an honorable life, a life above reproach?

In the Holy Bible, Daniel was an example of someone who did his best to live a life above reproach.

Daniel 6:4 tells us, "Then the other administrators and high officers began searching for some fault in the way Daniel was handling government affairs, but they couldn't find anything to criticize or condemn. He was faithful, always responsible, and completely trustworthy" (NLT).

When other people look at your life, what do they see? Do you live your life in such a way that others can find nothing to criticize or condemn?

In 2 Corinthians 6:3, Paul tells us, "We live in such a way that no one will stumble because of us, and no one will find fault with our ministry" NLT).

Our Christian witness is what the world sees of Jesus. It is important that we walk in obedience to Him. It is important that we live honorable lives that are pleasing to Him so that others may see Christ in us and desire a life with Him, too.

May we live an honorable life, following after Christ with every ounce of our being so that others may see the difference that He makes.

NOVEMBER 14

The Power to Change Lives

The same Good News that came to you is going out all over the world and changing lives everywhere, just as it changed yours that very first day you heard it and understood about God's great kindness to sinners.

—COLOSSIANS 1:6 (TLB)

God's truth changes lives. It doesn't just change them a little bit either. The difference God makes in us is dramatic.

Second Corinthians 3:18 tells us, "So all of us who have had that veil removed can see and reflect the glory of the Lord. And the Lord—who is the Spirit—makes us more and more like him as we are changed into his glorious image" (NLT).

God's power is so vast, so incredible, that there are not even words to describe it. He is all-powerful.

Have you witnessed this power?

Often we give up on people or write them off as a hopeless cause. But with God, there are no hopeless causes. We must only desire to be changed and believe He has the power to do the changing.

Consider the power to change in the life of Saul, aka Paul, as recounted in scripture. Acts 9:1 tells us that Saul was threatening Christians with every breath, and that he was eager to kill them. Yet God's transforming power turned him into a preacher in Damascus just a few days later.

Do you believe in God's power to change lives?

May we never doubt our omnipotent and loving heavenly Father, or His power to change lives.

NOVEMBER 15

Don't Stop

I am expecting the Lord to rescue me again, so that once again I will see his goodness to me here in the land of the living. Don't be impatient. Wait for the Lord, and he will come and save you! Be brave, stouthearted, and courageous. Yes, wait and he will help you.

—Psalm 27:13–14 (TLB)

In this age of war and terrorist attacks, it is often hard for us to see any goodness at all.

Yet it is precisely at those times of strife and conflict that God's goodness can be most evident. One example of this was recounted by a young Parisian woman involved in the November 13, 2015, terrorist attack on Paris.

This woman played dead for over an hour in a concert hall to avoid being one of the many massacred by gunmen that night. She told how a kind stranger covered her head when she began to whimper, shielding her. Another stranger hugged her and told her it was going to be all right, when she finally made it out of the concert hall.

A stranger even welcomed her into her home and brought her fresh clothing so that she would not have to go home in clothes bloodied by the slaughter. And many have showered love upon her.

It is the goodness of the Lord. It still exists, and it is in places we don't often look or realize.

Do you believe? Do you believe in the goodness of the Lord and in His power to save?

Don't stop believing. Don't ever stop believing. May the name of our Lord be praised forevermore.

NOVEMBER 16

The Joy of Forgiveness

"Blessed and to be envied," he said, "are those whose sins are forgiven and put out of sight. Yes, what joy there is for anyone whose sins are no longer counted against him by the Lord."

—Romans 4:7–8 (TLB)

My mother was always a great forgiver.

I still remember breaking one of her favorite dishes as a youngster. I went blubbering into the kitchen to tell her, and I could see that she felt every bit of my remorse. She wrapped her arms around me and hugged me, and with tears of empathy in her own eyes, she said, "It's okay, Prissy. I forgive you. Come on. I'll help you clean up the mess."

I knew she meant it, and though I still felt badly about what had happened, I felt a tremendous amount of joy in knowing my mother had wiped my slate clean. There was nothing I wouldn't do for her.

It is that way with our heavenly Father, too. He feels what we feel. He knows the remorse we feel when we sin.

Hebrews 4:15 tells us, "This High Priest of ours understands our weaknesses, for he faced all of the same testings we do, yet he did not sin" (NLT).

When we come before our loving heavenly Father to ask His forgiveness, He understands, and He wipes our slate clean before Him.

O what joy!

Is there anything you wouldn't do for Him?

NOVEMBER 17

Rightly Related to Him

Clearly, God's promise to give the whole earth to Abraham and his descendants was based not on his obedience to God's law, but on a right relationship with God that comes by faith.

—Romans 4:13 (TLB)

Are you in a right relationship with God?

Right relationships don't come just as a result of obedience. There is much, much more. It is possible to obey someone you can't stand. You can obey someone and spit behind their back. That is not a *right* relationship.

Right relationships grow and develop in an atmosphere of trust. Do you trust Him?

Until you get to the point where you trust God completely with your life, your day, your future, and your desires, you will never be rightly related to Him, and your relationship will fail to grow into the amazing gift that God intended it to be.

Luke 12:21 tells us, "Yes, a person is a fool to store up earthly wealth but not have a rich relationship with God" (NLT).

So, where and how are you spending your time?

If your priority is anything or anyone other than Jesus, then your priorities need some adjusting.

You will be amazed by the difference Jesus makes in your life when you are in a right relationship with Him.

NOVEMBER 18

Get in Line

I will take the line and plummet of justice to check the foundation wall you built; it looks so fine, but it is so weak a storm of hail will knock it down! The enemy will come like a flood and sweep it away, and you will be drowned.

—Isaiah 28:17 (TLB)

In a marching band, it is extremely noticeable when one person steps out of line. It makes the whole band look bad.

It is the same within God's church.

When we step out of line with God's Word, His truth, we make all Christians look bad. In everything that we say and do, others are watching, and we are teaching them—whether we like it or not.

Titus 2:7 says, "And you yourself must be an example to them by doing good works of every kind. Let everything you do reflect the integrity and seriousness of your teaching" (NLT).

Are you out of line?

If you need help getting back in line, that help is ready and available for the asking.

Remember that James 1:5 tells us, "If you need wisdom, ask our generous God, and he will give it to you. He will not rebuke you for asking" (NLT).

May others find your life to be a shining example of all that God desires.

NOVEMBER 19

Family Photos

Now we know so little, even with our special gifts, and the preaching of those most gifted is still so poor.

—1 Corinthians 13:9 (TLB)

O the joy of taking family pictures.

Each year in November, I torture my family by forcing them to wear matching shirts or sweaters for the annual Christmas picture. There is much whining and many questions and statements like, "Why do I have to wear this? It's not even cold outside!" or "Not again!" My personal favorite is, "Are we going to do this *every* year?" One year I forgot to make the appointment in time to have pictures done by the photographer, so we had to take the pictures at home. The disappointment was deafening (and a bit comical).

A picture may be worth a thousand words, but the pictures only tell part of the story. If you look at a Christmas picture of my family, you will have a very incomplete picture of who we are.

Here on earth, our understanding of things that God has planned and created is quite limited. We make decisions based on this limited picture that we have. But our picture and understanding are both incomplete. This is but another reason why it is critical that we trust Him. First Corinthians 13:12 tells us, "Now we see things imperfectly, like puzzling reflections in a mirror, but then we will see everything with perfect clarity. All that I know now is partial and incomplete, but then I will know everything completely, just as God now knows me completely" (NLT).

O the joy that one day we will have the whole amazing picture.

NOVEMBER 20

When Your Car Breaks Down on the Road of Life

Three times I was beaten with rods. Once I was stoned. Three times I was shipwrecked. Once I was in the open sea all night and the whole next day.

—2 Corinthians 11:25 (TLB)

I often wonder just what God was doing in the life of Paul that night and day he was adrift at sea.

Was He speaking softly to Paul's heart in the quiet beneath the stars? Or perhaps He was revealing some small piece of His divine plan.

God always knows just exactly what we need and when we need it, though we fail to understand all that He is doing in and through our lives.

One New Year's Eve, my brother's car broke down on the road from Canada to Texas. We were college students returning to school after visiting our parents during Christmas break. Fortunately, there was a mechanic's shop that happened to be open all night so the mechanic could work on our car. I did a lot of praying and wondering about why this happened on this particular night and in this particular small town. I'll probably never fully understand all of the reasons. But what I do know is that God got my attention long enough to speak softly to my heart.

And I listened.

Is your car broken down on the road of life? Perhaps you've been adrift for more than a whole night and a day. Is God speaking softly to your heart?

Maybe it's time you listened.

NOVEMBER 21

Rising Above Your Circumstance

No matter what happens, always be thankful, for this is God's will for you who belong to Christ Jesus.

—1 Thessalonians 5:18 (TLB)

Have you ever noticed that when you stop dwelling on and talking about your own problems, they somehow seem to get smaller?

I have often found this to be true.

If we fail to be grateful in every circumstance, then we have a tendency to allow our circumstances, rather than God, to control us. And if we are allowing our circumstances to control us, there is a pretty high likelihood we will allow sin, rather than God, to control us, too.

Do you ever do that?

Paul knew the secret of rising above his circumstances. In Philippians 4:12, he tells us, "I know how to live on almost nothing or with everything. I have learned the secret of living in every situation, whether it is with a full stomach or empty, with plenty or little" (NLT).

Do you know the secret?

The secret is simply depending upon God for our every need, through every battle, and in each and every circumstance.

Hosea 12:6 says, "So now, come back to your God. Act with love and justice, and always depend on him" (NLT).

May we depend on Christ to help us rise above every circumstance that comes our way.

NOVEMBER 22

Learning to Love

And as we live with Christ, our love grows more perfect and complete; so we will not be ashamed and embarrassed at the day of judgment, but can face him with confidence and joy because he loves us and we love him too.

—1 John 4:17 (TLB)

I recall asking God to teach me how to really love people—the way that He does—when I was twenty-one years old. I prayed this same prayer for several nights in a row, not really understanding what I was asking for, as is often the case.

In the years that have followed, God has placed me in many difficult situations, sometimes with some very difficult people—people who are very hard to love.

And He teaches me.

I'm not always the model student, but He is always the perfect instructor. He patiently and lovingly guides me. And He brings just the right people across my path to point me in the right direction, and to encourage me when I need it most.

He's not the kind of coach or personal trainer to bring you a bag of M&M's before your workout, as that would be counterproductive. God means business. And I am very glad of this. The results are always worth the pain.

Often I fail to realize just how difficult it can be for others to love *me*, too. What about you?

Father, may you continue to teach us to love. Amen.

NOVEMBER 23

Inch by Inch

Guide me with your laws so that I will not be overcome by evil.

—Psalm 119:133 (TLB)

There's an old saying that goes, "Inch by inch, anything's a cinch." But that saying is incomplete.

Only when God is at the helm and is guiding our steps do things become *cinchy*.

We must remain rooted and grounded in God and His Word daily to avoid being overcome by the evil that is all around us in this dark world. We can't allow Satan to deceive us into thinking we can do things on our own, with our own strength.

Sometimes our steps along the path seem to slow or stagnate, and in our impatience we are tempted to *help* God move things along. But we must be careful not to interfere in God's plan, lest we get ourselves off course and jeopardize His best for us.

God's timing and way is always perfect. He is never early and never late.

Luke 1:78–79 tells us, "Because of God's tender mercy, the morning light from heaven is about to break upon us, to give light to those who it in darkness and in the shadow of death, and to guide us to the path of peace" (NLT).

May we daily remember His tender mercy, His love, and the light He gives to guide us.

NOVEMBER 24

Give Thanks

"Oh, give thanks to the Lord and pray to him," they sang. "Tell the peoples of the world about his mighty doings."

—1 Chronicles 16:8 (TLB)

First Chronicles 16 tells us a beautiful story of celebration. King David has brought the Ark of the Covenant back to Jerusalem and placed it into the tent he has prepared for it. David longs to give the Ark of the Covenant the proper care and placement it had not received under the reign of King Saul.

David is so grateful for God granting the safe return of the Ark that he blesses the people in the name of the Lord, and gives every man and every woman in all of Israel a loaf of bread, a cake of dates, and a cake of raisins.

Afterward, David shares a song of thanksgiving and praise with Asaph and his fellow Levites. After the celebration ends and all of the people return to their homes, David returns to his home to bless his own family.

Do you celebrate God's loving provision and faithfulness in your life?

"Give thanks to the Lord, for he is good! His faithful love endures forever" (Psalm 118:29 NLT).

May we remember Colossians 3:16, which tells us, "Let the message about Christ, in all its richness, fill your lives. Teach and counsel each other with all the wisdom he gives. Sing psalms and hymns and spiritual songs to God with thankful hearts" (NLT).

And may we always give thanks.

NOVEMBER 25

Walking with God

Enoch lived 365 years, walking in close fellowship with God. Then one day he disappeared, because God took him.

—Genesis 5:23–24 (NLT)

Do you long to walk with God?

The account in Genesis of God walking in the Garden of Eden with Adam and Eve in the cool of the evening is completely foreign to us. We often feel as though our loving Father is very far removed from us, and we long to touch Him, to be with Him, to commune with Him

Yet, much like Adam and Eve who ran and hid from God when they heard Him walking in the garden when the cool of the evening breezes came (Genesis 3:8), we have a tendency to run and hide. More often than not, this is on account of our sin. It is also often due to our lack of faith and understanding.

Yet if we know and understand the true nature of God, then we know that He longs to have fellowship with us, to be with us, to dwell among us.

Psalm 23:4 tells us, "Even when I walk through the darkest valley, I will not be afraid, for you are close beside me. Your rod and your staff protect and comfort me" (NLT).

James 4:8 reminds us, "Come close to God, and God will come close to you. Wash your hands, you sinners; purify your hearts, for your loyalty is divided between God and the world" (NLT).

Are you coming close to God? "Just a closer walk with Thee. Grant it, Jesus, is my plea."[5]

---

[5] Author unknown.

NOVEMBER 26
He Never Changes

But whatever is good and perfect comes to us from God, the Creator of all light, and he shines forever without change or shadow.

—JAMES 1:17 (TLB)

The world is constantly changing.

An example of this change is seen in the public perception of the sin of homosexuality. Prior to 1973, homosexuality was considered a mental disorder by the American Psychiatric Association, the American Psychological Association Council of Representatives, and the World Health Organization. Homosexuality was declassified by the American Psychiatric Association in 1973, by the American Psychological Association Council of Representatives in 1975, and by the World Health Organization in 1990.[6]

To further illustrate this change, the *Journal of Sexual Medicine* now suggests that homophobia is the illness that needs to be cured.[7]

According to God's Word, the practice of homosexuality is still considered sin, and it always will be (Leviticus 18:22; 1 Corinthians 6:9–10). Psalm 103:17 tells us, "But the love of the Lord remains forever with those who fear him. His salvation extends to the children's children" (NLT).

What a joy and a comfort to know that God our Father never changes. He remains the same. And His steadfast love endures forever. Amen.

---

[6] "Homosexuality and psychology," *Wikipedia*, accessed December 12, 2016, https:// en.wikipedia.org/wiki/Homosexuality_and_psychology.

[7] Eric Metaxas, "Diagnosing Dissenters: Is Homophobia a Disorder?", October 28, 2015, accessed December 12, 2016, https://www.breakpoint.org/bpcommentaries/ entry/13/28370.

NOVEMBER 27

Gathered Together

And I tell you this—whatever you bind on earth is bound in heaven, and whatever you free on earth will be freed in heaven. I also tell you this—if two of you agree down here on earth concerning anything you ask for, my Father in heaven will do it for you. For where two or three gather together because they are mine, I will be right there among them.

—Matthew 18:18–20 (TLB)

The power available to us as God's children, united in His love, is miraculous and awesome, for His kingdom is all around us.

Often we fail to realize that He is living and working among us. We see Him as some distant deity in the highest heavens. But the Holy Bible tells us something different.

Psalm 46:7 declares, "The Lord of Heaven's Armies is here among us; the God of Israel is our fortress" (NLT).

He is here among us.

Do you see Him? Do you know that He is near?

As we gather together in the name of Jesus Christ, at every opportunity may we focus on knowing Him and doing His will. May we pray that we are one, united in our love for Him and for each other.

And may we fully realize and be good stewards of the power He avails to us through knowing Him and being His, with hearts full of thanksgiving for all that He has proven to be.

NOVEMBER 28

God's Bountiful Provision

For God, who gives seed to the farmer to plant, and later on good crops to harvest and eat, will give you more and more seed to plant and will make it grow so that you can give away more and more fruit from your harvest.

—2 Corinthians 9:10 (TLB)

I grew up in a home that was poor in the way of worldly goods, but I had a family rich in faith. I never had need of anything that God did not provide.

In fact, in all of my days I have never had need of anything that God did not provide. And as I grow older, God increases the resources available to me, filling me with a longing to be generous to others, as He has been with me.

Psalm 65:9 tells us, "You take care of the earth and water it, making it rich and fertile. The river of God has plenty of water; it provides a bountiful harvest of grain, for you have ordered it so" (NLT).

Second Corinthians 9:8 says, "And God will generously provide all you need. Then you will always have everything you need and plenty left over to share with others."

If you have need, ask our generous God. And when He grants your request, share with others in need, having the same generosity that He has lavished upon you, so that those with whom you shared may thank God for your generosity.

And may we always overflow with thanksgiving toward our loving and generous heavenly Father.

NOVEMBER 29

His Mighty Servants

God speaks of his angels as messengers swift as the wind and as servants made of flaming fire.

—Hebrews 1:7 (NLT)

One day as I was traveling to work early in the morning, my car was hit by a driver whose car was spinning out of control. The impact knocked my car over two lanes, into the freeway barricade, and then back to the middle of the freeway. All of the air bags deployed except for the one in the steering wheel, which my chest hit with such force that my necklace was broken. The other driver fled the scene.

Three wonderful Good Samaritans stopped to help me that day: a nurse, an eighteen-wheeler driver who blocked traffic, and a gentleman who had taken down the information of the man who hit me.

After a trip to the emergency room, I left without a scratch on me. My car was totaled, but I was not.

God sent mighty angels to protect me that day, and I saw His hand in action. There was no denying His love and His favor.

Do you know that He does that for us every day?

I think that sometimes we fail to see, or else we forget, His loving protection of us. I am grateful for these times to remember and be grateful.

Luke 4:10 tells us, "For the Scriptures say, 'He will order his angels to protect and guard you'" (NLT).

May we shine the light He has given us so that all the world may know His love.

NOVEMBER 30

The Rescuer

I will cry to him, "Arise, O Lord! Save me, O my God!" And he will slap them in the face, insulting them and breaking off their teeth.

—Psalm 3:7 (TLB)

I love the honesty of this verse. Have you ever felt like David in this passage of scripture?

I have.

God knows our heart. It serves no good purpose to fail to be honest with Him. We know that vengeance is God's, and sometimes we just want Him to act on our behalf.

The beautiful thing is that He promises to do just that.

In Psalm 91:14 is this promise: "The Lord says, 'I will rescue those who love me. I will protect those who trust in my name'" (NLT).

Psalm 13:5 tells us, "But I trust in your unfailing love. I will rejoice because you have rescued me" (NLT).

Is there an enemy you need to be rescued from today? Put your hope in God, our Savior, the One who rescues us.

Psalm 18:17 says, "He rescued me from my powerful enemies, from those who hated me and were too strong for me" (NLT).

And Psalm 144:2 tells us, "He is my loving ally and my fortress, my tower of safety, my rescuer. He is my shield, and I take refuge in him. He makes the nations submit to me" (NLT).

He did that for David, and He can do that for you, too.

DECEMBER 1

Evergreen

He is like a tree planted along a riverbank, with its roots reaching deep into the water—a tree not bothered by the heat nor worried by long months of drought. Its leaves stay green, and it goes right on producing all its luscious fruit.

—Jeremiah 17:8 (TLB)

What kind of tree are you?

Does the tree of your life produce fruit in season and out? Do your roots reach deep into the water, keeping you productive in times of heat or long months of drought?

What about your leaves? Are they evergreen?

Psalm 1:3 tells us about those who delight in the law of the Lord, meditating on it day and night. It says, "They are like trees planted along the riverbank, bearing fruit each season. Their leaves never wither, and they prosper in all they do" (NLT).

In order for our lives, our trees, to stand the test of time and endure 'til the end, we must be rooted and grounded in God's love and in God's Word, with an unshakable faith in the person of Jesus Christ.

Do you have that?

If not, you can start today. It's not too late.

First Corinthians 15:58 says, "So, my dear brothers and sisters, be strong and immovable. Always work enthusiastically for the Lord, for you know that nothing you do for the Lord is ever useless" (NLT).

May your tree be evergreen, ever-bearing, and pruned for everlasting life.

DECEMBER 2

Guarded

Above all else, guard your affections. For they influence everything else in your life.

—Proverbs 4:23 (TLB)

This evil fallen world in which we live is a dangerous place.

Try as we may to be careful and diligent, we, operating on our own effort, are often deceived and deeply wounded by those with wicked motives. Yet we cannot spend our entire lives in hiding. We must examine what God's Word tells us about being guarded.

Psalm 34:7 comforts us with these words: "For the angel of the Lord is a guard; he surrounds and defends all who fear him" (NLT).

Proverbs 2:8 says, "He guards the paths of the just and protects those who are faithful to him" (NLT).

Proverbs 13:6 tells us, "Godliness guards the path of the blameless, but the evil are misled by sin" (NLT).

So we see that a continued focus on our Lord and Savior, and a reverential fear of Him, provides the best possible guard we could hope for.

First Corinthians 16:13 tells us, "Be on guard. Stand firm in the faith. Be courageous. Be strong" (NLT).

May the peace of God guard your heart and mind as you live in Christ Jesus (Philippians 4:7).

DECEMBER 3

Eager to Serve

Feed the flock of God; care for it willingly, not grudgingly; not for what you will get out of it but because you are eager to serve the Lord.

—1 Peter 5:2 (TLB)

Are you eager to serve God?

The Holy Bible tells us in Matthew 23:11, "The greatest among you must be a servant" (NLT).

Even Jesus came not to be served but to serve others. His life demonstrated this repeatedly.

Matthew 20:28 and Mark 10:45 tell us, "For even the Son of Man came not to be served but to serve others and to give his life as a ransom for many" (NLT).

Each day of His life, Jesus was a servant to others, from healing the sick and disabled, and washing the disciples' feet, to giving His very life as a sacrifice for your sins and mine.

Having such an example, we should be eager to serve our generous, kind, and loving heavenly Father.

May we remember the words of Joshua 22:5, which tells us, "But be very careful to obey all the commands and the instructions that Moses gave to you. Love the Lord your God, walk in all his ways, obey his commands, hold firmly to him, and serve him with all your heart and all your soul" (NLT).

DECEMBER 4

I Have Resolved

I am determined to obey you until I die.

—Psalm 119:112 (TLB)

Each and every day we have a choice to make. That choice is whether or not we will choose God's way or our own.

When we accept Jesus Christ as our Savior, sin no longer controls us like it did in the past. We are now free to follow the Holy Spirit. He has written His laws upon our heart. Yet we still have the ability to overrule the Spirit living in us, choosing to sin. And God loves us enough to convict us of this sin, through His Spirit. We must choose daily to obey Him, to follow Him.

There is a beautiful hymn entitled "I Am Resolved" by Palmer Hartsough, published in 1896. The first and last verse and refrain are as follows, reminding us of our need to be resolute in following after Christ:

I am resolved no longer to linger,
Charmed by the world's delight.
Things that are higher, things that are nobler,
These have allured my sight.
Refrain:
I will hasten to Him,
Hasten so glad and free;
Jesus, greatest, highest,
I will come to Thee.
I am resolved, and who will go with me? Come, friends, without delay;
Taught by the Bible, led by the Spirit, We'll walk the heav'nly way.
May we resolve to follow Him each and every day of our lives.

DECEMBER 5

Saturated with Him

After this prayer, the building where they were meeting shook, and they were all filled with the Holy Spirit and boldly preached God's message.

—Acts 4:31 (TLB)

How well are you acquainted with God's Word?

Have you read it? Do you know it? Do you know it well?

We need to allow God's Word to saturate our lives, to permeate every part of us. When we do this, our faith will begin to grow. When our faith grows, the Holy Spirit will begin to permeate our lives. When the Holy Spirit permeates our lives, others will see the light of Christ in us. When others begin to see the light of Christ in you, they will be drawn to Christ within you, like moths to a flame. His light is attractive.

Titus 2:9–10 tells us, "Slaves must always obey their masters and do their best to please them. They must not talk back or steal, but must show themselves to be entirely trustworthy and good. Then they will make the teaching about God our Savior attractive in every way" (NLT).

When we are saturated with Him, we will find it easy to obey Him and our lives will demonstrate the genuine beauty of all that He is.

Luke 11:36 says, "If you are filled with light, with no dark corners, then your whole life will be radiant, as though a floodlight were filling you with light" (NLT).

Is His light filling every corner of your life?

May we each be found saturated with Jesus so that the sponge of our life can contain no more of Him. May He overflow to everyone around us.

DECEMBER 6

Oozing God

So I pray for you Gentiles that God who gives you hope will keep you happy and full of peace as you believe in him. I pray that God will help you overflow with hope in him through the Holy Spirit's power within you.

—ROMANS 15:13 (TLB)

Does your life ooze God?

What I am referring to here is the effortless production of fruit in a life wholly committed to Christ.

It looks something like this: You walk up to the Jennifer tree, and before you even speak a word to her, an apple or orange bonks you on the head. Her very demeanor is quietly effervescent with joy. She listens to your need and commits it to the Father with such confidence that you know the prayer has already been answered, without even being spoken.

Do you know anyone like that?

God wants us to ooze Him out of every pore of our being.

Scripture tells us in Matthew 22:37, "Jesus replied, 'You must love the Lord your God with all your heart, all your soul, and all your mind'" (NLT).

Do you love Him like that?

When we love Him like that, we will seek to please Him, and others will see Him in us.

May you overflow with confident hope through the power of the Holy Spirit.

DECEMBER 7

Evil Is Not a Person

For we are not fighting against people made of flesh and blood, but against persons without bodies—the evil rulers of the unseen world, those mighty satanic beings and great evil princes of darkness who rule this world; and against huge numbers of wicked spirits in the spirit world.

—Ephesians 6:12 (TLB)

Evil is not a person.

I have a tendency to forget this truth sometimes. It is a blessing that God's Word reminds us that the evil we are fighting against in this world is spiritual.

Knowing this, we must not dismiss evil. We must wage war against it—not him or her, but the evil within him or her.

How do we do that?

Scripture tells us in Ephesians 6:11, "Put on all of God's armor so that you will be able to stand firm against all strategies of the devil" (NLT).

Ephesians 6:13–17 tells us exactly what the armor looks like, and Ephesians 6:18 adds, "Pray in the Spirit at all times and on every occasion. Stay alert and be persistent in your prayers for all believers everywhere" (NLT).

Are we doing what scripture tells us to do here?

May we get serious about putting on God's armor every single day, like putting on our clothing in the morning.

We can't afford not to.

DECEMBER 8

A Little Dab Won't Do Ya

May you always be doing those good, kind things that show you are a child of God, for this will bring much praise and glory to the Lord.

—Philippians 1:11 (TLB)

Many people today want a dab of this religion and a dab of that one—never really committing to anything, so as not to impose upon their own selfish desires. But you can't have just a dab of Jesus. He is an all-or-nothing God. And it is for our benefit that He requires this.

Exodus 34:14 tells us, "You must worship no other gods, for the Lord, whose very name is Jealous, is a God who is jealous about his relationship with you" (NLT).

Jesus wants all of us, and He longs to give us all of Him, by way of the Holy Spirit. Without receiving all of Jesus, we cannot receive all that He has to offer. Without giving Him all of ourselves, we miss out on the full measure of blessing that He longs to give us.

Ephesians 1:3 tells us, "All praise to God, the Father of our Lord Jesus Christ, who has blessed us with every spiritual blessing in the heavenly realms because we are united with Christ" (NLT).

We must have the courage to speak this truth to those around us who believe they can serve many gods, as there is only one true and living God.

Jeremiah 10:10 says, "But the Lord is the only true God. He is the living God and the everlasting King! The whole earth trembles at his anger. The nations cannot stand up to his wrath" (NLT).

May we give Him all that we are so that we may be all He desires us to be.

DECEMBER 9

Hush Up

Don't talk so much. You keep putting your foot in your mouth. Be sensible and turn off the flow!

—Proverbs 10:19 (TLB)

As a youngster full of chatter, I found it a good thing to have a great-grandmother who knew well the truth of this verse. She would say, "Hush up," when my cousins and I got to talking so much that we were out of control. I am grateful she loved us enough to say it.

Often we run our mouths out of nervousness. Sometimes we run our mouths because we have an urge to expel every thought in our head, to vent. This is dangerous and often sinful, as it exhibits a lack of self-control.

The words we speak should edify others and build them up. That doesn't mean we should never speak a truth that is negative, as speaking painful truth at the right time is often the most loving thing we can do for a person.

As scripture tells us in Ephesians 4:29, "Don't use foul or abusive language. Let everything you say be good and helpful, so that your words will be an encouragement to those who hear them" (NLT).

Do you have someone in your life who will hush you up when you need it? If not, you can ask God to hush you up when the flow is out of control.

Psalm 141:3 says, "Take control of what I say, O Lord, and guard my lips" (NLT).

May God be the guard over your lips and mine, now and always.

DECEMBER 10

Scrubbed Clean by God

But who can live when he appears? Who can endure his coming? For he is like a blazing fire refining precious metal, and he can bleach the dirtiest garments!

—Malachi 3:2 (TLB)

I don't know about you, but I love clean. Whether it is a clean car, a clean house, clean clothes, a clean body, or clean dishes, I love clean.

God does, too.

But more than anything, He loves a clean heart.

And He is the only One who can give us a clean heart. Do you long to have a clean heart? God can give you one.

In Psalm 51:10, David writes, "Create in me a clean heart, O God. Renew a loyal spirit within me" (NLT).

We can't possibly know all of the sins we have lurking within our own heart (Psalm 19:12), but we can come before God, trusting in Him to wash us clean from sin.

Hebrews 10:22 tells us, "Let us go right into the presence of God with sincere hearts fully trusting him. For our guilty consciences have been sprinkled with Christ's blood to make us clean, and our bodies have been washed with pure water" (NLT).

May we trust in God, committing every ounce of our being to Him, so that He can scrub our hearts clean from sin.

DECEMBER 11

Our Great Intercessor

And the Father who knows all hearts knows, of course, what the Spirit is saying as he pleads for us in harmony with God's own will.

—Romans 8:27 (TLB)

There are many instances in which I do not know or understand what God's will may be. It is at these times when I am so very grateful to have the Holy Spirit, who pleads to the Father on my behalf in harmony with God's own will.

The Holy Bible tells us in Hebrews 7:25, "Therefore he is able, once and forever, to save those who come to God through him. He lives forever to intercede with God on their behalf" (NLT).

What a blessing to know that when we accept Jesus Christ as our Savior, He lives forever to intercede on our behalf! And this intercession is always in harmony with God's will for our lives.

How could we ever ask for more?

Are you struggling when it comes to what to pray for and how to pray? Take heart in the fact that you have a great intercessor to pray in harmony with the Father's will on your behalf.

Romans 8:26 says, "And the Holy Spirit helps us in our weakness. For example, we don't know what God wants us to pray for. But the Holy Spirit prays for us with groanings that cannot be expressed in words" (NLT).

May we allow the Spirit to intercede on our behalf when we don't know how to pray or what we ought to pray.

DECEMBER 12

God's Cure for Depression

When they walk through the Valley of Weeping, it will become a place of springs where pools of blessing and refreshment collect after rains!

—Psalm 84:6 (TLB)

Do you ever get down in the dumps, depressed about your circumstances?

No matter how bad your circumstance, there is someone else who has it worse, or has had it worse, than you.

When we focus on our own problems, we become very self-focused. We tend to make our issues the center of our own little universe, and we dwell there.

But God wants something much better for you and for me. He wants us to share His light with others, regardless of our own circumstances. When we do this, our own burdens become lighter and less important. And we have someone to bear them for us and with us.

Galatians 6:2 tells us, "Share each other's burdens, and in this way obey the law of Christ" (NLT).

In Matthew 11:28, we find a promise from Jesus: "Then Jesus said, 'Come to me, all of you who are weary and carry heavy burdens, and I will give you rest'" (NLT).

Are you ever depressed?

Share the burden of someone else in need, and give God your burden. He will carry you.

DECEMBER 13

Hope Beyond Hope

So, when God told Abraham that he would give him a son who would have many descendants and become a great nation, Abraham believed God even though such a promise just couldn't come to pass!

—Romans 4:18 (TLB)

Do you ever feel as though things are hopeless?

Perhaps you are in a situation that you have prayed about for too many years to count and nothing seems to change. Or maybe you believed you heard God's voice promising something of Abrahamic proportions to you, but you've yet to see with your physical eyes even a hint of its fulfillment.

Take heart, friend.

Scripture tells us in Proverbs 23:17–18, "Don't envy sinners, but always continue to fear the Lord. You will be rewarded for this; your hope will not be disappointed" (NLT).

Jesus calls us to walk by faith, not by what we see with our physical eyes (2 Corinthians 5:7). It is only by believing that we are able to please God (Hebrews 11:6).

And it is in this believing that God fills us with His hope.

Romans 5:5 reminds us of one of God's comforting promises in this regard. It says, "And this hope will not lead to disappointment. For we know how dearly God loves us, because he has given us the Holy Spirit to fill our hearts with his love" (NLT).

May God's love for you, as it did for Abraham, fill you with a hope beyond hope.

DECEMBER 14

Because of Trust

It is clear, then, that God's promise to give the whole earth to Abraham and his descendants was not because Abraham obeyed God's laws but because he trusted God to keep his promise.

—Romans 4:13 (TLB)

As a little girl, I obeyed my father when he asked me to do something. I had no fear of him and no reason not to trust him. I had no experience one way or the other.

"Jump!" he said as I stood at the end of the diving board at the local swimming pool. And when I jumped, he caught me. Time and again, he proved himself to me as worthy of being trusted. As my trust for my father grew, my love for him grew, too. There was nothing I wouldn't do for him.

The same is true of any relationship we have. Without trust, there really isn't much of a relationship.

All good relationships must be based on trust in order to thrive and grow. This trust begets love, and love produces a desire to please through obedience. Obedience without love is halfhearted.

When we have a close relationship with God, He writes His law of love upon our hearts. He has proven Himself worthy of our trust time and time again, instilling in us a deep love and a desire to please Him.

Isaiah 26:8 says, "Lord, we show our trust in you by obeying your laws; our heart's desire is to glorify your name" (NLT).

May this law of love written on your heart draw you into a right relationship with God because you trust Him.

DECEMBER 15

Patience Perfected

So let it grow, and don't try to squirm out of your problems. For when your patience is finally in full bloom, then you will be ready for anything, strong in character, full and complete.

—James 1:4 (TLB)

In our instant-gratification, get-it-done-yesterday, information-superhighway world, it seems that patience is in shorter supply than it's ever been before.

Proverbs 25:15 says, "Patience can persuade a prince, and soft speech can break bones" (NLT).

Patience is still one of the proofs that the Holy Spirit is controlling your life. Is He in control of your life today, or are you the one controlling your life? Second Corinthians 6:6 tells us, "We prove ourselves by our purity, our understanding, our patience, our kindness, by the Holy Spirit within us, and by our sincere love" (NLT).

We must learn to endure hardship, as this endurance builds character and integrity. It instills the kind of wisdom that only a dependence on the Holy Spirit in control of our lives can bring.

Second Corinthians 6:4 says, "In everything we do, we show that we are true ministers of God. We patiently endure troubles and hardships and calamities of every kind" (NLT).

Second Timothy 2:12 warns us, "If we endure hardship, we will reign with him. If we deny him, he will deny us" (NLT).

May we allow the Holy Spirit to fully develop patient endurance in our lives so that we may be complete in Him.

DECEMBER 16

Practicing What We Preach

He replied, "Yes, but even more blessed are all who hear the Word of God and put it into practice."

—Luke 11:28 (TLB)

There is a man at my office who is very difficult to work with. He manages by intimidation, is very judgmental of others, and spends most of his time in questionable, unexplained "meetings" outside the office. And nearly every sentence from his mouth contains a four-letter word beginning with the letter *f*.

You can imagine my surprise, and the surprise of others in my office, when he announced one day that he was a Christian and had been for many years. Perhaps he has not read Ephesians 4:29.

People such as this man are the reason why so many people run the other way when they hear the word *Christian*.

Are we practicing what we preach?

Are we proving that we are followers of Christ by the way we live (Matthew 3:8)?

We can listen to what God calls us to do until His eternal kingdom comes, but until we put it into practice, it is impotent.

James 1:22 tells us, "But don't just listen to God's word. You must do what it says. Otherwise, you are only fooling yourselves" (NLT).

May we be doers of God's Word, and not hearers only, having the courage to lovingly confront and call out others who fail to practice what they preach.

DECEMBER 17

Hide It Under a Bush? Oh No!

Another time he asked, "Who ever heard of someone lighting a lamp and then covering it up to keep it from shining? No, lamps are mounted in the open where they can be seen."

—Luke 8:16 (TLB)

Once upon a time, there was a very special woman who went by the nickname, Nony. Her parents divorced when she was very young. She lived with her mother until the day her mother died. After that, Nony lived alone, having never married.

Nony had God's light in her life, but she considered those around her to be uninterested in Him. The people around her were mostly heathens. Besides, she was sure that those people didn't look at life or anything else the same as she did.

She smiled a lot, but she kept God all to herself, neatly tucked into her pocket and undisturbed. She never talked of Him, and rarely talked to others at all, about anything.

As Nony grew older, her demeanor began to change. She smiled less—a lot less. She seemed unhappy. Even when others reached out to her, she hardly even acknowledged their thoughtful gestures.

The light of God's love was being snuffed out. There was no oxygen for it in that pocket where she kept it hidden.

The Holy Bible tells us in 2 Timothy 1:6–7, "This is why I remind you to fan into flames the spiritual gift God gave you when I laid my hands on you. For God has not given us a spirit of fear and timidity, but of power, love, and self-discipline" (NLT).

May we fan the flames of love that God has planted within us until the whole world sees His light.

DECEMBER 18

Esther Dove

"Lord," he said, "now I can die content! For I have seen him as you promised me I would. I have seen the Savior you have given to the world."

—LUKE 2:29–31 (TLB)

My father tells the story of a woman named Esther Dove who was dying of cancer. Her sister, Vivian, contacted my father to come and pray with her.

When my father arrived at the home where Esther was staying, she said, "Pastor, I contacted an evangelist to pray for me to be healed, and I still have cancer. I'm dying, and I want to be healed." Esther had not been able to get out of bed without assistance for quite some time.

My father asked her some questions and learned that Esther had not accepted Christ as her personal Savior. When she learned this, she wanted to receive Christ, and prayed to ask Him into her heart right then and there. She was very excited, believing that His Holy Spirit had come to dwell inside her. She got up from the bed and danced around as though there was nothing wrong with her.

In the days that followed, doctors treating Esther Dove pronounced her miraculously cured of the cancer that had been ravaging her body. Her husband, Cash, was so amazed that he, too, accepted Christ as his Savior.

Esther lived happily as a child of God for ten more years. God took her home by way of a heart attack. There was never any recurrence of the cancer.

We may not all be miraculously cured like Esther, but we may share His salvation with all people so that He may be glorified now and always.

DECEMBER 19

Giving and Receiving

And I was a constant example to you in helping the poor; for I remembered the words of the Lord Jesus, "It is more blessed to give than to receive."

—Acts 20:35 (TLB)

It is the season of the year when we focus our attention on gift-giving. But shouldn't we focus the same attention on giving all year long? Our Jesus did.

It isn't the dollar value of the gift that is important, but rather its impact.

Sometimes a warm sincere smile, a kind word, and a genuine interest in someone else is the best gift we could ever give to a person.

Or what about the last cookie? Is there someone you know who needs it more than you do?

Luke 6:38 tells us, "Give, and you will receive. Your gift will return to you in full—pressed down, shaken together to make room for more, running over,

and poured into your la you get back" (NLT).

. The amount you give will determine the amount

Do you have a generous heart?

Psalm 37:21 says, "The wicked borrow and never repay, but the godly are generous givers" (NLT).

May we hold nothing back. May our generosity in all things be evident to everyone we meet.

DECEMBER 20

Go Tell It on the Mountain

Has the Lord redeemed you? Then speak out! Tell others he has saved you from your enemies.

—Psalm 107:2 (TLB)

Do you share your faith in Christ with others?

If you have a relationship with Jesus Christ, and if He has changed you, transformed you, then it is cruel to keep that information all to yourself. It is like having the cure for cancer and not telling anyone about it.

He is the solution to every problem we will ever face in all of life. That is huge.

Mark 6:12 tells us, "So the disciples went out, telling everyone they met to repent of their sins and turn to God" (NLT).

Since we are His disciples, we must do the same thing.

Matthew 28:19–20 commands us to: "Therefore, go and make disciples of all the nations, baptizing them in the name of the Father and the Son and the Holy Spirit. Teach these new disciples to obey all the commands I have given you. And be sure of this: I am with you always, even to the end of the age" (NLT).

And as David said in Psalm 71:15, "I will tell everyone about your righteousness. All day long I will proclaim your saving power, though I am not skilled with words" (NLT).

May we tell it on the mountain, in the valley, on the sidewalk, in the mall, in the airplane, on the bus, in the restaurant, on the elevator, and every single place that we go.

DECEMBER 21

The Year in Review

The Lord will work out his plans for my life—for your loving- kindness, Lord, continues forever. Don't abandon me—for you made me.

—Psalm 138:8 (TLB)

It is that time of year when Christmas cards come, many of which contain letters of the family's year in review. I often marvel at how perfect and amazing everyone seems in these letters, when my own year has often played out like a bad country song.

When we reflect on our life, some years are definitely better than others. But that doesn't mean that we've been forgotten by our loving heavenly Father.

Ecclesiastes 7:14 tells us, "Enjoy prosperity while you can, but when hard times strike, realize that both come from God. Remember that nothing is certain in this life" (NLT).

God has a wonderful plan for each one of our lives, and though some years are drastically different, either better or worse than others, He manages to weave them all together into this amazing tapestry called *our life*.

So, whether it has been a banner year or a bummer year, we can rest in knowing that God is still in control.

Job 23:14 says, "So he will do to me whatever he has planned. He controls my destiny" (NLT).

May we remember to praise Him regardless of our circumstance, knowing that He is in control of the good years and the bad.

DECEMBER 22

O Be Careful, Little Mouth, What You Say

And I tell you this, that you must give account on Judgment Day for every idle word you speak.

—Matthew 12:36 (TLB)

O the trouble our mouths can get us into . . .

We often speak too much, too often, and we are often too careless for our own good and the good of others. This passage of scripture reminds us that we will have to give an account for every idle word we speak.

The Holy Bible has a great deal to say about the words we speak. Even though we may have the best intentions, if our words are not Spirit-led, then we can end up in trouble.

Proverbs 15:28 says, "The heart of the godly thinks carefully before speaking; the mouth of the wicked overflows with evil words" (NLT).

James 3:7–8 tells us, "People can tame all kinds of animals, birds, reptiles, and fish, but no one can tame the tongue. It is restless and evil, full of deadly poison" (NLT).

Often giving full vent to our thoughts only serves to poison, wound, and damage those listening. But taking our heart cry to God and laying it at His feet is how we will find true peace and rest.

Proverbs 22:11 encourages us with these words: "Whoever loves a pure heart and gracious speech will have the king as a friend" (NLT).

May we remember to fill our lives with the Holy Spirit so that He will be poured out in every conversation that we have.

DECEMBER 23

O Come, Emmanuel

That day a man named Simeon, a Jerusalem resident, was in the Temple. He was a good man, very devout, filled with the Holy Spirit and constantly expecting the Messiah to come soon. For the Holy Spirit had revealed to him that he would not die until he had seen him—God's anointed King.

—Luke 2:25–26 (TLB)

Simeon was a devout Jew eagerly awaiting the Messiah. God had promised Simeon that he would not die until he saw the Messiah. On this particular day, the Spirit of the Lord led Simeon to the temple.

There, Simeon found Mary and Joseph dedicating the Messiah, Emmanuel, to the Lord, as was the Jewish custom with the firstborn son.

Simeon knew God's promise had now been fulfilled. He took the baby Jesus in his arms, praised God, and prayed as Luke 2:29–32 tells us: "Sovereign Lord, now let your servant die in peace, as you have promised. I have seen your salvation, which you have prepared for all people. He is a light to reveal God to the nations, and he is the glory of your people Israel" (NLT)!

Emmanuel, *God with us*, had come—the light revealing God to the nations.

Isaiah 9:6 foretold, "For a child is born to us, a son is given to us. The government will rest on his shoulders. And he will be called: Wonderful Counselor, Mighty God, Everlasting Father, Prince of Peace" (NLT).

Emmanuel had come, and His Spirit lives among us today. May we always praise Him, our *God with us*.

DECEMBER 24

The Eve of the Gift

For God loved the world so much that he gave his only Son so that anyone who believes in him shall not perish but have eternal life.

—John 3:16 (TLB)

'Twas the night before Christmas All over the earth
When God sent His gift Of infinite worth.
This gift was most precious; Nothing could compare. 'Twas given for all,
For the whole world to share
The only gift perfect For you and for me,
It was wrapped in a promise To set all people free.
We need only believe Him And turn from our sin.
His promise: to guide us, Life's race for to win.
So let's share this present, This gift of God's Son.
Pray that all may receive Him, Each and every one.

DECEMBER 25

O Holy Night

That night some shepherds were in the fields outside the village, guarding their flocks of sheep. Suddenly an angel appeared among them, and the landscape shone bright with the glory of the Lord. They were badly frightened, but the angel reassured them. "Don't be afraid!" he said. "I bring you the most joyful news ever announced, and it is for everyone! The Savior—yes, the Messiah, the Lord—has been born tonight in Bethlehem! How will you recognize him? You will find a baby wrapped in a blanket, lying in a manger!"

—Luke 2:8–12 (TLB)

O what a beautiful holy night it was in Bethlehem of Judea when our precious Savior, God in the flesh, came to live on earth, to dwell among us.

He was announced first to the shepherds, the lowest in class. It was a sign of His humility. He came for the Jew first, but He also came for the Greek, the Gentile.

He came for every man, woman, boy, and girl alive, and for all who would ever come after.

O what a holy and glorious night it was, and forever will be.

Have you shared Him today? Have you shared this gift that you've been given?

Are you stuck not knowing what gift to give this Christmas? This gift has already been bought, and there is none greater.

Won't you share Jesus with someone desperately in need of Him today? It will be the best gift they've ever received.

DECEMBER 26

A Legacy of Faith

But Abraham never doubted. He believed God, for his faith and trust grew ever stronger, and he praised God for this blessing even before it happened. He was completely sure that God was well able to do anything he promised. And because of Abraham's faith God forgave his sins and declared him "not guilty."

—Romans 4:20–22 (NLT)

We are blessed to have a legacy of faith.

Because of Abraham's faith, we too are counted as righteous when we believe in God and in the many promises He gives to us. It is a glorious and rich legacy to be a believer in God.

Do you see Him for all that He is? Do you receive Him and all of the fullness, massive power, and glory that He possesses?

Do you share Him in everything that you do, every word that you say, every thought that you think? Is your life so filled with Him that He constantly flows out from you?

Galatians 3:29 tells us, "And now that you belong to Christ, you are the true children of Abraham. You are his heirs, and God's promise to Abraham belongs to you" (NLT).

O that we might grasp the power of this magnificent legacy that is ours as children of God, true children of Abraham, disciples of Jesus Christ, our Lord.

DECEMBER 27

The Promise of Faith

So God's blessings are given to us by faith, as a free gift; we are certain to get them whether or not we follow Jewish customs if we have faith like Abraham's, for Abraham is the father of us all when it comes to these matters of faith.

—Romans 4:16 (TLB)

There is no amount of work, no level of good deeds, that can ever make us right with God. What makes us right with God is faith.

Only by faith can we have a right relationship with God our Father.

Not only did Abraham have faith that God would make him the father of many nations, but also, just when things seemed most hopeless, Abraham's faith grew stronger (Romans 4:20).

When things seem hopeless in your life, does your faith grow stronger? That is the example of Abraham.

Galatians 3:14 tells us, "Through Christ Jesus, God has blessed the Gentiles with the same blessing he promised to Abraham, so that we who are believers might receive the promised Holy Spirit through faith" (NLT).

And Galatians 5:5 says, "But we who live by the Spirit eagerly wait to receive by faith the righteousness God has promised to us" (NLT).

May we live by faith, knowing that God's promises are true, for there is no other way to please Him.

DECEMBER 28

A New Day Dawning

It is a wonderful thing to be alive!

—Ecclesiastes 11:7 (TLB)

If you are able to read this or have it read to you, then you have something to be thankful for. God has blessed you with a new day, and He has a reason for you to be alive this very day.

Praise Him for His goodness, and open your eyes to the opportunities He has placed all around you.

Colossians 4:5 reminds us, "Live wisely among those who are not believers, and make the most of every opportunity" (NLT).

In each new day, God presents us with countless opportunities to live out a life of faith.

Ephesians 5:16 exhorts us, "Make the most of every opportunity in these evil days" (NLT).

Life can be hard, and we can easily become discouraged if we take our eyes off of Jesus even for a moment. But take heart.

Second Corinthians 4:16–17 encourages us. It says, "That is why we never give up. Though our bodies are dying, our spirits are being renewed every day. For our present troubles are small and won't last very long. Yet they produce for us a glory that vastly outweighs them and will last forever" (NLT)!

May we sing to the Lord and praise His name, each day proclaiming that He saves (Psalm 96:2).

DECEMBER 29

Finish Line in Sight

But life is worth nothing unless I use it for doing the work assigned me by the Lord Jesus—the work of telling others the Good News about God's mighty kindness and love.

—Acts 20:24 (TLB)

Each day we are in a race against the forces of evil to do the work that God has called us to do. In this race, we must remember that evil will stop at nothing to trip us up, hoping to cause us to lose the race.

But we must not give up. We can't quit, because the body of Christ is dependent upon each of us doing our part.

Ephesians 4:16 reminds us, "He makes the whole body fit together perfectly. As each part does its own special work, it helps the other parts grow, so that the whole body is healthy and growing and full of love" (NLT).

We have the finish line in sight. Can you see it? Keep going! You're almost there!

And you don't have to go it alone.

Hebrews 12:1 encourages us by saying, "Therefore, since we are surrounded by such a huge crowd of witnesses to the life of faith, let us strip off every weight that slows us down, especially the sin that so easily trips us up. And let us run with endurance the race God has set before us" (NLT).

May God bless you. You're almost at the finish line.

DECEMBER 30

Steadfast to the End

Beware then of your own hearts, dear brothers, lest you find that they, too, are evil and unbelieving and are leading you away from the living God. Speak to each other about these things every day while there is still time so that none of you will become hardened against God, being blinded by the glamor of sin. For if we are faithful to the end, trusting God just as we did when we first became Christians, we will share in all that belongs to Christ.

—Hebrews 3:12–14 (TLB)

Steadfast, immovable, faithful to Christ.

Do you know someone like that? Are you like that?

Sadly, it is a rarity to find someone who is a true follower of Christ today, a faithful follower. Even in our pulpits we hear profanity and coarse jesting, and the congregation simply laughs.

But God's Word is not to be taken lightly. This scripture reminds us that we are to warn one another each and every day regarding the consequences of turning away from the one true and living God. We should admonish each other concerning the deceptive nature of sin. And we must encourage our brothers and sisters to remain faithful to the end. For if we are steadfast in our faith to the very end, we will share in all that belongs to Christ.

Is your heart soft? Do you trust God as firmly as when you first believed, or are you rebellious and in need of a heart transplant? Ezekiel 36:26 tells us that God can take a stony, stubborn heart and replace it with a tender, responsive heart that longs to be faithful.

May we invite Christ to soften our hearts today so that we may be steadfast to the very end.

DECEMBER 31

Open the Gates

Open the gates of the Temple—I will go in and give him my thanks. Those gates are the way into the presence of the Lord, and the godly enter there. O Lord, thank you so much for answering my prayer and saving me.

—Psalm 118:19–21 (TLB)

The majesty of these verses brings two beautiful and glorious pictures to mind. The first is of the awesome entrance into the Holy of Holies in the tabernacle, behind the veil—that place where our Lord and Savior took up residence in the Old Testament. The second is of the grand and awe-inspiring entrance into heaven.

In 1 Chronicles 9, we read about the four chief gatekeepers who were responsible for the rooms and the treasuries at the house of God. First Chronicles 9:27 tells us, "They would spend the night around the house of God, since it was their duty to guard it and to open the gates every morning" (NLT). Can you imagine the splendor each morning as the gates were opened?

Can you imagine that great and glorious day when the gates of heaven will be opened for you and for me? Are you filled with the same confidence and gratitude as David? There is a wonderful hymn entitled "What a Day That Will Be" by Jim Hill. The lyrics to the chorus are as follows:

> *What a day that will be*
> *When my Jesus I shall see*
> *And I look upon His face,*
> *The One who saved me by His grace.*
> *When He takes me by the hand*
> *And leads me through the Promised Land,*
> *What a day, glorious day, that will be.*

Yes, what a day, glorious day, that will be.

About the Author

Author Priscilla Doremus accepted Christ at the age of five and has written books, poems, and stories from a very early age. She is the author of *Prayers for Times of Crisis* and has a passion for sharing Christ through the written word.

Priscilla attended Baylor University, and has worked in the field of Insurance and Risk Management for many years. She has two children, and her family currently makes their home in Sugar Land, Texas.

For more information, visit Priscilla's blog at:
priscilla-joy.blogspot.com

www.ingramcontent.com/pod-product-compliance
Lightning Source LLC
Chambersburg PA
CBHW030902080526
44589CB00010B/102